ADOBE HOUSES FOR TODAY

FLEXIBLE PLANS FOR YOUR ADOBE HOME

Laura Sanchez
Alex Sanchez

SANTA FE

Computer graphics were drawn using AutoCAD Release 14, with 2D graphics by Laura Sanchez and 3D graphics by Alex Sanchez.

Photograph of authors by John T. Finger.

FIRST EDITION

10 9 8 7 6 5 4 3 2 1

Library of Congress Cataloging-in-Publication Data:

Sanchez, Laura.

Adobe houses for today: flexible plans for your adobe home / Laura Sanchez, Alex Sanchez.—1st ed.

p. cm.

Includes bibliographical references.

ISBN: 0-86534-320-9 (pbk.)

1. Adobe houses—Southwest, New.

2. Building, Adobe—Southwest, New. I. Sanchez, Al. II. Title

NA7224.6 .S26 2001

690'.8—dc21 2001031453

Published in

SUNSTONE PRESS
Post Office Box 2321
Santa Fe, NM 87504-2321 / USA
(505) 988-4418 / *orders only* (800) 243-5644
FAX (505) 988-1025
www.sunstonepress.com

IN MEMORIAM

Delfin Sanchez

Guadalupe "Lu" Martinez Sanchez

CONTENTS

ACKNOWLEDGMENTS / 9
INTRODUCTION / 11
CHAPTER 1. THE OLDEST BRAND NEW THING IN HOUSES / 17
The First New Mexico Adobes / 18
The Far Kingdom / 19
Newcomers from the East: Territorial and Mountain Styles / 24
A New Century: Revival, Depression, Revival / 29
A Happy, Holistic, High-Tech Heaven: The 1960s and 1970s / 34
Adapting to a New Millenium / 36
CHAPTER 2. ADOBE'S ADVANTAGES AND DRAWBACKS / 39
Safe at Home in Fort Adobe / 42
Adobe's Low Embodied Energy / 44
Thermal Mass, the Comfort Food of Architecture / 46
What About Adobe's Disadvantages? / 47
CHAPTER 3. HOW MUCH ENERGY DO YOU WANT TO SAVE? / 56
What Does It Mean, Being Green? / 57
The Energy Pie: Where the Money Really Goes / 57
The Big Players: Size, Fuel Type, Habits and Gadgets / 58
Heating, Cooling and the Building Skin / 60
The Solar Components / 64
Green Building Programs / 66
Sorting It Out / 69
CHAPTER 4. DESIGNING THE HEART OF A HOUSE / 70
Houses that Fit a Variety of Sites / 71
Houses that Fit Different Kinds of Families / 73
Houses that Fit a Wide Range of Budgets / 78
Houses that Maintain High Quality in Materials, Design and Comfort / 87

CHAPTER 5. THE PLANS / 93

Playing with the Plans / 93

The Plans / 99

CHAPTER 6. ARE WE ALMOST THERE? / 148

Where Do You Want to Live? / 148

Is This the Site that Suits You? / 155

What About Finances? / 159

The Bottom Line / 166

CHAPTER 7. ADOBE FROM THE GROUND UP / 167

Site Work / 167

Concrete / 170

Adobe Walls / 172

Framing / 174

Insulation / 176

Stucco and Plaster / 178

Windows and Exterior Doors / 180

Roofing / 182

Interiors and Kitchens / 184

Mechanical / 186

Electrical / 188

General Job Costs, Overhead and Profit / 189

APPENDIX: Working Drawings and Building Permits / 191

NOTES / 195

BIBLIOGRAPHY / 196

ABOUT THE AUTHORS / 198

ORDER FORM / 199

ACKNOWLEDGMENTS

More people than we can list enriched this book with their knowledge and help, but we would particularly like to thank the following.

For reading and commenting on the manuscript: John Finger, Sandy Schauer and Joseph Tibbets.

For offering expertise in history, building costs and technology and the housing market: Jay G. Davis, Tom and Ann Enea, Jim and Lefty Folkman, Anthony F. Gallegos, Paul G. McHenry, Richard Melzer, Felipe Otero, Bob Reule, Chuck Roberts, Alexandria Sanchez, Jerry Sanchez, Chris Vigil and Chris Williams.

For allowing us to take photographs and ask questions: Ralph Flores and Geri Rhodes, Mike Levison and Jenny Trindel, John and Diane Shoemaker, Michel Richard, Manuel Martinez, Perry Wilkes, La Puerta, Inc., Saxe-Patterson, Pojoaque Pueblo Museum and Visitors Center, Taos Historic Museums, Santa Fe Habitat for Humanity, and El Rancho de las Golondrinas.

INTRODUCTION

Down through the centuries earth-walled structures have housed more people than all other building materials combined. Today, though, only a small percentage of new homes are built of adobe. Why are we using this superb material at less than its full potential?

Our best guess is that adobe became trapped in its own mystique like an actor who once played Hamlet so splendidly that, afterwards, he was offered only Shakespearean roles. In the United States adobe houses have become typecast as expensive, high-maintenance, poorly-insulated, romantic relics of the past.

In truth, adobe is an amazingly versatile material. As we shall see in Chapter 1, for hundreds of years it dominated construction in the American Southwest and it can be used economically in a full range of structures. In recent years modern building techniques have further increased adobe's flexibility. A close look at adobe today dissolves most of the outdated myths that limit the material's use.

Myth #1: "Adobe requires too much maintenance. I remember visiting my grandfather's adobe house. Problems all the time! Every year we had to fix leaky roofs and replaster walls."

Adobe maintenance headaches were real and frequent—a hundred years ago. Today there's no reason to suffer such inconvenience unless your goal is replicating historical building techniques. In Chapter 2 we will look at adobe's physical qualities and the contemporary building techniques that complement them:

- Stabilized adobe bricks
- Roofs built with adequate drainage slope

- Cement exterior stucco
- Waterproof foundations

Myth #2: "Adobe walls don't have any insulating value so adobe houses are difficult to heat and cool."

In reality, adobe houses with double-glazed windows and modern roof insulation maintain a far more comfortable year-around temperature than frame houses. A 10" adobe wall with rigid 2" foam exterior insulation is all you need in a temperate climate. Chapter 3 digs into current myths about energy use and looks in detail at one of adobe's most desirable qualities—how well it works in solar homes.

In some quarters the perception persists that a solar-heated adobe house is an expensive hassle. It's true that the early days of solar technology produced some ridiculously complicated systems. However, the house designs shown in this book obtain a large portion of their heating from sunlight without the expense, complexity, and echo of exotic self-sacrifice once associated with solar-adobe homes.

Myth #3: "Personally, I'm not that crazy about the 'adobe look' with those tree trunk posts and viga ends sticking out everywhere."

Actually, we're not crazy about leaving the ends of *vigas* (roof beams made of tree trunks) exposed either. If not protected from rain, they rot. But more to the point, there is no single "adobe look." Pueblo Revival, or Santa Fe Style, originated early in the twentieth century in New Mexico and became typecast as the way adobes look, but it is only one of many adobe styles in the southwestern United States alone. The houses illustrated in this book are based on Pueblo and Mountain styles, but they can be finished to suit a variety of tastes as the following illustrations suggest.

According to myth, adobe can only be used in desert settings. The water-powered mills scattered through colonial New Mexico and other parts of the southwestern United States demonstrate that adobe structures do not require arid surroundings.This reconstruction of an historical mill at El Rancho de las Golondrinas south of Santa Fe, New Mexico, rises two and a half adobe stories above its stone foundation. *Photograph by author, courtesy of El Rancho de las Golondrinas.*

Orchard House as shown later in this book.

The basic form and floor plan of Orchard House can be adapted to many styles. Shown from the top, the currently fashionable "Anasazi" look, Post-Modern, Territorial, Mission, Pueblo and Mountain styles.

Myth #4: "Adobe construction is just too expensive. Doesn't an adobe house cost twice as much per square foot as a frame one?"

Not unless you want it to. It is true that huge, elaborately detailed adobe houses sitting on prime real estate cost a bundle but most of that expense results from the house's size, finish material, detailing and site-related costs rather than from using adobe.

Walls make up between 8% and 10% of a house's construction cost and about 5% of the total selling price of a house and lot. The cost difference between adobe walls and frame walls is even smaller.

We set out to make the houses featured in this book as flexible as possible. A major aspect of that flexibility is adjusting to

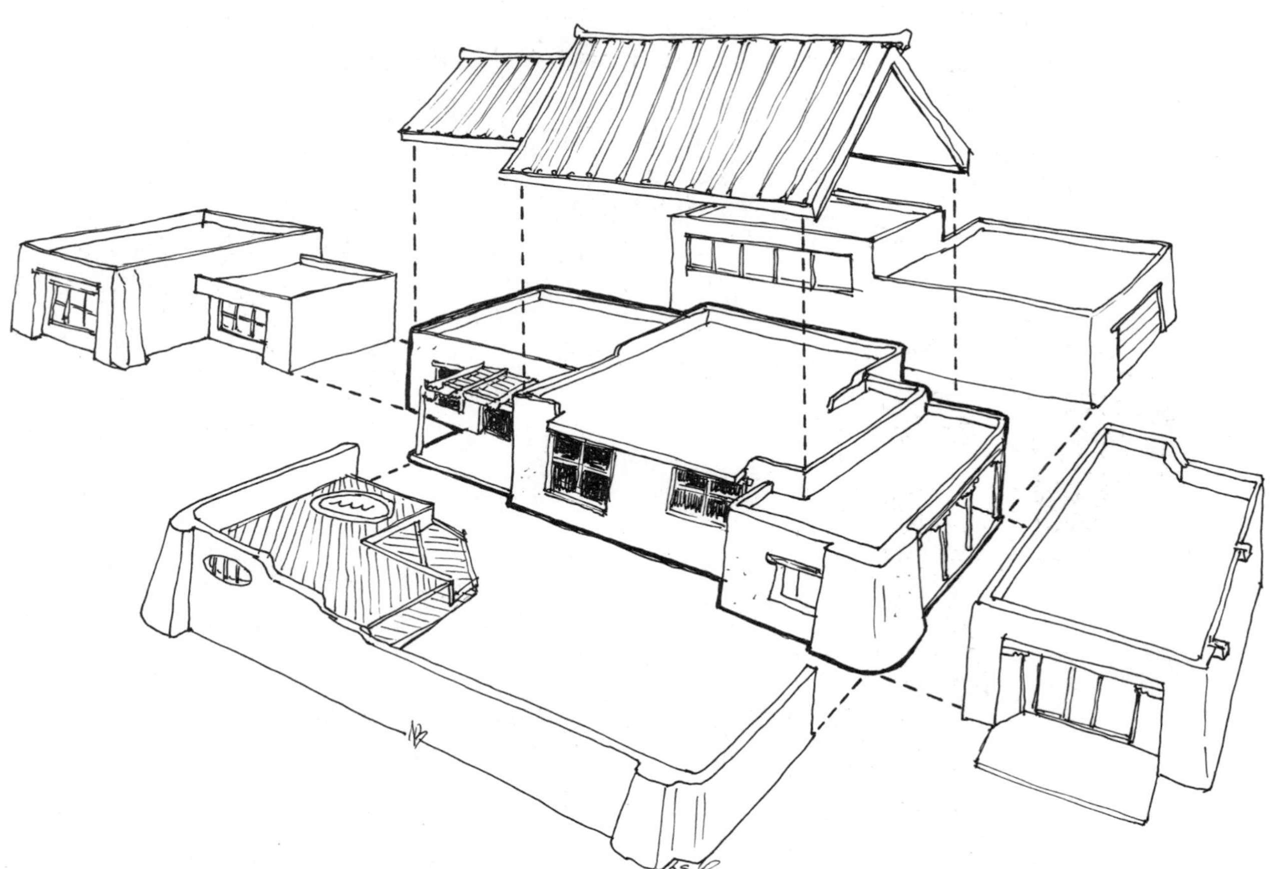

The basic core of Sun Hall House can wear a different roof or grow by adding the modules shown clockwise from the right: an owners' suite, outdoor living space, more bedrooms, a den and a garage.

a wide range of budgets. As we all know, it's much easier to increase the cost of a building project than to rein it in. We've done much of that hard work for you by distilling the twelve "Basic Houses" shown in this book into essential living spaces for an individual or small family. You can customize not only the layout, orientation and finish materials but also the size. The Basic Houses can grow to fit your changing needs.

The housing market today encourages us to buy far larger houses than we often want or need with the rational that someday in the future all that extra space might come in handy. In the meantime, these residential monsters can lead to unnecessarily huge mortgage payments and endless maintenance. The Basic Houses are designed for expansion so you can add space when *you* want or need it. Because the additions are planned from the beginning, they don't wreck the houses' looks, circulation and solar gain.

Adobe itself is an extremely versatile building material. But the designs sometimes imposed on it, along with outdated building techniques, can make it appear limited. In the following chapters we take a closer look at adobe myths and put together a "toolkit" of design guidelines, specific plans and construction processes that update and expand the possibilities of adobe houses.

1

THE OLDEST BRAND NEW THING IN HOUSES

If time travelers from the American Southwest of 800 years ago dropped in for a visit today, they would find much of your home mysterious and strange. Any walls built of adobe, though, would seem reassuringly familiar. The material has been used for almost a millenium in the southwestern United States and far longer in other parts of the world. Earth construction has been, in fact, the dominant human shelter ever since we started making buildings around 7000 B.C. Although earth-building traditions thrive in areas as unexpected as northern China and southern France, we'll stay in New Mexico for a brief look at the local version of adobe's long, versatile history.

An infinite variety of earth dwellings show up around the world.

A mosque beside the river Nile? No. The adobe Dar al Islam mosque beside the Rio Chama near Abiquiu, New Mexico.

Our time travelers would also be amazed at the Southwest's sprawling suburbs built of imported lumber, metal and brick rather than the earth around them. A region's building traditions evolve for logical reasons. Often the dominant building type is the most comfortable for a particular climate. Usually the most popular materials are locally plentiful. In the Southwest, the reasons for adobe's lasting popularity are easy to understand: lots of dirt, few trees.

THE FIRST NEW MEXICO ADOBES

A few miles south of Albuquerque, New Mexico, Isleta Pueblo sits beside the region's dominant river, the Rio Grande. On a visit to the pueblo to discuss aspects of their housing projects, we met Paul Lujan, an Isleta draftsman, on the highway outside the pueblo and followed him to the tribal offices. Paul had wisely avoided trying to give us exact directions. Isleta Pueblo existed long before cars (before horse-drawn wagons, for that matter) and its unmarked, winding streets serenely ignore the modern urban grid.

Above the rooftops rises the adobe bulk of St. Augustine Church, begun in 1613 and rebuilt in 1716. Adobe houses circle out from the church; like tree rings, the oldest are the closest in. But adobe homes are also going up amid frame houses and trailers in newer neighborhoods.

The word "Pueblo" has many meanings. In 1540 when Spanish explorers first entered New Mexico, they encountered people living in large, clustered apartment buildings of adobe and stone. Reminded of their own European and Mexican towns, the newcomers called the densely populated communities "pueblos." The word's primary meaning in Spanish is "village" but it also means "a people," and the multiple meanings still apply. "Pueblo" can refer to Native Americans of the Tiwa, Tewa, Towa, Zuni or Keresan language groups; to a "township" that is also a sovereign body, such as Isleta Pueblo or Sandia Pueblo; to a village itself as opposed to the land around it; or to the entire expanse of land owned by a particular tribe.

A thousand years ago the Anasazi people were building sophisticated complexes of stone masonry that still stand at Chaco Canyon in New Mexico, Colorado's Mesa Verde and smaller sites. When pueblo groups migrated into the Rio Grande valley around 1200 A.D., though, they began building houses with earth walls. Most early pueblo structures were made of coursed adobe. The builders placed handfuls of mud atop a cobble foundation to form a "starter" wall, or course, approximately 20" high and 10" wide. The mud was then shaped by hand into a smooth, compact mass. Once this lower course dried, the next course was added, and so on, until the walls reached the desired level, sometimes as high as three stories.[1]

It is unclear whether the molded sun-dried adobe bricks familiar today were used before the Spanish came. At any rate, after the arrival of Spanish settlers and priests, sun-dried brick began to dominate the area's architecture.

THE FAR KINGDOM

When they spoke of it at all, bureaucrats in baroque, cosmopolitan seventeenth century Mexico City referred to the land that would become New Mexico as the "Miserable Kingdom." It was poor, dangerous and utterly isolated—the most remote outpost of the Spanish Crown.

That isolation persisted through the Mexican Revolution and the opening of the Santa Fe Trail in 1821, survived the growing

Remnants of the oldest house in the United States survive near downtown Santa Fe, New Mexico. The house's lower walls of coursed adobe, built around 1200 A.D., are the last trace of the earlier Pueblo of Analco.

Just down the street from the oldest house stands the first church building begun in the United States, San Miguel Chapel. The oldest part of the adobe structure dates from 1610.

Several centuries of New Mexico architectural styles line a Santa Fe alley. Brick coping from the Territorial era tops the parapets of the nearest dwelling while the center house displays the simple masses of pueblo buildings. Modern construction lies beneath the stucco of the far structure.

Then as now, builders supported the roofs of adobe structures with beams made of whole tree trunks (*vigas*) such as these in a lumberyard near Española, New Mexico.

commerce and settlement that followed the United States's takeover in 1848, withstood the railroad's arrival in 1880, and persisted through statehood in 1912. Not until after World War II did much of New Mexico finally wander into the modern American world. Left to itself for centuries, the area developed unique building traditions that still thrive today.

The dwellings of Spanish Colonial New Mexico grew along with the households they sheltered. As marriages and births increased the size of families, new rooms were built onto the ends of a house for extra living quarters. In larger houses the added rooms eventually enclosed a central patio, a pleasant layout used in some of the "Basic Adobe" expansion plans shown later in this book.

Until the second half of the nineteenth century, building styles and methods changed little from those of the pueblos: earth walls topped by *vigas* and roofed with smaller trunks or branches that supported in turn a layer of earth for insulation. Large dwellings served, in effect, as forts. Few windows pierced the outer walls. Often the only opening was the *zaguan*, a gate with double doors wide enough to admit a wagon into the safety of the enclosed courtyard.

The Hacienda de los Martinez, begun around 1804 near Taos, is one of the few New Mexico buildings to retain its colonial appearance. The original four rooms to the left of the *zaguan* were eventually expanded to twenty-one rooms that housed the family, servants, workshops, storage areas and chapel. Today the house, furnished much as it was in its hey-day, is a part of the Taos Historic Museums system.

The Hacienda de los Martinez. *Photograph by author, courtesy Taos Historic Museums.*

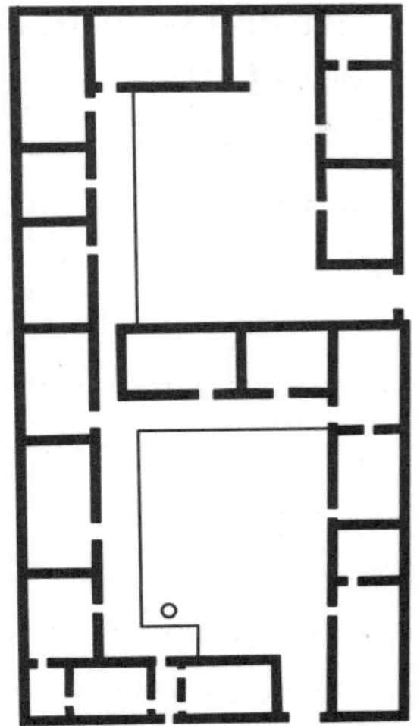

The floor plan of the Martinez house shows rooms arranged around front and rear *placitas*, or courtyards. Except during the worst weather, daily living took place outdoors in these courtyards and the *portales*, or porches, around them. *Sketch by author, courtesy Taos Historic Museums.*

A tunnel-like adobe passageway connects the two Martinez *placitas*. The front courtyard served family and trading activities; the rear courtyard was used for servants' quarters and workshops. *Photograph by author, courtesy Taos Historic Museums.*

NEWCOMERS FROM THE EAST: TERRITORIAL AND MOUNTAIN STYLES

The Territorial style took its name in retrospect from the United States's 1850 annexation of New Mexico as a territory. Although features of the style soon appeared in newly built U.S. military installations, the building fashion only became dominant after the coming of the railroad in 1880. Along with milled lumber, glass and fired brick, the trains brought news of enticing and elaborate building styles popular in the outside world.

Greek Revival detailing, already passé in the eastern United States, blended with adobe to produce the Territorial style. Exteriors combined adobe's soft contours and warm colors with painted, precisely milled columns trimmed head and foot. Windows grew larger and more numerous. Both doors and windows acquired elaborate pediments, jambs and sills. Another new arrival, fired red brick, protected the tops of parapets from rain. Contact with the East also popularized a new type of floor plan, a squarish layout with rooms opening off a central hallway. The new, compact floor plans were often topped with pitched roofs.

During the Territorial era porches moved from courtyards to front yards and windows showed off the fashionable new millwork.

Built around 1860, the Padre Gallegos house in downtown Santa Fe, New Mexico, combines the traditional courtyard layout with Territorial wood trim and brick-topped parapets.

Compact floor plans such as used in this Socorro, New Mexico, house became increasingly popular in the late nineteenth and early twentieth century.

Another Socorro house with a square layout shows Victorian influence in the trim of the porch posts.

On the heels of the neoclassical influence, late Victorian revival styles arrived one after another, collided with adobe and local ingenuity, and brought forth buildings rich and strange. In 1880 the Santa Fe Railroad wanted to extend its tracks south of Albuquerque through Los Lunas, New Mexico. The desired route ran through the lands of the powerful Luna-Otero clan, directly, in fact, through the existing Luna home. As part of the right-of-way settlement, the railroad agreed to build the Lunas a new house in whatever style they preferred. The widely traveled family decided on

Lunas's new house built by the railroad.

a mansion like ones they had seen in the South—built of adobe, of course.

Although New Mexico's high altitude valleys are often chilly, rainy, and surrounded by forests, mountain dwellers still built frequently with adobe. In rural and mountainous areas, a third distinct style arose in the late nineteenth and early twentieth centuries, the Mountain style.

When milled lumber and corrugated metal roofing arrived by rail, Mountain style houses began to acquire steeply pitched "tin" roofs that shed the heavy snows. The trend intensified during World War II when local men sent home military paychecks to pay for the expensive new roofs.

Mountain style porch and window details were plainer versions of Territorial millwork. The elements blended into simple but well-proportioned houses that usually followed the single-file room layout, either straight or L-shaped. If building sites allowed, houses were situated with a long side facing south to be warmed by the winter sun. The Mountain style adapted adobe—a material associated with desert landscapes—to survive a colder, wetter climate.

"Mountain" houses weren't always in the mountains. This house is in La Joya, New Mexico, near the Rio Grande. It shows the classic single file of rooms and a long porch.

Many Mountain style houses were L-shaped with a porch in the L. The porch floor and eave height of this house near Velarde, New Mexico, indicate the high ceilings that gave the houses a distinctive profile.

Today the Mountain style is enjoying a rivival, as are other New Mexico traditions such as the art of carving and painting traditional religious images, or *santos*. On a hill near the village of Chimayo, wood carver and *santero* Manuel Martinez is building a new studio in the traditional Mountain style. The building and its future contents will complement each other.

The new studio of Manuel Martinez.

Manuel Martinez stands beside the exterior staircase to the attic of his studio. In the old days, attic space under the steeply sloped rafters of Mountain houses was used to dry and store food. Manuel uses the attic for more work space.

A NEW CENTURY: REVIVAL, DEPRESSION, REVIVAL

At the end of the nineteenth century, New Mexicans were erecting adobe buildings in any European revival style that became fashionable. Then, in the early years of the twentieth century something very different happened. The state's inhabitants stopped chasing after exotic foreign styles and began reviving their own local architecture.

The late architectural historian Jerome Iowa cites buildings on the University of New Mexico's Albuquerque campus as the first examples of the Pueblo Revival style. In 1906, college president William G. Tight and members of a local fraternity built a round, underground chamber in conscious imitation of the round, underground kivas used by pueblo religious societies. Then in 1908 Hodgin Hall, the school's first academic building, was remodeled from its original Romanesque style to look like a small three-story pueblo.[2]

The UNM Kiva (or "Estufa") survives, now isolated between two streets.

Although Hodgin Hall's form could hardly be more different from that of the Kiva, both originated in the same Pueblo Revival enthusiasm.

The Sagebrush Inn, built in the late 1920s in Taos, New Mexico, is an exuberant example of commercialized Pueblo Revival style from its buttresses to the "mission bell" over the entry area.

The appeal of Pueblo Revival's sculptural massing, sensuous surfaces and rugged detailing made the "new" style immediately popular, particularly with newcomers. It soon came to symbolize New Mexico and still does today under the alias Santa Fe Style, but the revival had an unforeseen consequence. Earlier, New Mexicans built imported styles in adobe. The Pueblo Revival period began the practice of applying "adobe style" to materials other than adobe.

Yet even while adobe style was migrating to other materials, adobe construction found a new role during the Depression years in large-scale government projects. On May 1, 1935, people from Oklahoma and northern New Mexico gathered for a public lottery in Valencia County, south of Albuquerque. Their farms had been wiped out by drought; their hopes were pinned on being one of forty-two families whose names would be drawn that day. The families who won the lottery won the chance to buy one of forty-two farm-size parcels of government-owned land along the Rio Grande. Each parcel would include a house made of adobe, the ubiquitous local building material.

The federal government's Resettlement Administration oversaw the project but the WPA (Works Progress Administration) cleared the land, made the adobes and built the homes.[3] The area eventually became the village of Bosque Farms and these first houses acquired the nickname "Bosque Originals." They are so prized for their thick adobe walls, pleasant proportions, wide window trim and *viga* ceilings that forty-one of the forty-two homes still exist today, a remarkable survival record.

Even while the WPA was erecting the Bosque Originals and adobe public buildings in Pueblo Revival style, architect John Gaw Meem launched the Territorial Revival style. Like its inspiration, Territorial Revival combined flat roofs, simple volumes, stucco finish and crisp, painted wood detailing. The style's components were so easy to expand into large-scale public buildings and so simple to translate into frame and concrete block that only rarely were Territorial Revival buildings made of adobe.

After World War II, Territorial and Pueblo Revival styles were widely adapted in the region for mid- and low-cost houses built of wood frame or structural clay tile. Builders and developers looked at the flat roofs and simple woodwork and saw an inexpensive way to trim out a building. Adobe style became completely divorced from adobe construction.

A Bosque Original today. With the exception of the front window shades, the house has undergone little exterior remodeling.

A block down the street from the Territorial era Padre Gallegos house shown previously, this Territorial Revival building houses Santa Fe's public library and a police substation.

The "Roundhouse," New Mexico's state capitol, throws a curve at typically straight-edged Territorial Revival style.

End of the trail for adobe styling? "Pueblo" style manufactured housing has appeared in recent years, at times complete with protruding *viga* ends.

A HAPPY, HOLISTIC, HIGH-TECH HEAVEN: THE 1960S AND 1970S

In New Mexico "The Sixties" brought not only upheavals in political and social philosophies but experiments in house design and technology. Local and immigrant young people looking for more environmentally sensible ways to live discovered adobe and used it to construct amoeba-shaped dwellings, homes topped by geodesic domes, bottle houses, can houses and half-buried hobbit hutches. More than progressive beliefs drove the infatuation with adobe. Most of the new builders possessed little construction experience or cash; adobe was a forgiving material and cheap if you made your own bricks.

Meanwhile, the energy crisis of 1973 spurred traditional adobe builders to investigate solar heating. They discovered (more accurately, rediscovered) that passive solar design was a natural partner for adobe construction. The trends merged. South-facing windows and a wood stove cost far less to install and operate than a central heating system, and solar heating appealed as a clean, off-grid energy source.

The new adobe experimenters sought a life in harmony with the natural world. Ironically, their efforts benefited from groundbreaking, high-tech research in solar-adobe performance underway at the Los Alamos National Laboratory. Los Alamos scientists built adobe test cells to collect accurate data, monitored the effect of adobe as thermal mass and calculated solar savings fractions. Through various channels, the information quickly made its way to solar-adobe builders. The design ferment produced effective solar-adobe styles still built today.

This compound near Taos, New Mexico, exhibits the classic components of 1960s and 1970s building experiments: greenhouse spaces, clerestories, domes and other nonrectangular structures.

Though its finish work is more refined, this adobe house south of Taos, New Mexico, drew its basic design straight out of the 1970s.

ADAPTING TO A NEW MILLENIUM

The ten-unit compound designed by architect John Midyette.

In the southwestern United States, adobe use began in multifamily housing and that function has revived in recent years. Among adobe condominium complexes built since the 1970s is this ten-unit compound designed by architect John Midyette on Bishop's Lodge Road in Santa Fe. Adobe's ability to resist fire and to buffer noise make it well suited for the separation walls required between dwelling units.

The tower at the Pojoaque Pueblo Museum and Visitors Center challenges the perception that adobe structures can only be low and sprawling. Pojoaque is located centrally among the six Tewa-

Pojoaque Pueblo Museum and Visitors Center.

speaking pueblos in northern New Mexico. The three-story tower houses the Poeh Arts Program, which offers students from the pueblos traditional art instruction incorporating the Tewa world view. The small windows in the tower establish sight lines to other existing or vanished pueblos.

A Habitat for Humanity home.

Santa Fe, mecca of the multi-million dollar adobe estate, is also home to affordable adobe houses. On the west side of town, five Habitat for Humanity homes like this one cluster on a single, sloping lot—the best-looking Habitat houses around. As with all Habitat projects, donated materials, volunteer labor and cost-effective size helped keep expenses down. An adobe pressing machine speeded up brick production. But perhaps most important, the Habitat group was willing to challenge the current mythology that there's no way to build affordable houses in adobe.

Architect Knight Seavey designed his house to curve around a commanding, boulder-strewn site in the foothills of the Sandia Mountains overlooking Albuquerque, New Mexico. The house takes advantage of adobe's plasticity and acknowledges historical forms without resorting to stereotyped imitation.

Even as adobe takes on new roles, its traditional uses endure. Outside of science fiction, humans have yet to achieve time travel but old adobe houses easily perform the feat, sailing smoothly on through style fads and technical innovations. Part of the durability of adobe houses results from their mystique—they are often treasured and maintained by a succession of owners. Part of the durability results from the comfort, safety and sculptural malleability that give adobe an edge over other building materials. In the next chapter, we'll meet an adobe time traveler and explore the physical properties that give adobe its advantages.

2

ADOBE'S ADVANTAGES AND DRAWBACKS

In the year 1692, young Captain Ignacio Roybal rode north through the Kingdom of New Spain with the forces of Diego de Vargas. The members of the expedition, which started from present-day El Paso, Texas, did not know what they would find if and when they reached their destination, present-day Santa Fe, New Mexico. Twelve years earlier during the pueblo revolt, all Hispanic inhabitants of New Mexico had been killed or driven south of El Paso.

After several years of sporadic fighting the Spanish regained control of the area. Around 1705 Ignacio Roybal began building a house north of Santa Fe. Then in 1757 Don Ignacio, full of years and honors, died. Of the house, his will says only that it "consists of seventeen rooms, and in one of these there is a spinning wheel/ loom for weaving coarse wool."[1]

But we know the house was built of adobe because portions of it still stand and because in 1705 Don Ignacio had no other practical choice of building material. Almost 300 years later, Don Ignacio's great-great-great-great-great-great grandson, author Alex Sanchez, has lots of choices but, like many others in the southwestern United States, prefers to live in an adobe house.

The aesthetic and psychological qualities of adobe houses have long beguiled artists and travelers as well as the houses' owners. The material's organic, sculptural quality shows up in features as prominent as a massive buttress or as subtle as a one-degree bend in a wall. And the cool, quiet peace, the sense of solidity and permanence, that characterize earth-built dwellings is not imaginary. Thick exterior walls moderate changes in temperature, reduce sound transmission from the outside world and survive onslaughts that demolish less durable construction.

The Ignacio Roybal house today. The original building probably formed a quadrangle enclosing the well whose housing is visible in the center of the photograph. No doubt the house looked more like the Martinez house shown in Chapter 1 when first built but it has been extensively remodeled over the centuries.

A portion of the north side of the Roybal house with its present day Territorial trim.

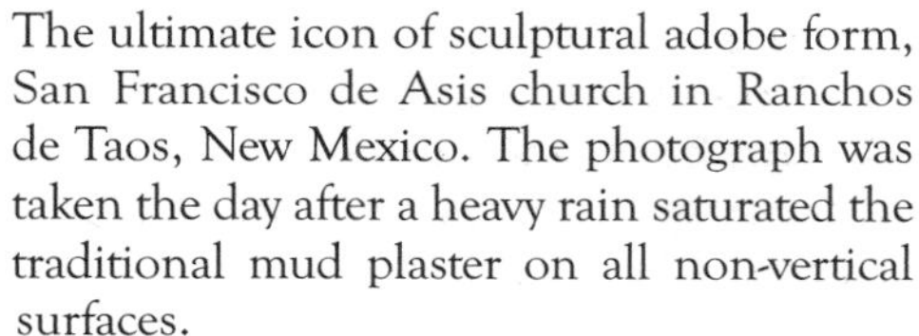

The ultimate icon of sculptural adobe form, San Francisco de Asis church in Ranchos de Taos, New Mexico. The photograph was taken the day after a heavy rain saturated the traditional mud plaster on all non-vertical surfaces.

Sometimes the organic (well, animate) quality of adobe and stucco goes over the top, as happened on this playful Santa Fe fence.

In this chapter we turn from adobe's subjective, sensory qualities to objective data about its performance as a building material. The first sections of the chapter look at adobe's safety, environmental efficiency and thermal comfort. The last section examines qualities often cited as drawbacks of adobe construction to see which are real problems and which are misconceptions.

SAFE AT HOME IN FORT ADOBE

In a world where the media tell us far more than we want to know about dangers and disasters, adobe walls make secure ramparts against the outside world. Adobe doesn't burn, blow away or turn to Swiss cheese under gunfire.

Every year fires kill more Americans than all natural disasters combined. National Fire Data Center figures show that 80% of those deaths occur in homes. Anything that reduces the risk is worth a look. Fire can make an adobe house unlivable because the house's contents and wood components will burn. Yet odds are high that a fire in your adobe home won't take you with it. Two characteristics reduce fire danger in adobe structures: slower flame spread and non-toxic materials.

Traditional New Mexico *hornos* are beehive-shaped ovens made from adobe and used for baking bread and roasting meat. These adobe "fire-boxes" point up the obvious—masonry walls don't catch fire. An adobe wall has a four-hour fire rating; that is, it takes more than four hours for fire to affect the strength of the wall. Perhaps more important, adobe walls reduce the amount of combustible surface available to fires started by cooking, heating or faulty wiring.

According to the National Fire Protection Association, 75% of people killed in fires die from inhaling smoke and poisonous gases. Adobe exposed to fire does not produce the toxic smoke and fumes that, combined with lightning-fast spread, make mobile home fires so lethal.

We often assume that we don't need to worry about home fires because we live in the United States, an advanced country with stringent building codes, community fire departments and a relatively new housing stock. In reality, Federal Emergency Management Agency statistics show that the United States leads the industrialized world in fire-related injuries and deaths. So far, no one has pinned down

Hornos at the Hacienda de los Martinez. Mud plaster mixed with straw covers the adobe walls of the ovens. Plywood protects the openings when the *hornos* are not in use. *(Photograph by author. Courtesy the Taos Historic Museums.)*

exactly why. Possible suspects include relatively isolated homes, the heavy use of noxious synthetics in U.S. houses, the huge number of mobile homes, and a national fondness for arson.

Adobe's weight gives it another life saving quality—wind resistance. The afternoon we were roughing out text about wind and adobe, the evening news announced that a severe storm had just ripped through the small village of Tomé, New Mexico, about six miles south of our house. The coincidence compelled us to go check out the damage.

Amazingly, no one was seriously injured by the storm but water covered sections of road and leaves ripped from cottonwoods littered the landscape. We reached ground zero—a neighborhood of mobile homes behind the Tomé post office. Trees had fallen, power lines had snapped. Siding was peeled away from trailers like torn wrapping paper. The roof of one home had blown completely off and its walls were splayed open like a stomped shoebox. Another trailer had been dumped upside down thirty feet from its foundation.

On the other side of the highway, an old adobe house peered from under the fallen trees that almost covered it; the house walls had suffered no damage.

A linear foot of frame wall finished with stucco and gypsum board weighs about 180 pounds, and a mobile home wall can be significantly lighter. A linear foot of adobe wall with stucco and plaster weighs a minimum of 950 pounds. It won't blow away.

And to end on a lurid note, there's gunfire. An essay in a 1998 issue of *The New York Times Magazine* provoked a good bit of indignation in New Mexico. The article's author, a recent arrival, asserted that the sublime physical beauty of Taos concealed a dark and dangerous soul. Local crime statistics and edgy run-ins with residents had stoked the author's fears. Eventually a friend's experience sent her to the gun shop: "A friend called to tell me that at 3:00 A.M. she woke to gunshots under her window, and when police arrived they found six bullet holes in the adobe wall of her house."[2]

The point of this story is the phrase "bullet holes *in* the adobe wall." The bullets did not penetrate through the wall, nor did they penetrate the writer's friend. Anecdotal evidence of adobe's protective quality is supported by statistical data. In 1998 Joseph M. Tibbets of the Southwest Solaradobe School performed bullet penetration tests on adobe. On average, bullets from a range of firearms—Glock 40 caliber, FEG 380, and Colt 45 pistols, as well as 9mm rifles and a 20-gauge shotgun—penetrated an unplastered adobe wall less than 2".[3]

ADOBE'S LOW EMBODIED ENERGY

The true cost of the energy used to produce a material—the total BTUs required to extract, refine, ship, manufacture, package, transport and install a material—is called its embodied energy quotient. (BTU stands for British Thermal Unit, the amount of heat required to raise the temperature of one pound of water one degree Fahrenheit. One BTU is approximately the amount of heat produced by burning one wooden kitchen match.) Adobe has a very low embodied energy quotient, only 2,500 BTUs per brick. How low becomes apparent when adobe is compared to a roughly equal volume of other masonry materials:[4]

2 adobes (1120 cubic in.)	5,000 BTU
1 concrete block (1024 cubic in.)	29,018 BTU
14 common red bricks (1120 cubic in.)	189,980 BTU

Adobes require little energy because their manufacture is so straightforward and because most bricks are used within fifty miles of where they are made. Traditionally, adobes are made by digging sand and clay soils, mixing them with water (and recently, emulsifiers), pouring the mix into ladder-shaped forms and letting the adobes dry in the sun. Newer manufacturing methods use a machine to pressure-form damp dirt into durable bricks. Machine-made adobes use more energy, but they are still BTU misers compared with other wall materials.

Ideally, the crew at an adobe yard loads finished bricks onto a truck, drives to a building site and parks alongside a wall. Then the builder's masonry crew mounts the truck bed and lays the adobes directly into mortar on the rising wall.

Adobe manufacturing in New Mexico. From the foreground, a stack of ladder-shaped forms for molding the adobes, newly made bricks, and beyond, adobes turned on edge to finish drying.

A mason laying adobes from the delivery truck.

THERMAL MASS, THE COMFORT FOOD OF ARCHITECTURE

A 1981 issue of *Architectural Record* included a short article titled, "From Teepee to Solar-Heated Mobile Homes: Experimental Houses for New Mexican Indians."[5] The article described a pilot program then underway at Tesuque Pueblo north of Santa Fe. The goal was to encase a mobile home entirely in adobe, strip the south side of the trailer down to the studs, install a Trombe wall and glazing, put on a new roof, install storm windows over the original trailer windows, insulate the outside of the adobe and stucco the whole thing for a "hacienda-like appearance."

Yes, well. Let us briefly note that we have never seen New Mexico Indians living year-round in "teepees," and that building in adobe from scratch would have been easier. More to the point, the article acknowledges that comfortable, economical heating requires thermal mass.

Great-Granny was manipulating thermal mass on winter nights when she heated a brick and stuck it under the bed covers to keep her feet warm. Heat always migrates from warmer to cooler materials, whether air, wood, water, metal, adobe or shivering human flesh. When solar or furnace heat warms the air in your house, that heat slowly seeps into various materials—the thermal mass—within the enclosed space. Then, as the air in the room cools, the materials gradually release their stored heat into the air in an attempt to equalize

The doorway reveals the width of the adobe walls that provide thermal comfort for this new house.

temperatures. Denser materials generally absorb, store and release heat more effectively. Adobe works well as thermal mass because it is about four times as dense as the densest component of frame walls, the wood studs.

Thermal mass makes a house comfortable because it "evens out" both short-term and long-term temperature swings. You may be all too familiar with short-term swings if you live in a house built of lightweight materials. The furnace comes on for half an hour, the house gets uncomfortably hot. The furnace shuts off, cold creeps back immediately.

Longer 24-hour temperature swings occur in climates where night and day temperatures differ significantly. (In central New Mexico, daytime highs and nighttime lows commonly differ by 30 to 40 degrees Fahrenheit.) Sufficient thermal mass greatly reduces a house's heating and cooling costs in these climates. In summer, opening windows at night allows a house to expel heat and remain cool for most of the next day. In winter, thermal mass allows efficient solar heating, a subject explored in more depth in Chapter 3.

WHAT ABOUT ADOBE'S DISADVANTAGES?

A handful of negative images have become so attached to adobe that they discourage potential builders from investigating the material. Most of these perceived problems, however, result from using out-of-date construction materials and methods.

Leaky Roofs

Flat roofs on old adobe houses often leaked. The weight of the thick layer of soil used for roof insulation caused beams to sag so that rain ponded in the middle of the roof and seeped through. Ponding leaks also plague newer asphalt-coated flat roofs if they are built with no drainage slope at all. But competent residential contractors no longer install truly flat roofs. Over *viga* or beam ceilings, slope is built up with tapered insulation or additional framing members that create a slanted top surface. The top members of "flat" roof trusses have drainage slope built in. With sufficient slope and proper detailing at parapets, valleys and skylights, there's no more reason for the roof to leak over an adobe house than over a frame one.

Along the back parapet you can see a slight slope from the central ridge of this "flat" truss roof that directs water to the *canales* (or scuppers) in the parapets.

Melting Walls

Old houses often suffered damage resulting from walls that rested at ground level on cobble foundations; water "wicked" up from wet ground into unstabilized adobe. Today the bottom course and often an entire wall are built of stabilized or semi-stabilized bricks. Walls are now supported at least 6" above the ground on concrete or concrete block foundations. These practices generally eliminate problems. If a building site is very damp or has a high water table, a foundation wall mopped with bituminous waterproofing and a footing drain will prevent damage as effectively for adobe structures as for other building materials.

Traditional unstabilized adobes are made of clay, sand, water and possibly straw. Fully stabilized adobe bricks include between 5% and 12% asphalt emulsion. Semi-stabilized bricks include about half that amount. The emulsion very effectively prevents water damage. Building codes require stabilized adobes in some situations. For instance, the New Mexico code requires fully stabilized adobes for the first course of a wall. Most adobes manufactured today are fully or partially stabilized, as are the mortars used with them. Adding cement to the mud mix will also stabilize the adobes but the cement additive is more expensive than asphalt.

For twenty years this stack of semi-stabilized adobes has sat in the authors' back yard, completely unprotected from the weather and basically undamaged.

Walls of semi-stabilized brick line a river bridge approach in Albuquerque. Although the walls are fully exposed to weather and splashed by passing traffic, they have held up satisfactorily.

On the other hand, unstabilized adobe can deteriorate rapidly as this west-facing fence demonstrates. Unstabilized, machine-compressed bricks are particularly vulnerable if left exposed.

High Upkeep Exteriors

In the old days, adobe exteriors were replastered every year or so with the same mud that formed the adobes. No cement or plastic-based stucco was available. The mud plaster bonded completely with the underlying bricks and the mud produced a subtle, sensuous finish that cement can never match. But the frequent plastering, usually done by women, took a lot of work. Even with replastering, roof drains that allowed water to splash on the base of the walls caused erosion, and rain gradually wore down the parapets. Today's standard stucco finishes last as long on adobe houses as on frame ones.

Opinions vary sharply about using cement stucco instead of mud plaster on adobe. The argument is that if small cracks in the stucco admit water, the less permeable stucco can trap the moisture, not only damaging the adobe wall but also concealing the damage under an apparently sound surface. Semi-stabilized bricks, however, are resistant to the type of moisture damage reported on historic buildings of made of unstabilized adobe. Waterproof foundations and 2" rigid insulation applied to the exterior side of the bricks also protect walls from moisture. On any stucco-finish building, however, it is wise to patch cracks as soon as possible to reduce the chance of damage.

Applying the base coat of cement stucco to wire netting on an L-shaped adobe column. Stucco is usually applied in three separate coats.

Another potential problem is that nothing bonds very well with adobe bricks except mortars and plasters of similar composition. Applying the stucco over a wire netting or mesh helps compensate for the lack of natural bonding.

As with any structure, exposed wood at windows, doors and trim requires maintenance. Today, though, metal windows and metal or vinyl cladding on wood windows have practically eliminated the upkeep on the windows themselves. Newer, better sealing techniques used for double glazing have cut leaking and condensation problems dramatically.

Inadequate Insulation

The idea that you can't adequately insulate adobe walls comes not from adobe but from ideas about insulation that have no factual basis. The next chapter addresses adobe, solar heat, and myths and misconceptions about energy use in detail.

High Cost

Yes, an adobe house can cost well into seven figures, but it doesn't have to. As discussed throughout this book, the house's cost depends primarily on size, design and finish material choices rather than on the use of adobe *per se*. Having said that, let us add that some elements of adobe houses will cost more than comparable wood frame equivalents under any circumstances:

This Socorro, New Mexico, house has preserved the handsome, if high-maintenance, trim at gable and bay but replaced the original windows with newer, more efficient ones.

Exterior walls: A framing crew usually erects a house's exterior wood stud walls in a couple of days, while an adobe crew may take a week or more to lay up masonry units. How much this adds to the bid varies greatly depending on local wages.

Insulation and stucco: Applying rigid insulation to the exterior of adobe walls costs about 2-1/2 times as much per square foot as installing batt insulation between the studs of a frame wall. Adobe exteriors also require a greater amount of stucco to smooth out surface irregularities that don't appear in ruler-straight, sheathed frame walls.

Electrical wiring: Instead of one visit, an electrician usually needs two trips to an adobe job, one to lay horizontal wiring runs between courses as the walls go up and another for overhead wiring once the roof is framed. How much adobe walls boost a bid depends heavily on an electrician's familiarity with and liking for adobe.

The bottom line? The cost of exterior walls generally totals around 5% of the total cost of a house and lot. A variance in wall costs doesn't make that much difference in the overall budget.

No Adobe Supply Nearby

Yes, this truly is a stopper. We're not such rabid Missionaries of Mud that we insist on adobe for readers who live hundreds of miles from the nearest adobe yard. If that's your situation, you don't have much recourse other than making your own adobes, using an adobe pressing machine or building your house of another material. After considerable investigation, Rastra seems the best alternative for mass-wall houses.

Not long ago friends in Taos told us, "Iron Mike's building a Rastra house."

We were extremely interested because we were tracking down data and experiences with various materials used to build 10" to 16" thick walls. We headed for the property of Mike Levison and Jenny Trindel south of Taos in the small community of Talpa. In a deep green pasture sloping to a tree-lined stream, we found a house with the lovely, simple proportions of traditional New Mexico adobes, a house made of material invented thirty years ago in Austria.

"Rastra" is the brand name for panels made of 85% recycled polystyrene and 15% cement. Hollow cores run horizontally and vertically through the panels. After Rastra units are placed in position and bonded with glue, the cores are filled with concrete and reinforcing to form a structural grid. Standard wall panels are 15" tall, 10' long and between 8" and 14" thick.

Tests conducted by the manufacturer list 70,000 pounds per linear foot as the load that an un-reinforced, concrete-filled wall will support before it collapses. Recent testing suggests a Rastra wall resists earthquake stresses seven times better than a wood-frame wall with solid sheathing.[6] As for insulation value, preliminary data indicate that a 10" Rastra wall has an R-value of 24, more insulation than you need in all but the coldest climates.

Mike and Jenny's house in Talpa.

Because Mike wanted the soft-edged, sculptured look of adobe, he trimmed the sharp corners of the Rastra at doors and windows with a saw and rasp.

"Iron Mike" did not get his nickname from winning Tough Man Contests or steering ships, but from designing and fabricating metal furniture. He is accustomed to working at a high level of craftsmanship and considers Rastra a relatively easy material to use. Wiring installation requires simply cutting a kerf into the panels with the tip of a chain saw and then gently tamping the wiring into the slot. Wood plates bolted to the top of the walls support the rafters.

A ledger board bolted to the wall supports porch framing.

In New Mexico a contractor-built Rastra wall "sandwich" with stucco and plaster costs between 10% and 15% more per square foot than a completed adobe wall. "Cost" includes more than money directly out of your pocket. Although Rastra's use of recycled expanded polystyrene foam is admirable, Rastra has a greater environmental impact than adobe. *Environmental Building News* points out that a Rastra wall uses slightly more cement than a concrete wall of the same thickness.[7] Cement manufacture is energy-intensive and releases significant amount of carbon dioxide.

3

HOW MUCH ENERGY DO YOU WANT TO SAVE?

"Green building" practices can have a big impact, positive or negative, on your budget. Green, or environmentally aware, houses are sometimes characterized as expensive hassles, partly because the most elaborate, photogenic showcase homes get the most publicity. Yet green houses can be great money savers that reduce both your utility bills and your maintenance headaches. Conservation features like those used in the Basic Houses bring you direct financial, health, comfort and community benefits without raising a house's price:

- Living in a green home minimizes utility bills
- Using green materials eliminates the "sick building" syndrome
- Green homes put less stress on local power, water, and waste disposal services, lowering utility bills for everyone
- Green homes conserve resources used for building materials
- A green home can qualify for mortgage breaks
- Energy conservation ratings can boost a home's resale value an average of $8400[1]

In this chapter we talk a lot about costs but not because money is green building's only important aspect. Energy costs simply offer an objective score card that compares the outcomes resulting from various choices. We'll first look at what the term "green building" means, then take a closer look at energy conservation, its solar heating aspects and where the money spent on recurring energy costs actually goes. Using a typical energy conservation program and the Basic Houses as an example, the final section surveys the benefits and limitations of green building programs.

WHAT DOES IT MEAN, BEING GREEN?

As part of their millennial research, in 1998 the National Geographic Society produced a *Population & Resources Map*. The map uses beautiful graphics to lay out scary data.

Between 1960 and the millennium, world population doubled to just over six billion. By 2050 the United States population will further increase by 50% according to current projections. After that, estimates vary wildly. A birthrate that averages only two children per woman boosts the world's population to 10.8 billion by 2150. In the same time span a slightly higher birthrate of 2.6 children produces a jam-packed planet of 27 hungry billions. The current average world birthrate is 3.3.

Meanwhile, resources are shrinking. For instance, while Australia still has 4.5 acres of farmland per person, the more densely populated U.S. has "developed" its much greater area of arable land until only 2 acres per person remain. Asia, a preview of the crowded future, is down to .4 acres of farmland per capita.[2]

We don't want to beat the subject to death but however you analyze the figures, more and more people are chasing ever scarcer resources and facing ever greater pollution. And that is the underlying reason for green building.

Referring to the map's statistics, population expert Joel E. Cohen says, "What we get as we increase our population are increasingly difficult choices." Fortunately, green building becomes a part of the solution without being difficult at all.

In its broadest sense, the term "green building" includes large-scale issues such as neighborhood amenities, land use policies, shorter commuting distances, and renewable energy sources. In a narrower sense, green building concerns techniques and materials used in construction. In an even narrower definition, green building refers to meeting requirements that qualify a house for various federal, state, and private financing benefits.

THE ENERGY PIE: WHERE THE MONEY REALLY GOES

Green building's main goal is to reduce energy use but before we can stop wasting energy we need to know where the energy actually goes. Even when technically true, popular beliefs about energy are often nearly irrelevant. They need a "Yes, but," tacked onto the end. The sheer number of factors that determine a house's energy use creates a rich compost for misconceptions:

- Geographic location
- Orientation and microclimate
- Number, ages and habits of family members
- Local fuel costs
- Number and type of appliances and gadgets
- Building size, material and quality
- Method used for energy analysis

Tackling the huge matrix of energy-saving choices would have been impossible had we not discovered a magic tool: the Home Energy Saver, or HES. HES, an Internet tool for calculating home energy use, went online in March 1999. The program, sponsored by the Environmental Protection Agency and the Department of Energy, uses methods developed by Lawrence Berkeley National Laboratory. Don't let that scare you; HES is more fun to play with than most video games. If you don't have Internet access, it's worth the effort to go to a local library or Internet cafe to analyze your building project with HES. At the time of publication the website is http://hes.lbl.gov/hes. (At the time of publication, accessing the HES address requires that you leave off the usual "www.")

The HES Energy Advisor begins by showing you the energy cost difference between the average size, average age house in your zip code and a new energy-efficient house in your zip code. Then, you analyze costs for your house by customizing the "Average House in Your Area" figures to match your own home.

THE BIG PLAYERS: SIZE, FUEL TYPE, HABITS AND GADGETS

Next to "living over the shop," building a smaller house is the greenest thing you can do. Smaller buildings require fewer resources, disturb less land and use less energy throughout their lives. In the next chapter we look at how to distill a house down to the essence of livability, so that's all we'll say here about size.

Heating System Fuel Type

The second biggest factor in energy costs is the type of heating fuel used. In most of the American Southwest, electrical resistance heating currently costs several times as much per BTU as heating with natural gas. The situation varies wildly from region to region with the Northeast depending on heating oil, the Southeast favoring electricity and the Northwest in a current state of flux over dependence on hydroelectric power. Prices change from month to month. Whether you use municipal utilities or have fuel delivered is also a factor. Still, in most areas one fuel source is more economical than others. A good source for information about local and national energy costs is the Energy Information Administration website, found at www.eia.doe.gov at the time of publication.

Habits

Most of us have energy-wasting habits we never notice that can account for a large portion of the utility bill:

- Lounging around in T-shirt and shorts in January
- Leaving the thermostat on one setting (Programmable thermostats are great energy savers.)
- Running the washer and dryer to launder one shirt
- Forgetting to open and close shades, doors, and windows to control heat
- Leaving lights burning in empty or sunlit rooms
- Having kids or pets (We aren't suggesting you get rid of them; just train them regarding the link between open doors and lost heat.)

Gadgets

Even if you're a model of good energy habits, using lots of gadgets can wreck your utility budget. Here, the gadgets category includes both appliances and consumer electronics. Tracking down these sneaky little energy thieves is a lot easier with the HES program. The HES program is so detailed that you can easily check the cost effect of making a single change, for instance planting shade trees or changing to a more efficient water heater.

The compact, tightly constructed Basic Houses described in this book cost very little to heat. Their low heating bills emphasize the comparative importance of appliances and gadgets. For the Basic Houses, the energy cost of using standard appliances ran several times the cost of heating fuel. Even more surprising, consumer electronics ran up an energy bill twice the cost of heating fuel. And the gadgets calculation included only the more common items: coffee maker, microwave oven, toaster, vacuum cleaner, answering machine, audio system, color TV, computer, printer, VCR, video game, door bell, hair dryer, electric toothbrush, and ceiling fan.

"In some homes, conventional uses of energy are dwarfed by miscellaneous appliance loads," says Marla Sanchez, the lead author of a Lawrence Berkeley Laboratory study on small appliance energy use.[3] Sanchez notes that a heated waterbed can use more electricity than an efficient refrigerator. Warming the nation's waterbeds requires the electricity produced by two large power plants. Even worse, a great deal of energy is wasted by standby losses, the "leaking electricity" produced by items such as VCRs and instant-on televisions even when they are turned off. Alan Meier, a co-author of the 1998 report states, "More than $1 billion per year could be saved in the U.S. by reducing the standby power loss of every leaking appliance to one watt."

In short, while the nation watches and worries about the cost of heating fuel, the unnoticed, combined energy costs of residential appliances and gadgets has zoomed to approximately nine times the cost of residential heating fuel in moderate climates.

HEATING, COOLING AND THE BUILDING SKIN

Although it costs little to heat a small, well-built new house, there's still no point in allowing BTUs to escape through the building's exterior surfaces. Low infiltration, decent windows and adequate insulation reduce heat loss.

Infiltration

"Infiltration" refers to the frigid (or sweltering) outdoor air that leaks into your house replacing the comfortable interior air that you have paid to heat or cool. Infiltration is measured in terms of air changes per hour. An "air change" is the complete replacement of the house's air volume, which equals the cubic feet of interior space. Air changes per hour in new construction with carefully installed caulking, weather-stripping and vapor barriers range between .5 and .75.

Windows

When we talk about energy loss through windows, we're actually talking about four distinct factors:

- Total square feet of glass
- Which direction the windows face
- Air leaks around the windows
- The windows' R-Value (or U-value)

Proper design reduces energy losses from oversized windows on the wrong side of a house, and good quality windows and competent installation minimize leaks. "R-value" or "resistance value," which measures how well a given thickness of a material resists the passage of heat, depends on the design and materials of a window itself.

The higher a material's R-value, the greater its insulating ability. (U-value is the reciprocal of R-value. That is, you divide 1 by a material's R-value to get its U-value. An R-value of 20 equals a U-value of .05.) There is little difference in R-value between particular window brands in the same price range. In the past, window companies claimed R-values as high as 8 for their windows. A class action lawsuit regarding the effectiveness of sealants and inert gases sobered the industry. Today, most window companies claim realistic R-values between 1.9 and 2.9. Various special treatments such as Low-E (low-emissivity) coatings can increase window R-value.

Insulation

During the energy crisis of the 1970s, we developed a national obsession with R-values that still lingers. The myth persists that, if R-11 insulation in your walls saves heat and money, R-22 walls save twice as much and R-44 walls double your savings again.

Sadly, it doesn't work that way and many people have wasted

Old windows such as this one on a shop in Santa Fe, New Mexico, have lots of charm but not much insulating ability.

A modern window installed in a house under construction. Today's double-glazed, clad wood, vapor sealed, double-hung windows with thermal breaks have approximately three times the insulating ability of traditional windows.

lots of money over-insulating their walls. The energy (and money) you save by adding more wall insulation diminishes quickly. Starting with an R-value of zero, every increase of two units in R-value cuts the amount of heat lost through a wall by about half, as shown in the following chart. The amount of heat still escaping through the walls soon becomes so tiny that adding more insulation is almost pointless.

In moderate climates such as Albuquerque's, there is little benefit in insulating walls beyond R-11. The curve of diminishing returns varies slightly with climate but in all cases it is much lower than sales pitches for insulation imply. Contrary to popular superstition, an adobe wall with 2" of polystyrene insulation works very well in mild and moderate climates.

The left side of the chart shows how many BTUs each square foot of exterior wall loses over the course of a year. Along the bottom of the chart run R-values from 1 to 50. The lower curve shows how quickly the benefit of adding more insulation disappears in Albuquerque's climate. The upper curve shows the same pattern for much colder Madison, Wisconsin.

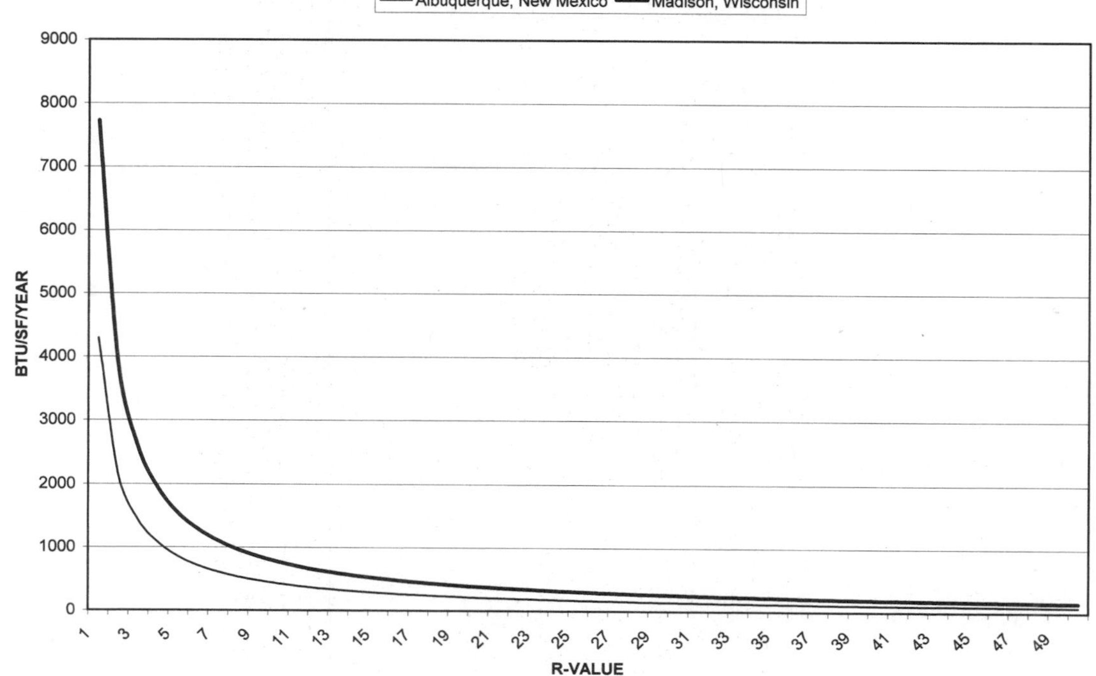

If you wish, Oak Ridge National Laboratory will calculate your optimum insulation R-values, using your zip code and your local fuel cost. At the time of publication, the website is www.ornl.gov/roofs+walls. Go to the Interactive Calculators section.

The recent fad for building with straw bales results in part from the claim that straw bale walls have an insulation value of R-60. In reality, recent, more accurate tests done at Oak Ridge National Laboratory show the most commonly used straw bale wall configuration yielding R-28. In any event, a wall R-value of 60 is unnecessary anywhere south of the Arctic Circle.

THE SOLAR COMPONENTS

With the Basic Houses, we set out to provide the greatest possible flexibility, keep costs low and eliminate unnecessary maintenance hassles. Limiting solar heating to the amount possible with standard design and construction helped achieve all three goals. Basic passive solar heating is simple. In addition to adequate insulation, an effective setup requires only three elements:

- Sunlight entering a building
- A shading device that blocks the sun in summer but not in winter
- A material that stores incoming heat and then releases it gradually

Solar Gain

In moderate climates the sun supplies between 40% and 50% of the Basic Houses' small heating load. Calculating this solar savings percentage begins with measuring a house's square feet of south-facing glass and its square feet of interior floor area. For instance, if a house has 11 square feet of south glass for every 100 square feet of interior floor area, it has 11% south-facing glass. Depending on several factors, in moderate climates that 11% glazing yields between 40% and 50% of the house's required heat. The same 11% qualifies a house for various energy efficiency ratings.

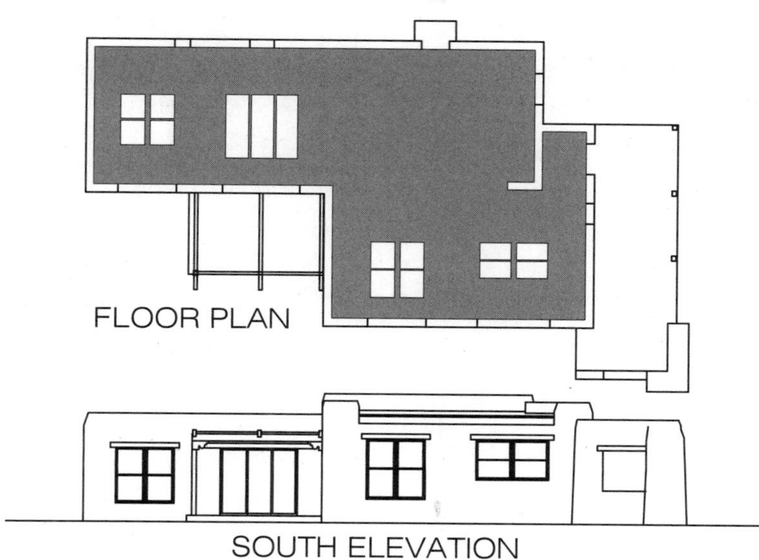

Sun Hall House has 107 square feet of south-facing glass, represented as white areas against the 908 square feet of interior living space, shown shaded. The resulting percentage of south-facing glass is just under 12%.

Shading Control

At Albuquerque's 35 degree latitude the summer sun rides high in the sky; at noon its rays strike the earth at a 78 degree angle. At midwinter, however, the sun is so low that the noon angle of its rays is slightly less than 32 degrees. A correctly sized shading overhang blocks the summer rays, yet allows the winter sun to shine under it and strike the window.

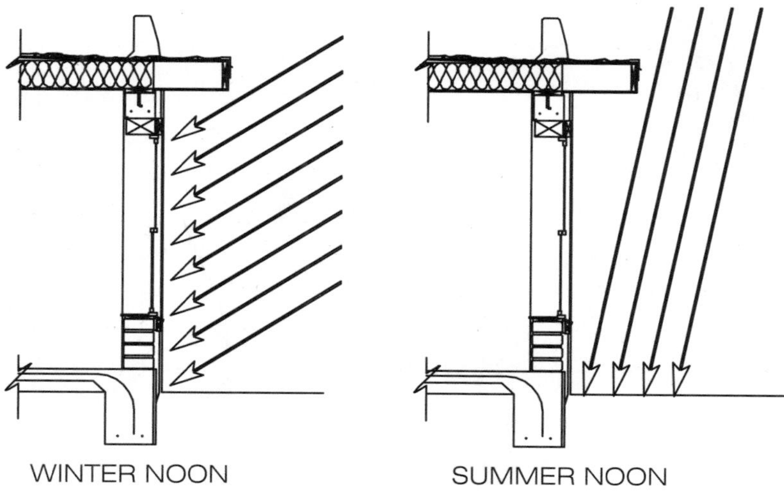

The two building sections show a south-facing adobe wall with a large window and a shading overhang. On the left, the arrows follow the 32 degree angle of the winter sun at noon and shine under the overhang. On the right section, the same overhang protects the window from the 78 degree noon angle of the summer sun.

In the 1970s, solar experimenters installed sloped glazing on many greenhouses and sunspaces. They wanted to place the glazing as nearly perpendicular to the sun's winter rays as possible to increase insolation (the amount of solar energy entering the structure.) Because it was difficult to shade adequately, sloped glazing caused overheating. And it almost always leaked.

Thermal Storage

Like south-facing glass and wall insulation, thermal mass was often oversized in the early days of modern solar construction. The result was dwellings so bulked up with water barrels, rock bins and mass walls that their interiors looked like tunnels through a storage basement.

With properly sized glazing, a mass floor such as the stained and sealed concrete floors used in the Basic Houses will moderate temperature swings. Using both adobe exterior walls and a mass floor assures thermal comfort.

Other flooring materials that work well at storing heat in areas of direct sunlight are tile, brick and a medium or dark colored linoleum. Thick carpeting, however, acts as insulation, interfering with heat absorption by the underlying concrete.

Even if your house is completely solar heated, many financial institutions will require a conventional heating system also. Mechanical/electrical plans for the Basic Houses show a system that uses the water heater as a boiler for a hydronic radiant floor. The system is less expensive than using a separate boiler and more comfortable and energy-efficient than a forced air system. Chapter 7 discusses hydronic systems in more detail.

If you want to use a wood stove for back-up heating, first check local regulations. Some urban areas have initiated "no-burn nights" to reduce air pollution. Also, the cost and availability of firewood vary greatly. If burning wood won't work in your area, consider a direct-venting, gas-fired fireplace.

GREEN BUILDING PROGRAMS

Various national and local programs promote green building. Many of them are based on the Environmental Protection Agency's Energy Star program. An Energy Star rating for your house can reduce your down payment, increase the mortgage amount you qualify for or reduce your interest rate.

Many green building programs use the national Model Energy Code as a benchmark for their certification standards. Generally, the programs aim for energy efficiency that exceeds Model Energy Code requirements by a certain percentage, using environmentally sound building materials and techniques along with energy-efficient appliances.

Green building programs vary from state to state and they are changing rapidly. Legislation that affects the home building industry is constantly under consideration. We can't predict the situation by the time you read this or what local conditions you may encounter. Check out the green building websites listed in More Information for updated data. The EPA's own website, www.epa.gov, also offers information in depth.

Efficiency Is Not Conservation

Energy Star-type programs promote efficiency but not necessarily conservation. Although they overlap, the two goals are different. Efficiency says to put good insulation in the roof of your 5,000 square-foot home; conservation says build a smaller house. Efficiency says to make sure your refrigerator and two freezers are energy-saving models; conservation says forget buying the second freezer.

Government sponsored conservation programs do not usually address size, a home's biggest conservation factor. Nor do they currently award points for location although some of the programs recommend building houses close to work and services.

Having said that, let us add that green building programs are a great step forward. They encourage the manufacture of materials that reduce toxicity and conserve resources; they encourage recycling during construction; all other things being equal, they cut home utility costs; and their rating systems can increase home resale value.

How a Green Building Program Works

The Home Builders Association of Central New Mexico sponsors the state's Green Star program. The program awards points for various features divided into four categories: water conservation, materials conservation and content, solid waste reduction, and energy conservation. To earn Green Stars, a house must earn a minimum number of points in each category. If a house earns 20 points, it wins a 1 Star rating. Thirty points wins a 2 Star rating, and so on.

The Green Star program also includes a list of substitutions for each category. The substitutions are important because they are tailored to local building practices, less dependent on buying costly extras, and based on choices made during the design phase.

The following features, already built in or possible with our Basic Houses, earn the number of New Mexico Green Star points shown. Your local program will differ but the list provides a general guide to the types of items covered.

WATER CONSERVATION

1 Toilets that use 1.6 gallons per flush or less

1 Shower heads that use 2.5 gallons per minute

MATERIALS: CONSERVATION AND CONTENT

2 Two engineered materials such as trusses and oriented strand board (OSB) or plywood sheathing

SOLID WASTE REDUCTION

4 Recycling on-site framing lumber waste.

3 Recycling on-site cardboard waste.

2 Adding an in-home recycling center such as a three-bin kitchen cabinet

ENERGY CONSERVATION

1-4 Window R-value upgrade

1 A water heater that operates at a minimum .57EF (Efficiency Factor) for 30 gallon capacity, .55EF for 40 gallon, and .53EF for 50 gallon

FROM SUBSTITUTION LIST

2 Centrally located water heater

1 Using locally produced products such as columns and corbels from local sources

2 Centrally located electrical panels

4 Home construction using a substantial portion of adobe, etc.

2 Extended shades or awnings over southern and western windows

2 Radiant floor heating

1 Ceiling fan
4 Solar gain design, that is, 11-25 SF of south-facing glass per 100 SF of floor area

You can quickly increase your point total by choosing items such as energy-efficient appliances, materials with low toxicity and recycled content, and low-water landscaping. Contact your state EPA office or local chapters of the National Association of Home Builders to find out about green building programs in your area.

Again, these programs change with every political wind. Albuquerque's Home Builders Association will change to another program by the end of 2001, the Department of Energy's Building America Program, which is more restrictive and more focused on high-tech solutions for conserving energy.

SORTING IT OUT

Energy dollars don't always go where one might expect, yet conserving energy often pays bigger returns than more conventional financial investments. Making wise energy choices involves so many factors that the process often gets bogged down in its own complexity. The following list sums up the type of options available for energy conservation, going from items with the most impact to those with the least:

1. Cut your commuting miles by working close to where you live. (Chapter 6 looks at this strategy in greater detail.)
2. Build a smaller house.
3. Use the most cost-efficient fuel available in your area.
4. Use energy-efficient appliances.
5. Get the gadget explosion under control.
6. Take advantage of solar heating and various natural cooling strategies.
7. Use good-quality double-glazed windows, caulking and weather-stripping.
8. Install adequate ceiling insulation.
9. And in a feeble ninth place, beef up wall insulation.

4

DESIGNING THE HEART OF A HOUSE

Our design goal for the Basic Houses was simple but fascinating: find the design choices that give homeowners the widest range of choices. We settled on four individual requirements that reinforce each other. After a quick survey of these design guidelines, we'll look in detail at the techniques that turn the theoretical requirements into actual building designs.

Houses that fit a variety of sites: While we can't design stock plans for specific sites, we made sure that the collection includes houses that fit different climates and surroundings and that can face whatever direction is necessary for solar heating.

Houses that adapt to different kinds of families: These days, few families fit the traditional profile of Dad, Mom and several at-home kids. The housing industry, though, still builds most of its models for these "typical" families instead of the singles, couples, single parents and retirees who make up a majority of households. The Basic Houses fit the smaller households that are becoming the new standard yet their flexible "pre-designed" expansions allow them to grow gracefully to meet changing circumstances.

Houses that fit a wide range of budgets: Most of us would agree that it's easier to add costs to your dream house budget than to cut them. With the basic houses, which cost between 1/2 and 2/3 the median house price, we've tackled the difficult end of the budget spectrum by selecting features that maintain quality and winnowing out features that add more cost than benefit. The houses are carefully designed so that you can indulge in the indescribable fun of adding the goodies that fit your personal vision and budget.

Houses that maintain high quality in materials, design, and livability: Cutting costs while keeping houses physically and visually satisfying depends on a central principle: put the money into the elements that endure. The cost savings obtained by initially building fewer rooms allow for generous communal spaces and quality materials.

For easier reference, we've given names to the twelve Basic Houses and you'll meet them all in Chapter 5. Round House, Coyote House, Orchard House and Corbel House are single-story with one bedroom in the basic version. Also single-story, High Valley House, Sun Hall House, Garden House and Ramada House have two bedrooms. Farm House, Balcony House and Deck House are two-story, while Pueblo House is designed to accommodate three independent living areas.

HOUSES THAT FIT A VARIETY OF SITES

The building site is perhaps the most important factor influencing the design of a home. It's even fair to say, "Don't start thinking about the design of your house until you know where you will build it." While we can't predict the views, size or microclimate of your building site, the designs include houses that function well for solar heating on almost any lot.

The Most Likely Site

Plans for the Basic Houses assume the most common site condition—a lot that slopes less than three feet across the immediate building area. The compact size of the houses allows them to fit comfortably on a greater variety of building lots than larger houses that crowd up against their property lines.

The conservative engineering design loads used—soil bearing, live, dead and wind—are adequate for most soil and weather conditions. Even so, consult your local building official or engineer about your specific site before building. Chapter 6 discusses site selection in detail.

Solar Tempering Your House

The one feature that demands a specific orientation is solar heating. The plan collection includes houses with front elevations that can face in several directions. The presentations in Chapter 5 include diagrams showing how each house can be situated on different lots while keeping the heavily glazed side facing south.

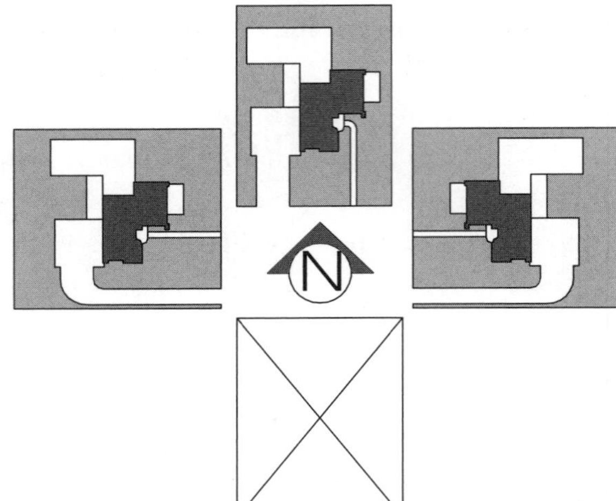

The site diagrams show how a house can fit on lots that face different directions without destroying solar gain.

The expanded version of Orchard House, with solar glazing down a side wall, fits well onto a narrow, deep lot. The expanded version of Farm House, which concentrates glazing on the rear walls, works well on wide, shallow lots.

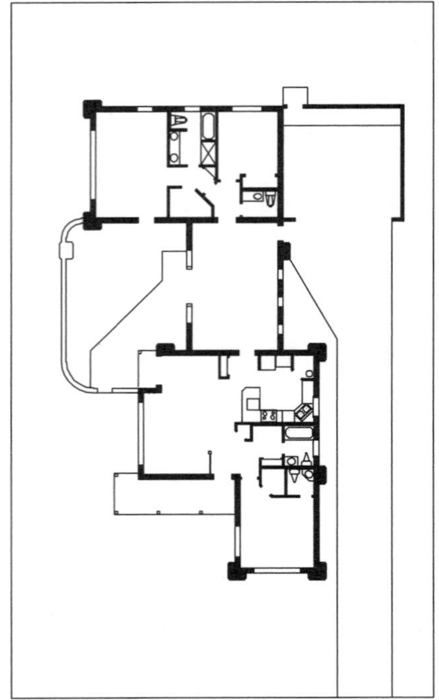

Orchard House

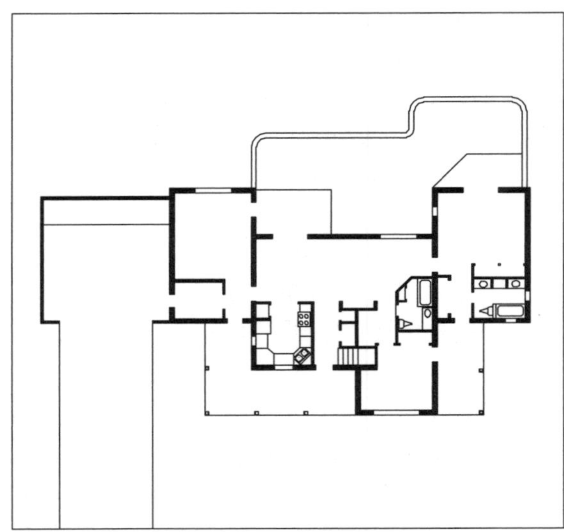

Farm House

Houses that face east or west can usually be placed on lots with narrower frontages because the longer, solar-gain side of the house runs back the length of the lot. East-facing houses can be "flipped" to face west and vice versa.

A building site that faces south presents the greatest challenge for solar design; large expanses of glass facing the street can turn your life into around-the-clock entertainment for the neighbors. Also, a south-facing orientation conflicts with the desire to open the rear (north side) of the house to the privacy of the backyard. The house designs that face south to the street include front patio walls for privacy.

Dwellings that are 100% solar heated tend to subordinate all other design goals to the need for south-facing glass. The Basic Houses compromise with south-facing glass square footage that averages 11% of the houses' inside living area. Eleven percent glazing supplies between 40% and 50% of the heating needed in mild to moderate climates.

Climates are classified as mild, moderate (or temperate) or severe based on a number of factors, the most important of which is degree days. "Degree days" are a measurement of local temperatures used to size heating and cooling systems. Albuquerque's moderate climate, for example, has 4,348 heating degree days per year. To find heating degree days for a location, the difference between the 65 degree inside temperature and the average outside temperature is calculated for each day of the heating season. These daily differences for a year are added to produce the total heating degree days figure. Degree days in U.S. locations range from 14,279 in Fairbanks, Alaska, to 0 in lucky Honolulu, Hawaii. The bibliography includes references listing degree days for your area.

HOUSES THAT FIT DIFFERENT KINDS OF FAMILIES

Everything changes but change itself, including families. (And here we're defining family as whatever collection of living beings you choose to call family—whether it's you, Spot and Fluffy or four generations of blood relatives.) The three areas where family change usually affects housing needs are size, room use, and accessibility.

Flexible Expansions

"Agglutinative architecture," a slightly silly term for some of the world's most pleasing dwellings, simply refers to buildings that have been added onto whenever the inhabitants need more space. Any house that survives long enough acquires additions. The additions may be graceful and efficient or awkward and inconvenient.

The Basic House plans use layouts, hallway routes, knock-out panels and high eaves to make expansion easy. This pre-planning eliminates problems that plague most additions: loss of solar heat and natural light, loss of access to porches and patios, messed-up circulation and awkward roof splices.

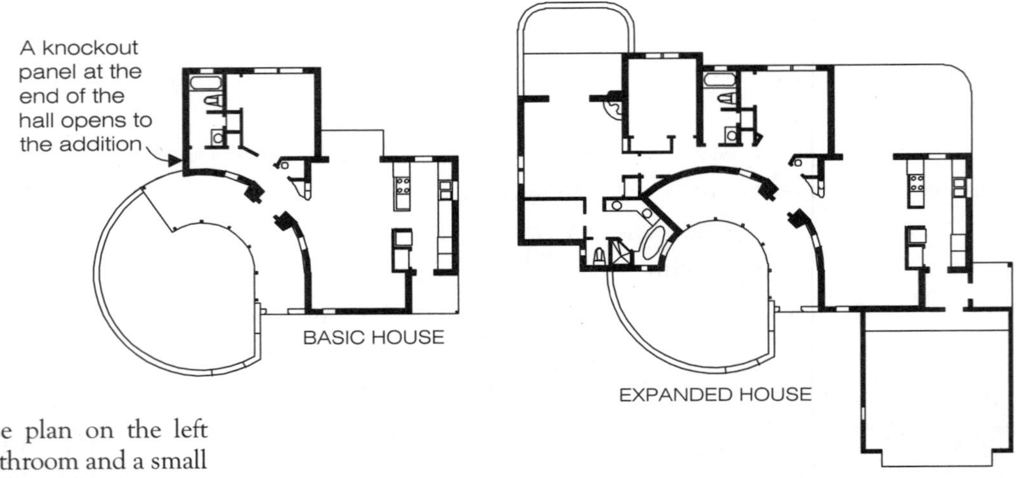

The basic Round House plan on the left shows a hallway to the bathroom and a small porch off the kitchen. When the house is expanded as shown on the right, a knock-out panel (door lintel and jambs built into the solid wall) opens the hallway to the new bedrooms. The kitchen porch becomes a utility room and route to the garage.

Most of the expansions shown add three types of space:

- A garage and storage/utility room. Typically, these areas attach near the kitchen and extend to the north of the house.
- A new living area that can be as formal or informal as you wish. In most of the basic houses, the kitchen, dining and living areas flow into each other. When a new living area is built the kitchen and dining areas can expand into the former living room space.

- A bedroom wing. The bedroom additions include a large suite and one or perhaps two secondary bedrooms. In two-story houses the upstairs usually becomes the new bedroom area. When the new bedrooms are built, the original bedroom can become an office, secondary bedroom, guestroom, parlor, den, media room or workout room.

Beyond the Standard, Single-Family Detached House

Ten of our Basic House plans are standard, detached, single-family houses. The last two, Plan #11 and Plan #12, address other situations.

Plan #11, Deck House, is designed for "zero lot line" properties. In an area zoned for zero lot line development, houses are built with one windowless side wall running along the property line. The arrangement allows for a larger side yard on a narrow lot. The basic plan includes a one-car garage. If lot covenants demand an attached two-car garage, the garage can expand across the front of the house, shielding the porch and second-floor deck from the street.

Deck House is designed so that its windowless north side can run along the property line, allowing a wider side yard on the heavily glazed south side.

Plan #12, Pueblo House, can shelter one family or accommodate three. The house features roomy living and dining areas next to a large eat-in kitchen and a utility room. Around these shared spaces fit one, two or three separate, independent living units.

The three units can combine to suit a large variety of living arrangements. Each unit can be a large bedroom suite, an independent "apartment" for one of several adults living in the house, a mother-in-law apartment, living quarters for a grown child, two smaller bedrooms, an office or a rental unit locked off from the main house.

Around the core of Pueblo House three apartments, a garage and eating patio can be plugged in.

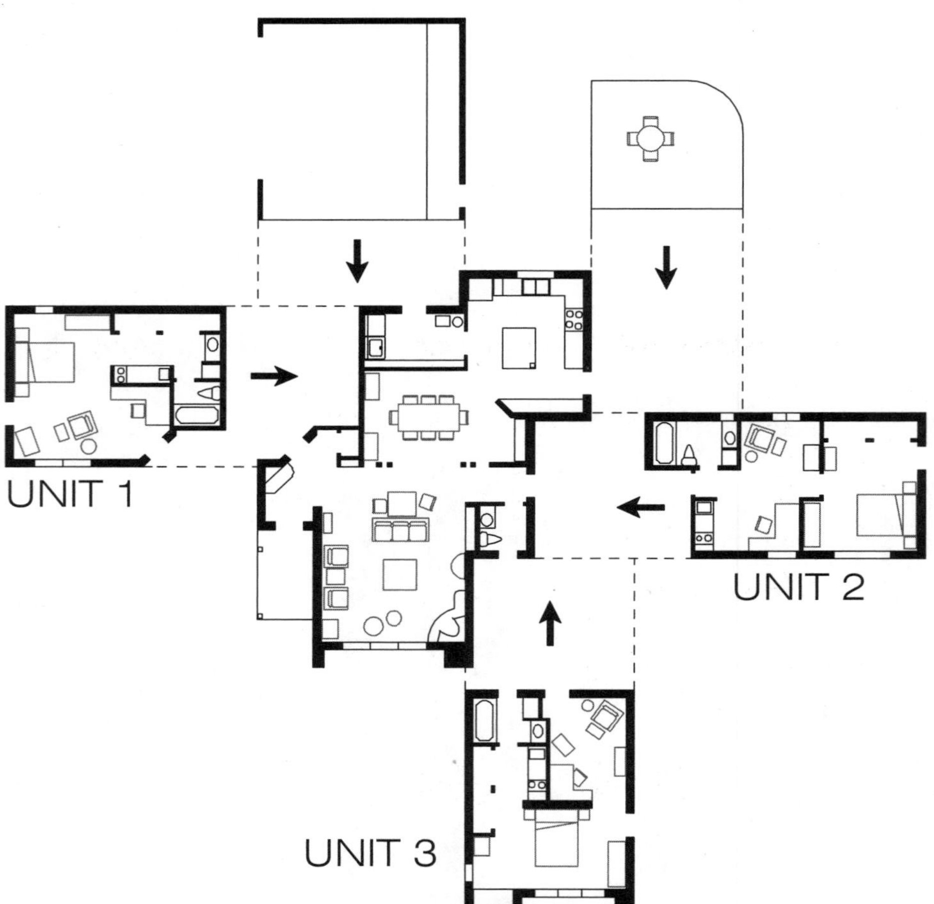

Plans #3, #4, #7, #10 and #12 also have wheelchair-accessible versions. The accessible versions require separate working drawings because the Basic Houses use every square foot of space. Allowing for wider clearances in doorways, bathrooms, halls, kitchens and pantries requires a bit of a trade-off, usually removing a closet, an extra half-bath or a laundry space. Accessible versions also specify outlets and switches at a more convenient level and require the contractor to install lavatories and kitchen work surfaces at a height designated by the owner.

On the left, the accessible version of Orchard House, Plan #3, has a larger bath with room for a combination roll-in/transfer shower. The kitchen and passage to the bedroom are barrier free. Ramps lead from the porch and patio.

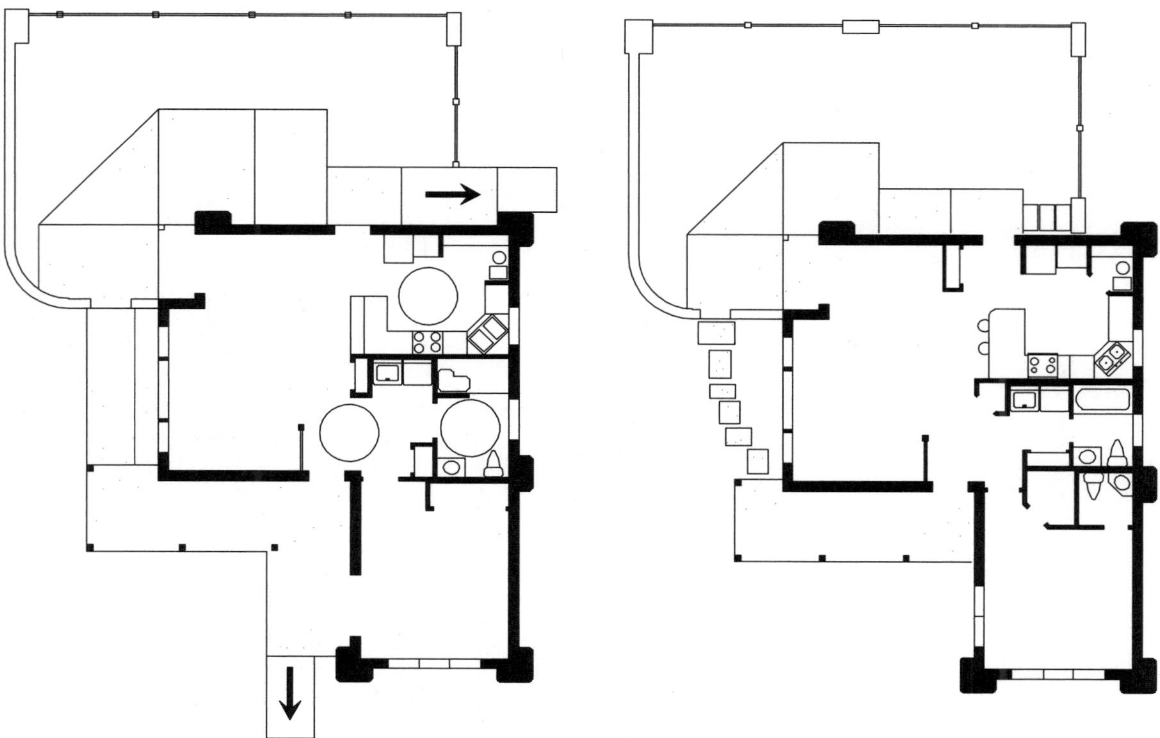

HOUSES THAT FIT A WIDE RANGE OF BUDGETS

The most important element of a house is the shape and size of its interior space. Once built, that interior space is difficult to change. Most of the Basic Houses' square footage and budget goes into roomy, high-ceilinged living/dining/kitchen areas. The plans also specify top-grade materials for foundations, windows, roofs, walls and outdoor living areas. To balance the budget, the designs use several cost-cutting techniques:

- Keep square footage small
- Leave personal details to the owner
- Minimize space needed for hallway circulation and mechanical equipment
- Forget "imperial" bathrooms
- Eliminate garages on the basic plans
- Keep building forms and structural systems simple

Small Square Footage

Whether a house seems small depends on what it's compared to. Levittown, the famous "first subdivision," was built just after World War II in Long Island, New York. Levittown houses averaged 800 square feet and sheltered families that averaged 4.2 people. But even Levittown seems roomy in Japan where, traditionally, a house considered suitable for a four-person family could be as small as 355 square feet. (Of course, the Japanese demand 24-hour use from rooms—bedrooms at night, then living areas once sleeping mats are rolled up in the morning.) In contrast, by 2000 the U.S. median home had grown to 2260 square feet to hold the two and a fraction people rattling around inside.

The Basic Houses fit somewhere between "too large" and "too small." The one-bedroom versions average 906 square feet; two bedroom versions average 1058 square feet. They are, in effect, freestanding apartment-sized dwellings. (Total square footage is calculated to the exterior structural surfaces of heated, finished space.)

There are two main ways to shrink a house's square footage—eliminate unneeded rooms or reduce the size of rooms that are too

Floor plans drawn at the same scale compare the 800 square foot Levittown model, a 360 square foot Japanese layout, and a 1109 square foot Basic House across the top row. A 2260 square foot median U.S. home takes up the bottom row.

big. Yes, too big. The usual rationales for very large rooms are that they're handy for impressing people and for gathering in large groups. Impressing people, a fascinating topic, is outside the scope of this book but let's take a closer look at the idea of gathering in large groups.

Good hosts have always known that seating more than eight at a dinner table causes people to split into different conversational huddles. The same split happens when people are simply sitting around. With more than eight in a group, several uncomfortable things may happen:

- Individuals battle for speaking time, interrupting each other
- The party turns into a monologue by the person most eager for the spotlight
- Other people become withdrawn
- Listeners are torn between different speakers
- People strain to talk louder than usual or others can't hear them

Except at formal meetings, people rarely coalesce in large groups. They split apart into more comfortable small groups that seldom need a space larger than about twelve feet by twelve feet. A house suitable for get-togethers may need several linked spaces for people to congregate, drifting from one conversation to another, but it doesn't necessarily need an oversized "great room."

Fine Trimwork "By Owner"

A recent book about houses maintains that custom detailing rather than enormous size makes a house feel like home. The book's theory is right, but unfortunately, elaborate, individualized trimwork carries a staggering price tag when included in a contract. Other than site-built casing around doors, working drawings for the Basic Houses include few custom details for several reasons:

- If we drew them in, they would be our personal touches, not yours.
- Because of their sculptural nature, earth-built walls look good—in fact, better—without a lot of decoration.
- Craftsman details are extremely expensive. And often trimwork can be added after you move in as your own woodworking project, a separate contract, or possibly a trade-off with a handy friend.
- If details are drawn and specified, they cost more than if they're added at the contractor's whim. Many builders have their own signature details—a *bas relief* in the stucco, a certain corbel pattern, *bancos* (benches) or stepped half-walls built from leftover adobes—that they will add for little or no extra cost. Talk it over; you may get some freebies.
- Often, a single splendid light fixture, door, carved beam or work of art so focuses a room that extra trimwork, if not coordinated with the focal feature, becomes distracting frou-frou. These key objects that fire your imagination and inspire your devotion may come from your own family history or from antique stores, boutiques, or salvage yards—but they won't come from us.

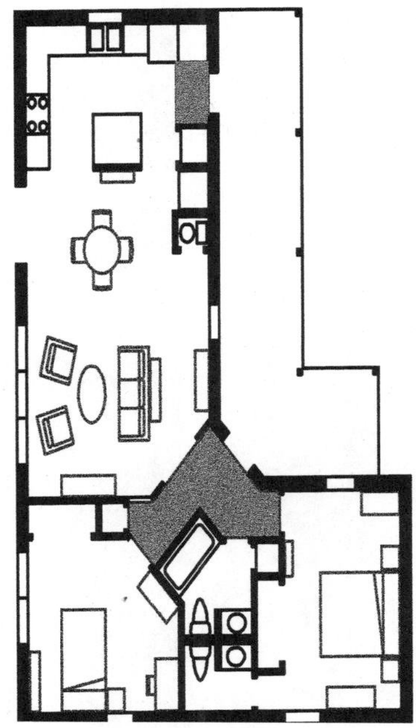

Fine wall sconces from a ceramics firm in Taos, New Mexico, can highlight interior or exterior walls.

Antique doors from a company in Santa Fe, New Mexico. Thousands of doors from both regional and Asian buildings are available in their salvage condition or refurbished and built into custom installations.

Handsome gates like these often dominate the street view of a home.

After saving money by choosing a small, energy-efficient house you might find yourself in the delightful position of having several thousand dollars extra for upgrades. You'll have your own priorities, but also consider the following items that greatly enhance a house's distinction for a relatively small expenditure:

- Upgrade interior doors to a paneled or tongue-and-groove style
- Upgrade kitchen cabinets and counter tops
- Use the finest available light fixtures in prominent places and simple, inoffensive ones elsewhere
- Add custom bookshelves, display shelves or other cabinetry

Minimum Space Devoted to Circulation and Mechanical Equipment

A house needs a certain amount of circulation space just so people can get from one room to another. The Basic Houses reduce costs by minimizing circulation space and making it perform multiple jobs. Frequently, circulation routes pass through rooms so the travel space adds to the room's volume. Where hallways are necessary, they often serve as a solar gain area or access to storage on either side.

Furnace enclosures require approximately ten square feet of floor space. Baseboard or in-wall unit heaters take up wall space needed for furniture, doors, windows and wall ornaments. The Basic Houses' single-boiler system for hot water and radiant floor heat reduces space needed for heating equipment.

Standard Bathrooms

Each of the Basic Houses has one full bathroom placed to serve bedrooms with privacy while still convenient to the house's public areas. Several of the one-story houses also show a space off the main bedroom that can be either a half-bath or an extra closet. Working drawings for the two-story houses include the information necessary to finish an upstairs bathroom. (The two-story house plans assume owners will finish the downstairs and move in, leaving the upstairs to be finished later.)

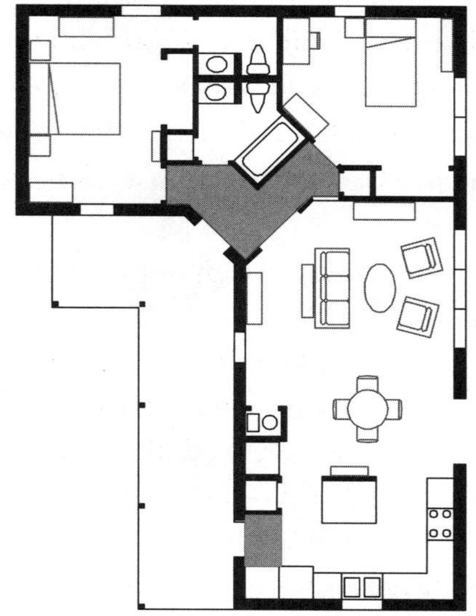

Shaded areas on the High Valley House floor plan show circulation spaces, which double as entries.

Bathrooms in the Basic Houses

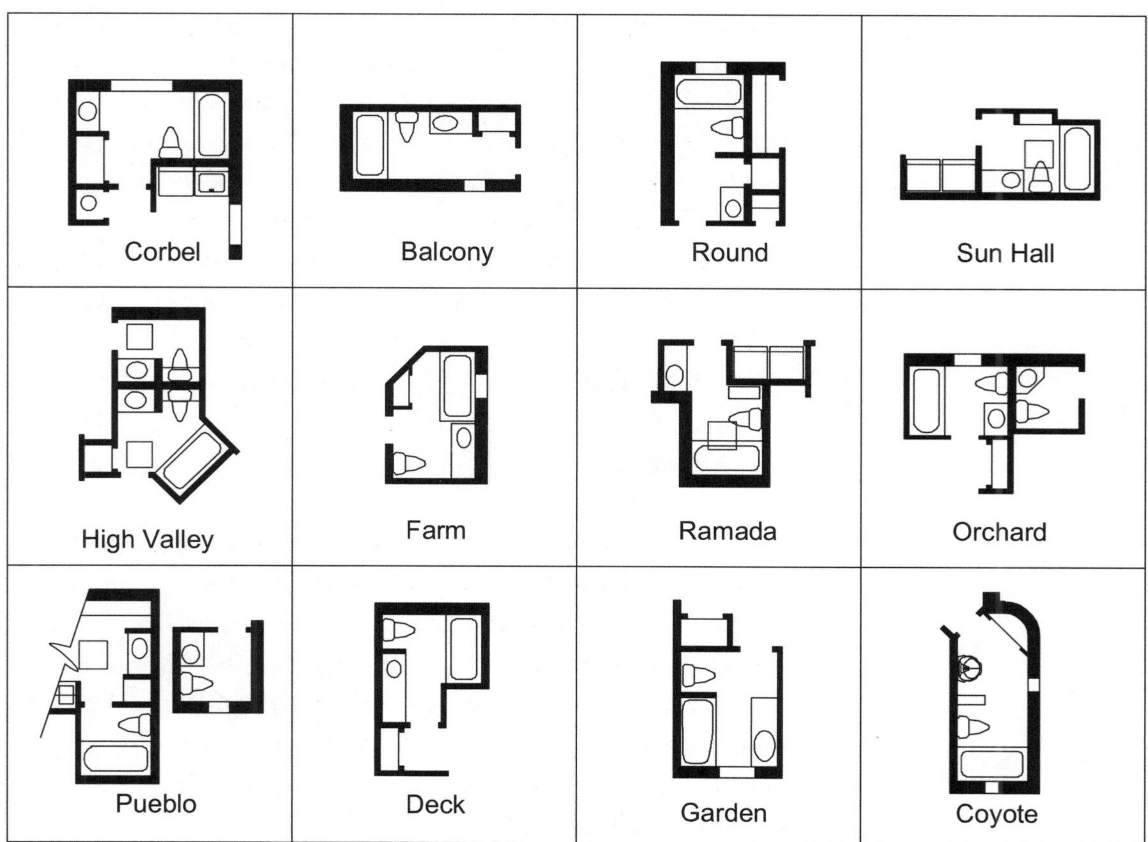

Opulent bathrooms with Roman tub, separate shower, bidet, exercise area, double sinks, fireplaces and big-screen TVs are real estate hot-buttons that pump up sales commissions and make fixture manufacturers happy. The Basic Houses' bathrooms fall short of imperial grandeur and here's why:

- A trophy bathroom can easily add an extra 30% to the price tag
- Keeping all those square yards of porcelain and marble spotless requires too much cleaning
- You can have a mega-bath when you add the owners' suite—by then you'll be older and more in need of long, hot soaks

No Garages

Okay, we love our cars and we love to store junk. Unfortunately, a garage can add as much as 20% to the cost of a Basic House. A garage also tightly controls how a house must be positioned on a lot. So plans for the Basic Houses don't show garages except for Plan #11, designed for zero lot line zoning.

If you really want a garage or if your property covenants demand one, check the expanded versions of the plans, which include double garages. The site placement diagrams show the houses with garages positioned on lots facing different directions.

Simple Structural Systems and Building Volumes

Stewart Brand, one of our most creative and provocative theorists of practically everything, has analyzed what makes a building function effectively through many generations—or become obsolete in a decade. To grossly simplify Brand's conclusions, the simpler a building's structure and surfaces, the better it performs, the longer it survives and the easier it is to alter or expand.[1]

These houses use standard, simple structural systems. Foundations consist of a single-pour slab with turndown footings. Except at buttresses, exterior walls are a single width of adobe set lengthwise. The truss roofs are designed with the fewest possible ridges, valleys, penetrations, dormers and linear feet of flashing. Interior walls and ceilings are finished with gypsum board and floors are carpet, linoleum and stained and sealed concrete. Because most rooms receive natural light through windows, skylights are largely unnecessary. Where applicable, building dimensions match the standard modular sizes of various materials to avoid waste.

Using straightforward structure encourages designs with simple volumes and coherent roof forms. The clean forms, in turn, save money. Elaborate trim, bay windows, cantilevers, pop-outs, telescope gables and numerous roof planes can make a small house cost as much as one twice its size. Instead, the Basic Houses rely on harmonious proportions for visual appeal.

In many considerations of housing costs and functions, the one-story versus two-story debate arises. Conventional wisdom says that a two-story house is less expensive than a single-story with the same floor area because it requires smaller areas of expensive roof and foundation. Often this is true, but not always:

- Contractors usually charge more for work above the first floor that requires scaffolding
- Mechanical and electrical work above the first story are more expensive
- A two-story house adds the cost of a stairway and second floor framing and decking
- Most surprising, the area of expensive exterior wall increases approximately 40% on a two-story house

While a two-story house may indeed cost less, the savings often result from fitting the house on a smaller, cheaper lot.

HOUSES THAT MAINTAIN HIGH QUALITY IN MATERIALS, DESIGN AND COMFORT

Now that we've all eaten our spinach, we can move on to the cake and ice cream. Certain types of features make a house a comfortable, enduring haven instead of an inflexible, continual irritation. While many desirable home features depend on individual taste, budget or location, the more universal ones mentioned here, along with adobe walls, add to almost any home's livability without adding drastically to construction costs.

Ample Outdoor Living Areas

The Basic Houses are liberally supplied with porches, patios and courtyards. Developed outdoor space is dramatically cheaper than interior heated space and often more pleasant. Whether you're inside or outside, outdoor living space visually expands the apparent square footage of a house.

A 9' by 39' porch stretches across the rear of Ramada House and turns the corner. Removable trellis boards shade the space in summer.

Porches wrap the north, east and west sides of Farm House.

Full Scale Kitchens

As people spend less and less time cooking, lifestyle magazines feature ever larger kitchens packed with every imaginable appliance, many of them imported. And now the marketing mavens push the two-cook kitchen, doubling your gadget requirements. Just keep asking yourself, "Who pays for it? Who cleans it up?" The "apartment" solution of tiny kitchens with no windows is less expensive, but even worse.

The kitchens of the Basic Houses boldly seize the middle ground. They are sized for houses of approximately 1800 square feet so that they will be adequate for a house when it is expanded. Open counter-top space on the 12 plans averages 38.5 square feet. With some of the kitchens, counter and storage space can be added without demolishing appliance hook-ups or walls.

The Basic House kitchens

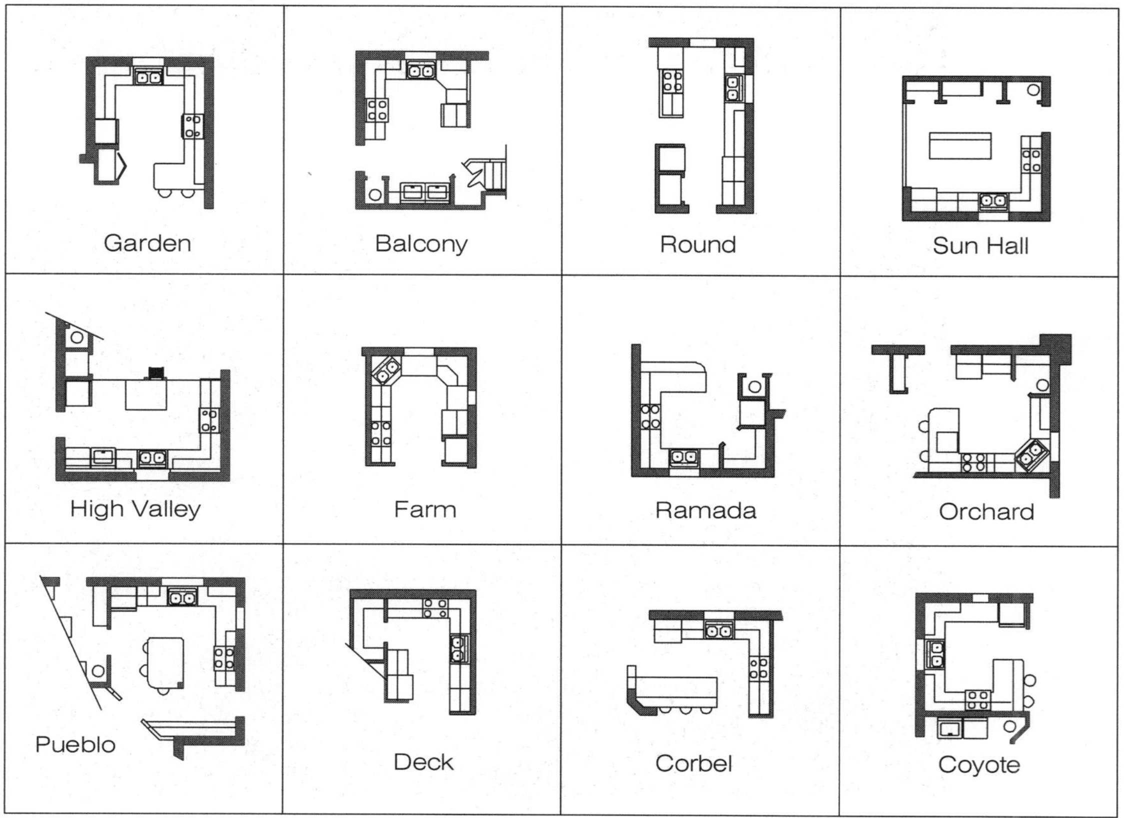

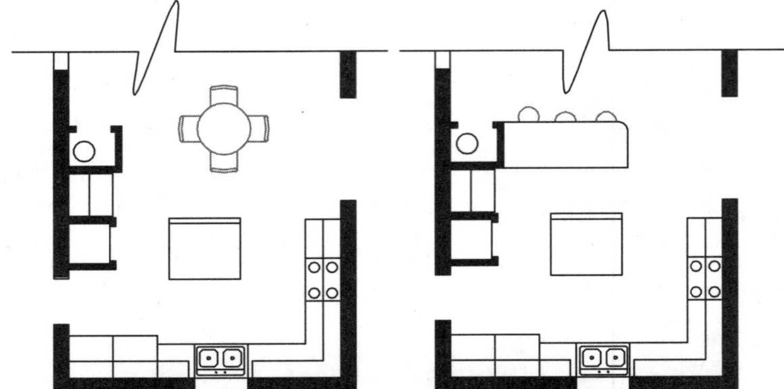

When High Valley House is expanded, you have the option of adding a large work/eating counter.

Adequate Storage

In addition to coat, linen and bedroom closets, the Basic Houses include generous kitchen cabinet space and either utility rooms or pantries. The expansion plans include large storage areas. Owners of the two-story houses can finish the downstairs and move in, then finish the upstairs as needed. In the meantime the upstairs makes a great storage area.

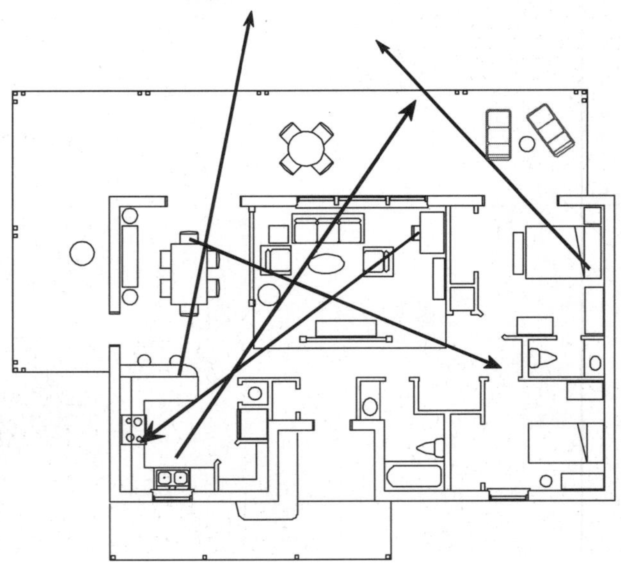

The arrows mark the direction of sight lines from various points in Ramada House.

Generous Windows, Long Sight Lines and High Ceilings

A room's feeling of spaciousness comes more from its sense of openness than its actual size. A closed-in room without windows gives the eye no openings to explore, no sense of distance; the mind feels as confined as the body. In such a room, your "line of sight" can be no longer than the room's longest dimension, the diagonal from one corner to the opposite. The Basic Houses avoid a confined feeling by using room layouts, half-walls and windows to create long lines of sight in each space while maintaining a sense of privacy.

In larger rooms, high or sloping ceilings create better proportions as well as psychological expansiveness. Each of the houses shown in this book has some areas with ceilings higher than the standard eight feet. In the two-story houses, portions of the upper level are open to the downstairs.

The main living area of Coyote House not only has glazing on three sides, but the openings flanking the interior adobe wall extend the diagonal views significantly.

The designs in this book juggle and tweak a lot of smaller options to open up one big option—the ability to build a high-quality home right now that fits your household. In the process, we've tried to keep the design parameters as flexible as a set of kid's building blocks. The following chapter includes the plan collection, both basic and expanded versions, and a sampling of ways you can further customize the designs.

5

THE PLANS

We called it "plan fever" when people showed up at our office with dazed expressions and red, irritated eyes. They had spent weeks, months—maybe years—looking through newsstand plan books, building magazines and "Home and Real Estate" sections, carefully studying hundreds of house plans without ever finding one that fit.

We all need to put a personal stamp on our homes. We all need, in different degrees, togetherness and privacy. A house works if it supplies the spaces we need to follow our daily routines with ease and pleasure. The flexibility designed into the Basic Houses allows you to tailor a plan to your lifestyle. These houses do not strive for the usual architectural goal of a building as a perfect, unchangeable object. Instead, we've treated the houses as a set of interlocking building blocks that you combine to your own satisfaction.

Computer aided drafting (CAD) has grown to dominate the architectural graphics field. CAD drawings are very easy to alter, whether presentation drawings like the ones in this chapter or working drawings like those shown in Chapter 6. A competent CAD operator can stretch a room with a single command. "Flipping" a set of working drawings to face east instead of west takes only a couple of hours instead of the days usually required by manual drafting. For this reason, working drawings for the Basic Houses were done with a computer, producing both hard copy printouts that resemble traditional blueprints and CAD files that can be changed to fit an owner's requirements.

PLAYING WITH THE PLANS

There are as many ways to customize houses as there are

individuals, yet several types of modifications show up again and again. This section applies three common alterations to the interiors of the Basic Houses and offers three ways to fit the exteriors to a particular building site.

Change Room Uses

Presentation drawings like the ones in this chapter use labels and furniture symbols to show standard uses for each room but the Room Use Police won't pound on your door if you choose otherwise. Think about your activities during the day and night. For instance, maybe you hate laundry and love photography; leave off a utility room's window, put a movable work surface over the washer and dryer and call the space a darkroom. Second bedrooms can serve as offices. Room uses can double up. If you eat at the kitchen counter 29 days out of every 30, use the dining table as a desk for those 29 days and clear it off for your monthly formal dinner.

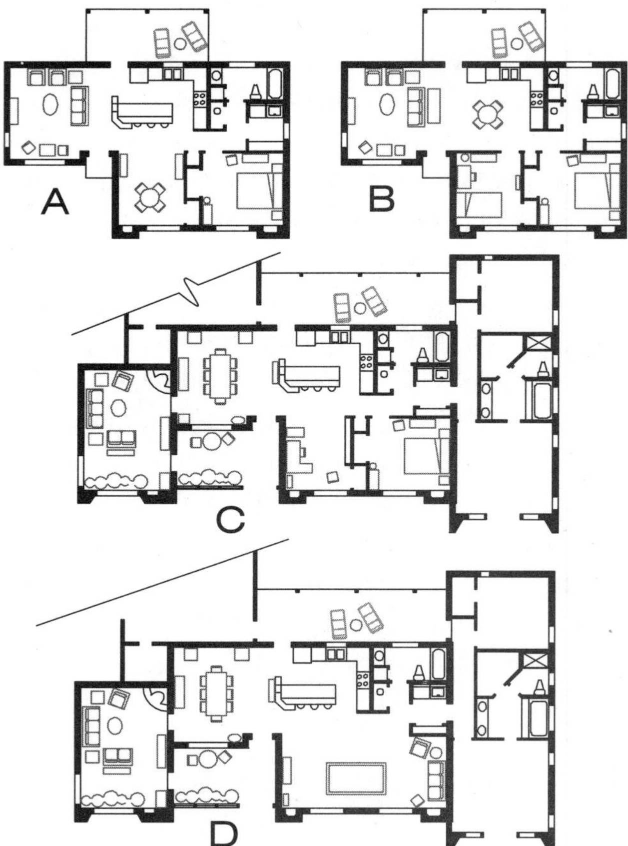

The basic version of Corbel House includes a separate dining room, as shown in version A. Alternately, it can have two bedrooms and a country kitchen as shown in B. The expanded version C can include four bedrooms or use the same space for three bedrooms and an office. Version D shows two bedrooms and a den large enough to hold a pool table.

Move Walls

Certain interior walls, called partition walls or non-bearing walls, have no function other than separating room spaces. At either the planning stage or when remodeling, you can reposition or remove partition walls without damaging a house's structure.

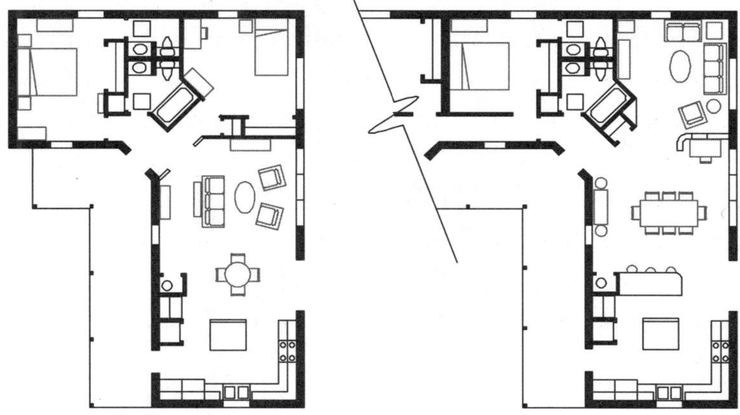

The left floor plan is the basic version of High Valley House. The plan on the right shows a portion of the expanded version. Removing the original partition wall that closes off the corner bedroom creates another living space.

Other interior walls, called bearing, structural or support walls, support the roof or upper floors. They cannot be moved unless some other form of structural support is substituted. Because of their simple roof framing, the Basic Houses have very few interior bearing walls. A roof framing plan, one element of a set of working drawings, will show which walls support the roof.

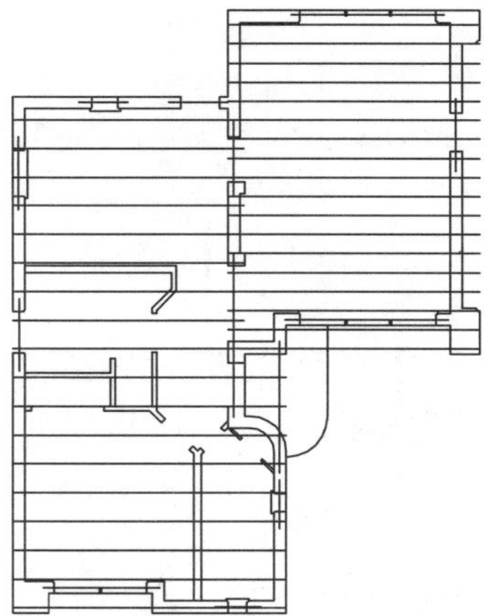

The simplified framing plan for Coyote House shows that the only interior bearing structures are the adobe wall between hall and living room and the lintels on either side.

Stretch Rooms

Suppose you want to enlarge a living area or bedroom by moving an exterior wall farther out. Depending on how the roof framing runs, it may be possible to make the roof larger by adding a couple more roof trusses at one end. However, if you need to make each truss longer to expand the room, the longer span may require stronger framing members. You should also check expansion plans to see how stretching a room might affect future additions to the house.

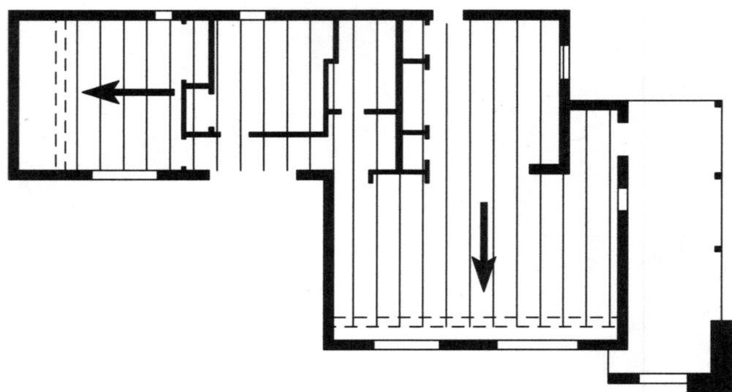

On the left side of Sun Hall House, the main bedroom is stretched four feet by adding two trusses. The living/dining area is stretched by using trusses that are two feet longer. The dashed lines show the original position of the walls.

Turn a Plan on the Lot

Because the Basic Houses are designed for solar heating, one particular side of each house must face south. But what if your building site requires that the heavily glazed side face another way? Most of these houses are designed so that more than one side can be the "front" of the house that faces the street. Check the plan's lot placement diagram to see if the house can switch its "front" side.

Flip Plans from East to West

Suppose you like Orchard House, designed to face east, but you own a west-facing lot. Putting the standard version of Orchard House on your lot would turn the heavily glazed side toward the north, destroying the house's solar gain. No problem. A designer competent with CAD software can simply flip, or "mirror," the various elements of the working drawings.

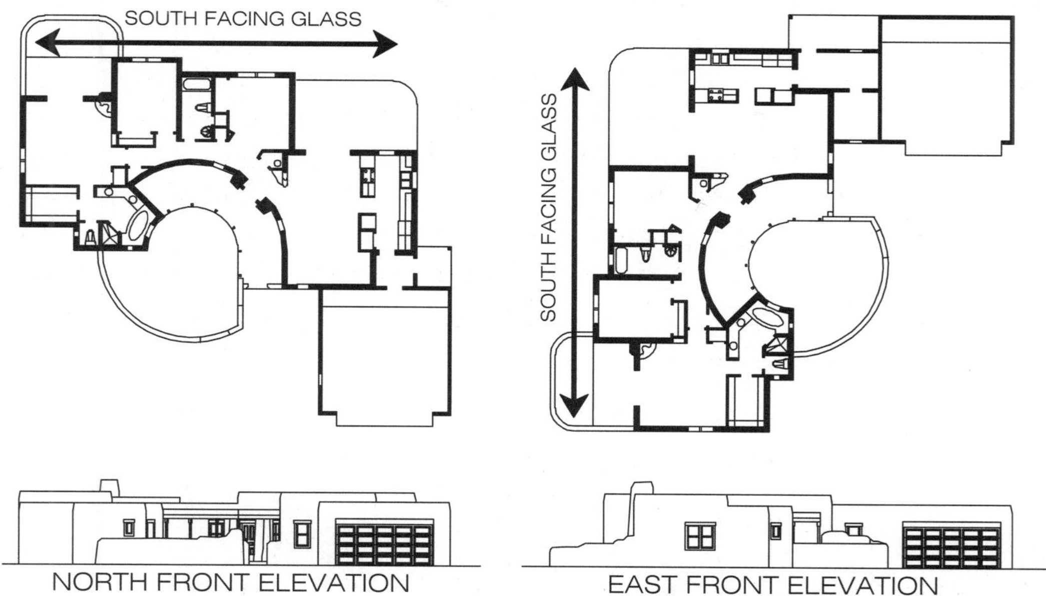

On the left, the standard version of Round House is designed for a lot that faces north and allows the heavily glazed rear to face south. On the right, the house is adapted for an east-facing lot by moving the garage door and adding storage and workshop spaces between house and garage.

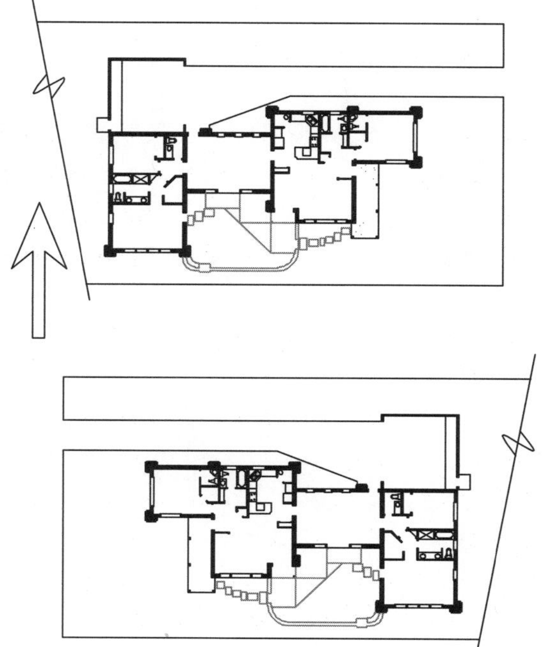

At the top is the standard version of Orchard House, designed for a lot that faces east. Below, the plan has been flipped to adapt it to a west-facing lot. The arrow points north.

Add a Different Expansion

The ways to expand these houses are almost limitless. For each, we designed an expansion that complements the basic house. However, your needs or the shape of your property may call for something completely different. The following illustration shows different possibilities for expanding Coyote House.

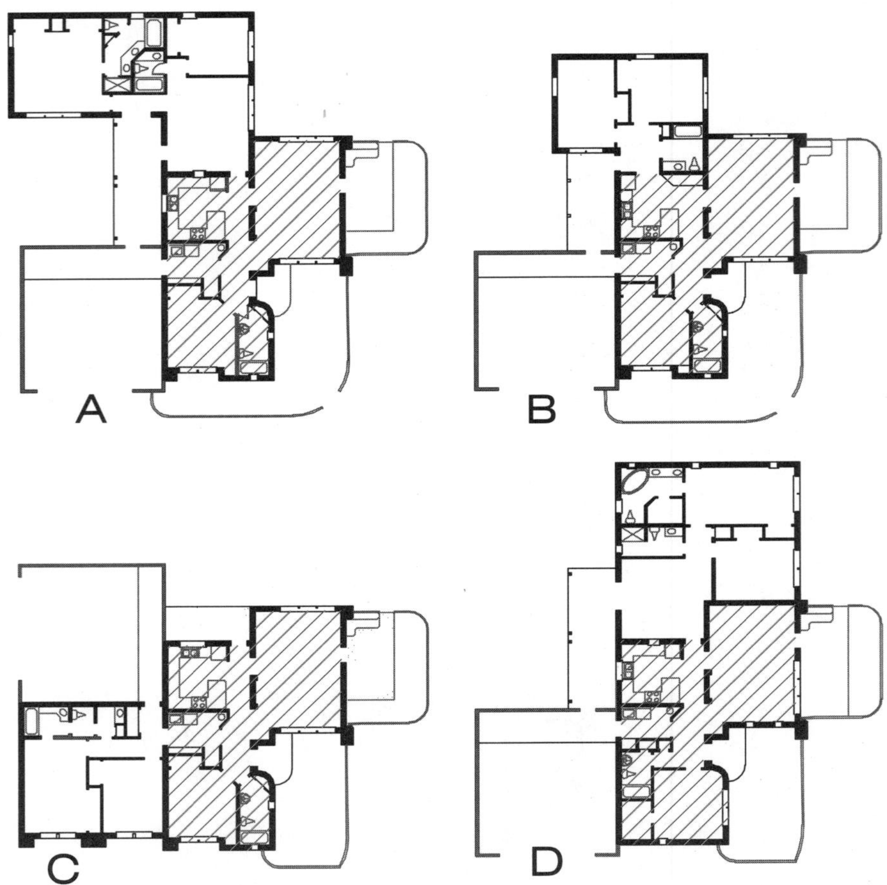

Version A shows the standard expansion of Coyote House—a garage, den or dining room, and two more bedrooms that form a courtyard. Version B deletes the dining room for a more compact footprint. Version C expands the house to the left to fit onto a wide, shallow lot. Version D moves the solar glazing from the front to the side to suit an east- or west-facing lot.

THE PLANS

This section presents the twelve plans. Each presentation includes a floor plan and elevations of the basic plan followed by the same elements showing an expanded version. Each presentation includes a lot placement diagram. For houses with an accessible version, the presentation shows the accessible floor plan in simplified form.

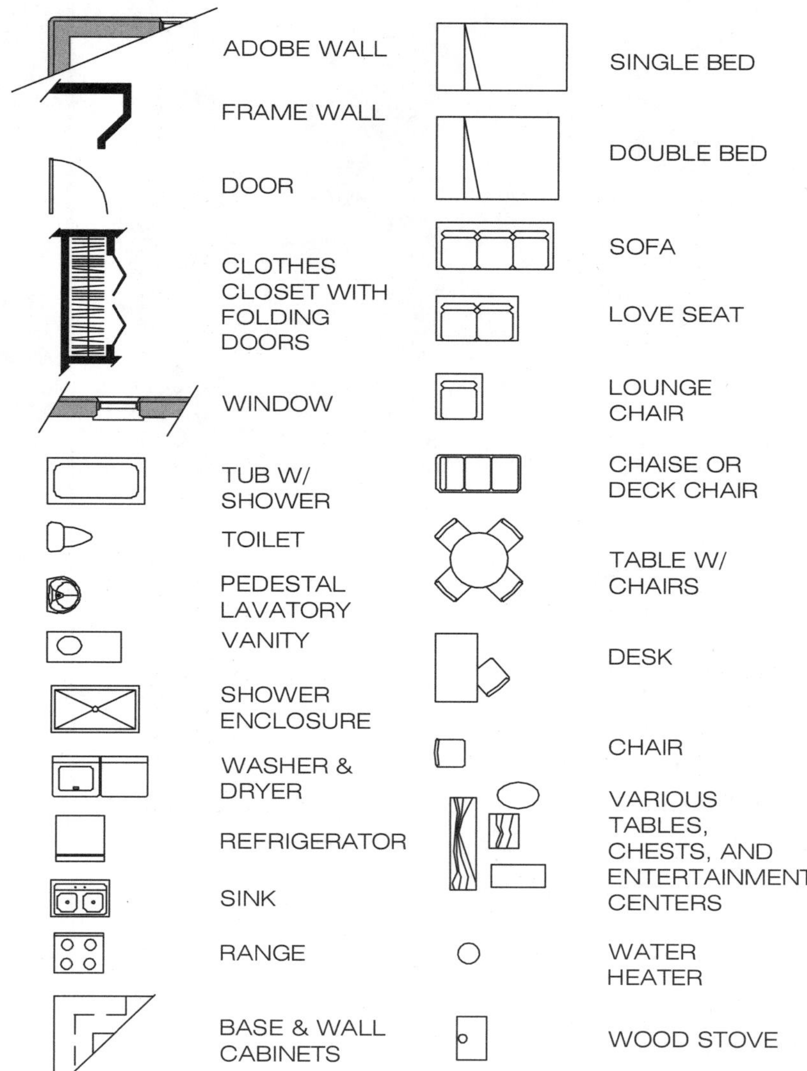

The presentation drawings use various symbols to indicate fixtures, appliances and furniture arrangements.

PLAN 1
ROUND HOUSE

The curved porch and courtyard of Round House create an outdoor living room with both sunny and shady sides. The courtyard gate leads along the porch to a front door flanked with buttresses.

From the entry, a curved hallway leads left to the bedroom and bath. To the right, a stepped adobe wall and *banco* frame a living and dining area with high ceilings and generous south-facing glass. An alcove off the living area can be either a private workspace or closed in for extra storage. Beyond a partial wall lies the kitchen with its own service porch.

Basic Rear (South) Elevation

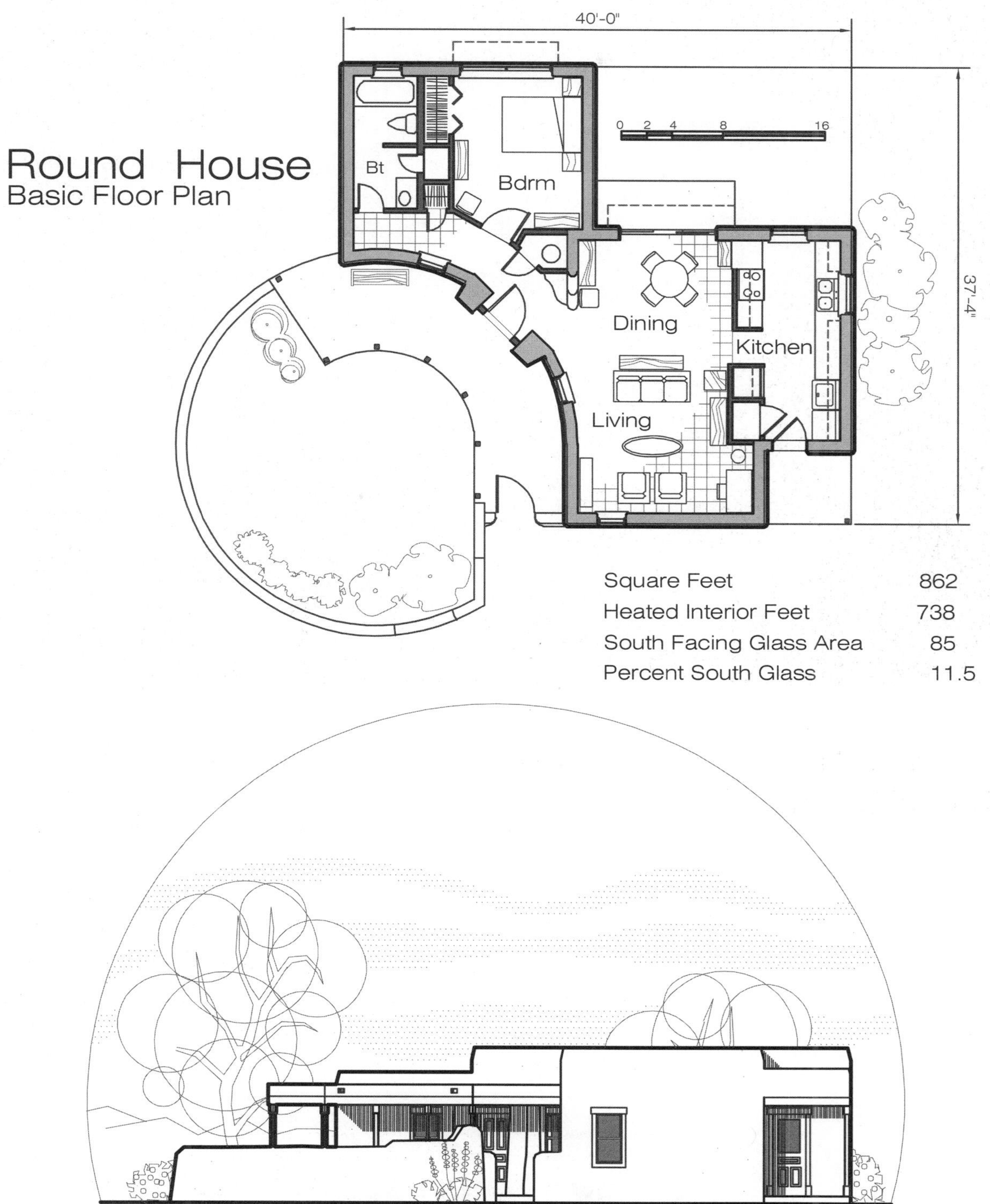

Basic Front (North) Elevation

The expanded house grows around the courtyard to include another bedroom and a large suite with fireplace and private courtyard. In the expansion shown, one wall of the original bedroom can become an opening that frames a study, formal living room or adult retreat.

At the other end of the house, the service porch turns into a utility/storage room leading to the garage. The illustration shows a garage for a house that faces north. For an east-facing lot, move the garage and door as shown previously.

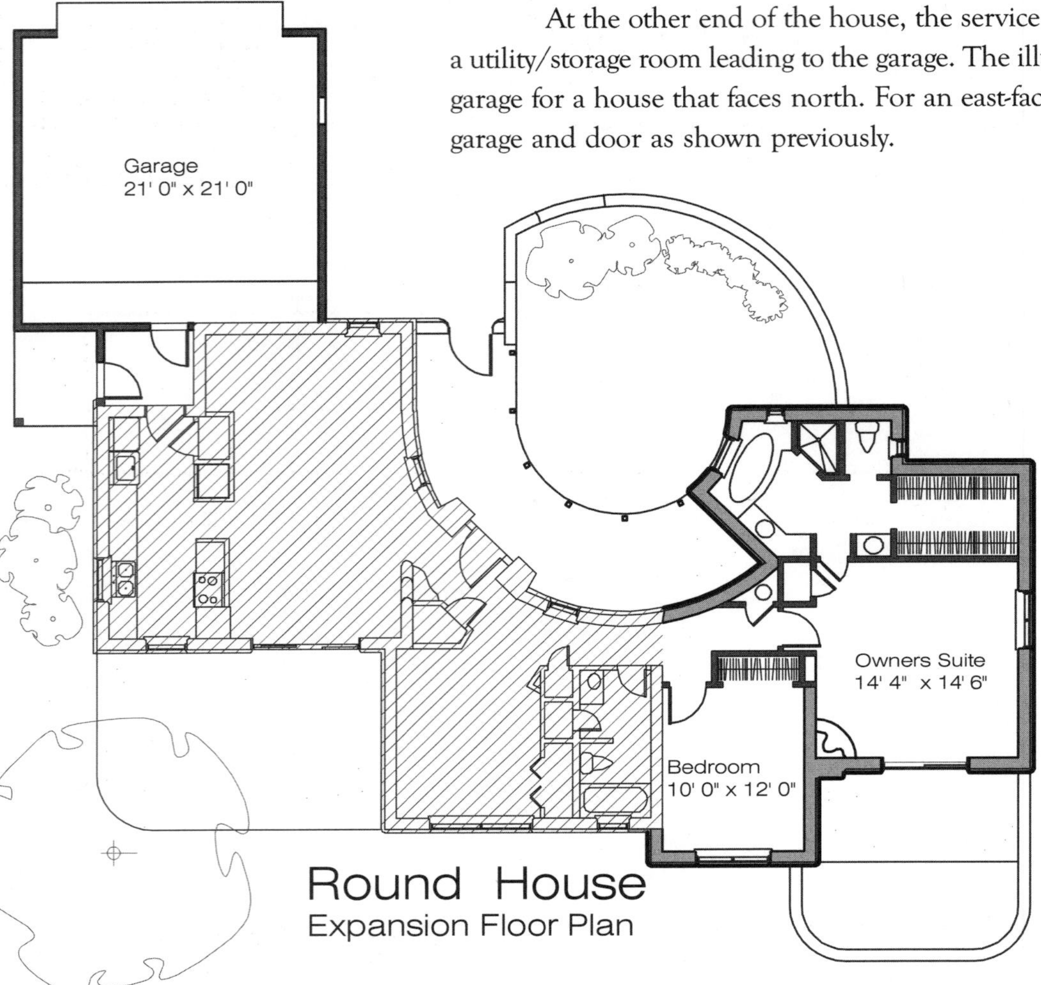

Round House
Expansion Floor Plan

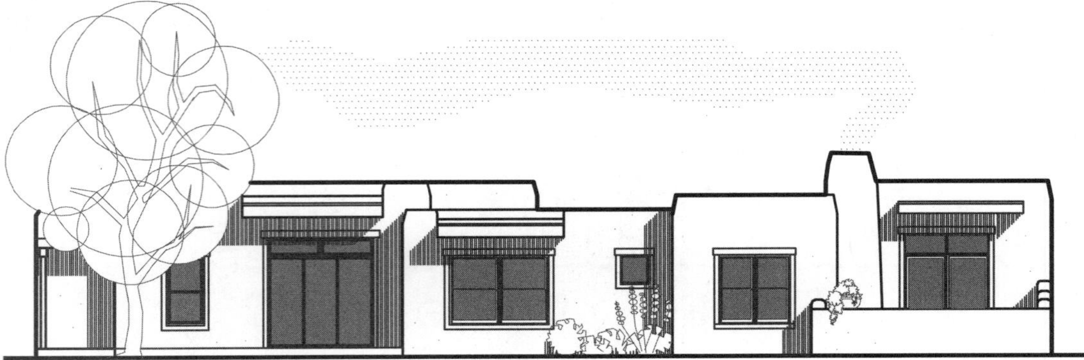

Rear (South) Elevation, Expansion

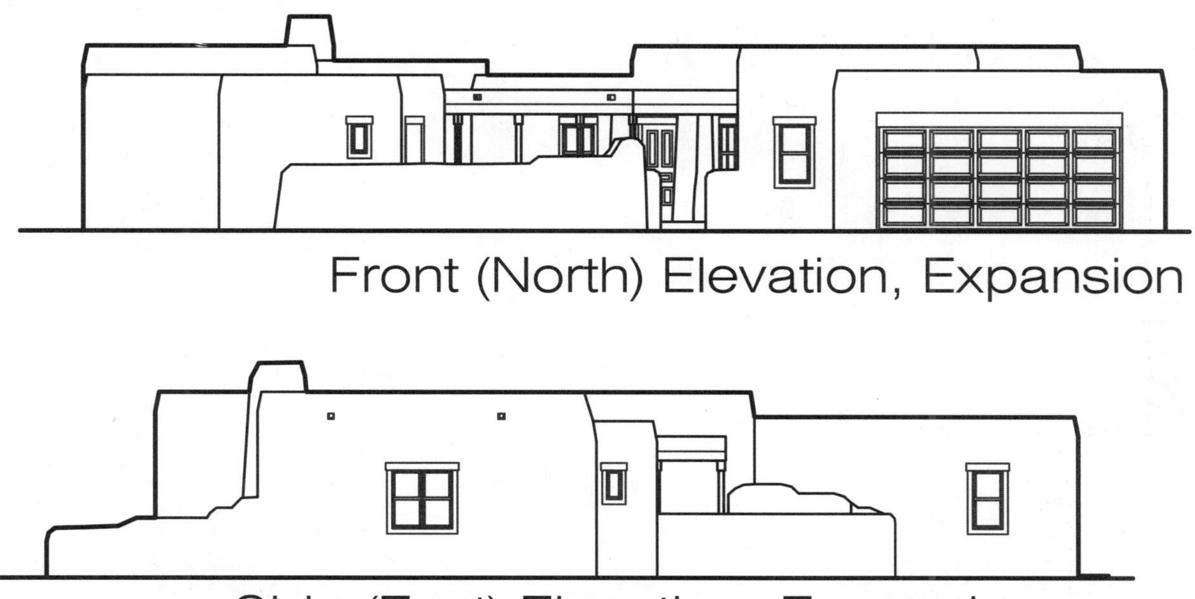

Front (North) Elevation, Expansion

Side (East) Elevation, Expansion

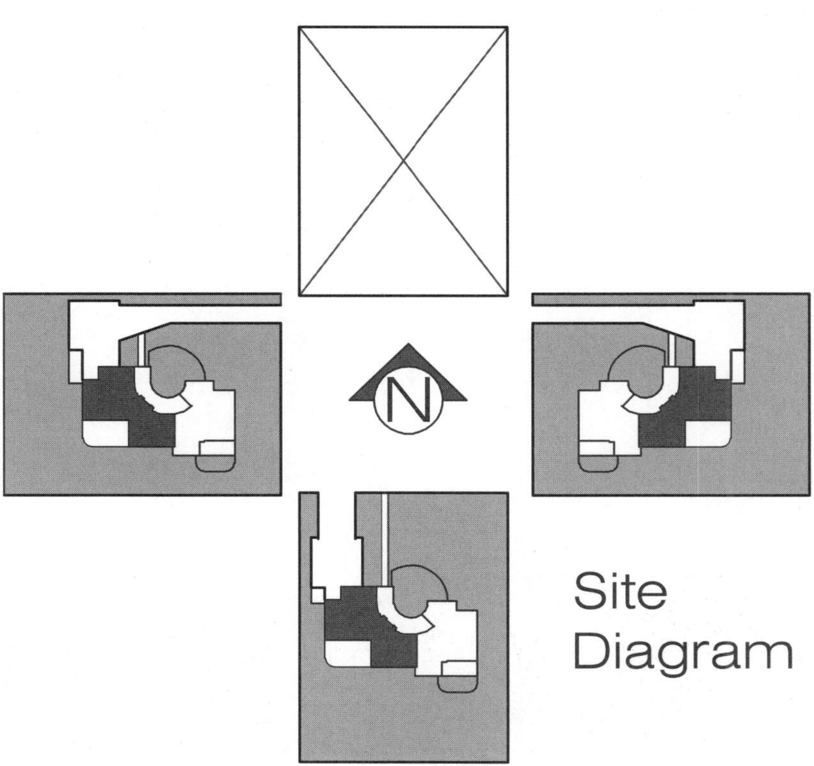

Site Diagram

PLAN 2 COYOTE HOUSE

Coyote House isn't designed for four-legged residents; it's named for the traditional "coyote" fence made from trimmed branches and saplings with the bark left on. The fence adds a rich texture that complements the clean lines of the building and shields the south-facing front of the house from the street.

The front door opens onto an angled entry hall with a skylight. To the left, a sunny bedroom and a bath make up the private zone of the house. To the right, space flows into a large, solar-heated living and dining area with a ceiling that rises to 11.5'. An exterior door leads to the patio on the east. The utility room and a kitchen with eating counter are located across the hall.

Basic Side (East) Elevation

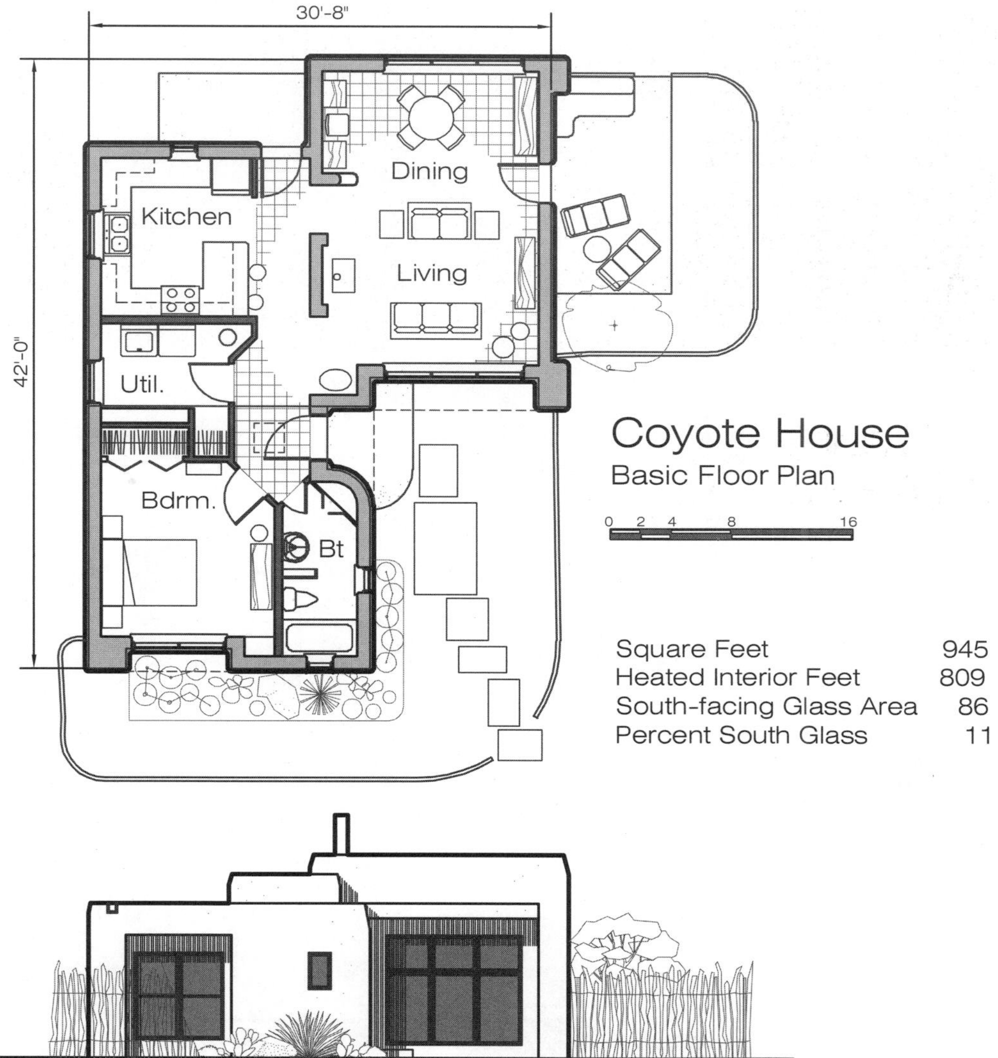

Basic Front (South) Elevation

In the expanded house, the original bedroom can become an office, guestroom, or study. The utility room becomes a convenient route to the garage. The original kitchen doorway opens onto a new family room or dining room, and the north kitchen window becomes a pass-through.

The new garage and new bedroom wing form a sheltered courtyard facing west. This outdoor area is accessible from the garage, family room and owners' suite. A clerestory into the dining room and large windows into the owners' suite provide solar heating for the added areas.

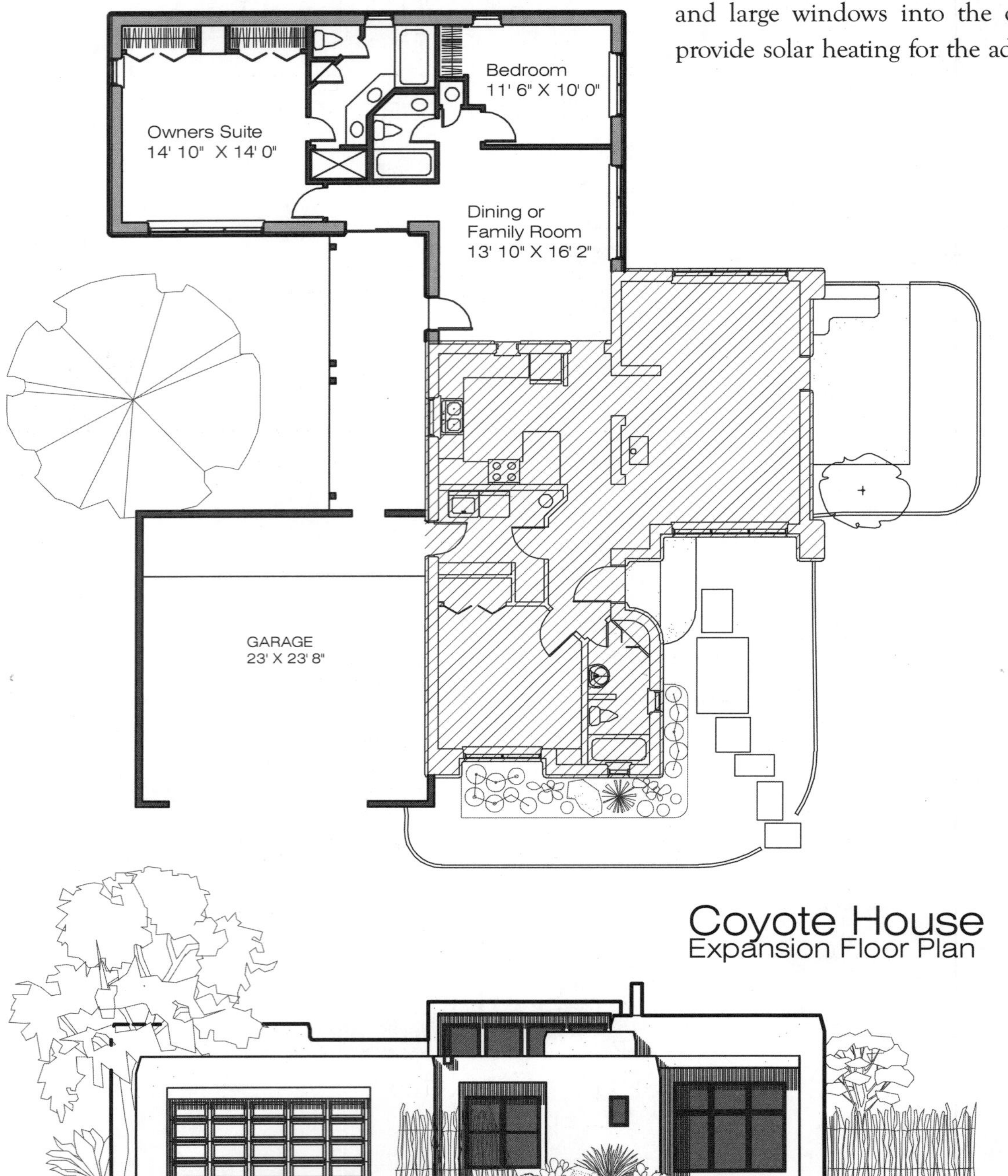

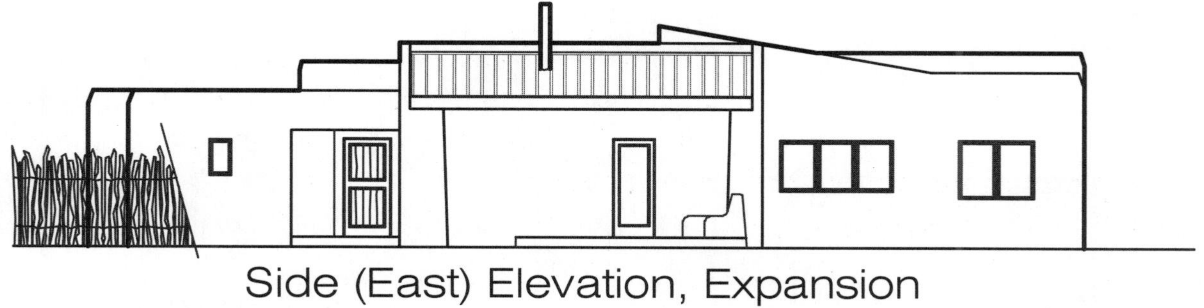

Side (East) Elevation, Expansion

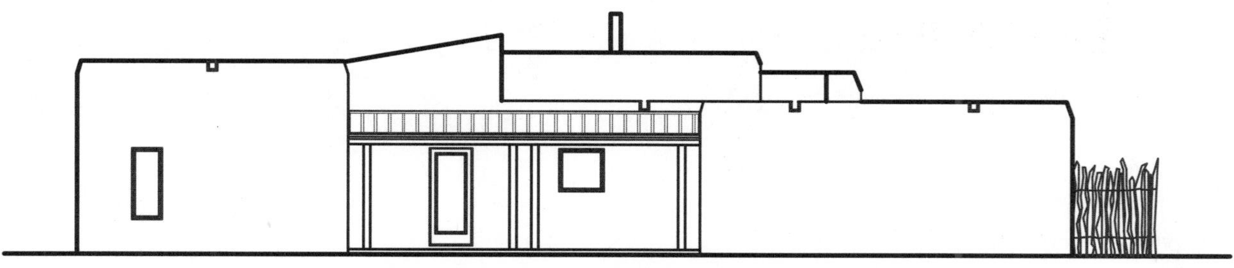

Side (West) Elevation, Expansion

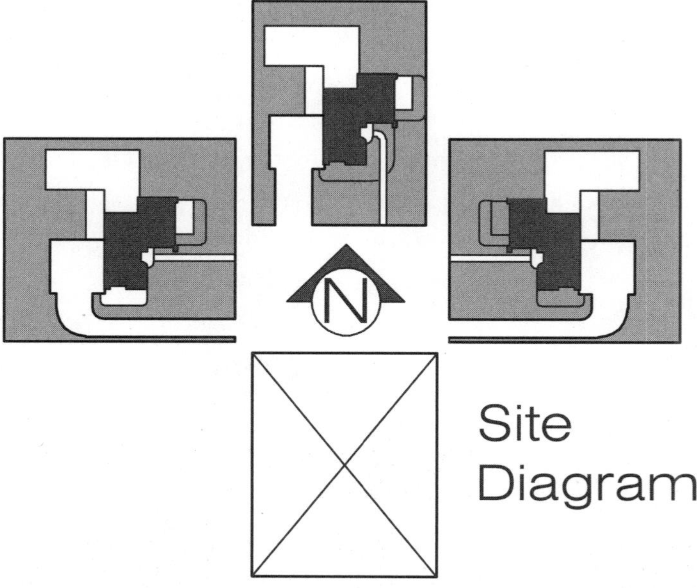

Site Diagram

PLAN 3
ORCHARD HOUSE

The shady front porch of Orchard House makes a good place to greet the day if the house faces east or to watch sunsets if it faces west. A short path leads from the porch to an outdoor living area behind the house. Just inside the front door, a compact entry provides access to bath, storage and a bedroom isolated from the main living area. Extra space off the bedroom can be a half-bath as shown, or a second walk-in closet.

All ceilings are higher than standard; the vaulted trusses in the living and dining room rise to nearly 12'. The kitchen, with pantry, eating counter and skylight, opens to the dining area, yet is shielded from the front door. The wheelchair-accessible version modifies the pantry and eating counter for easier use, as well as the laundry, bath, and patio areas.

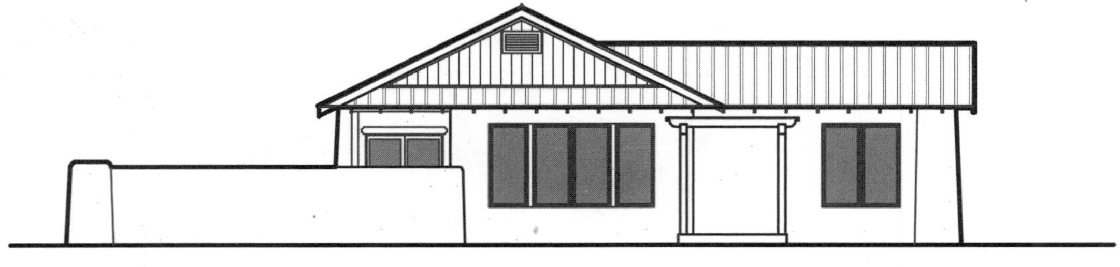

Basic Side (South) Elevation

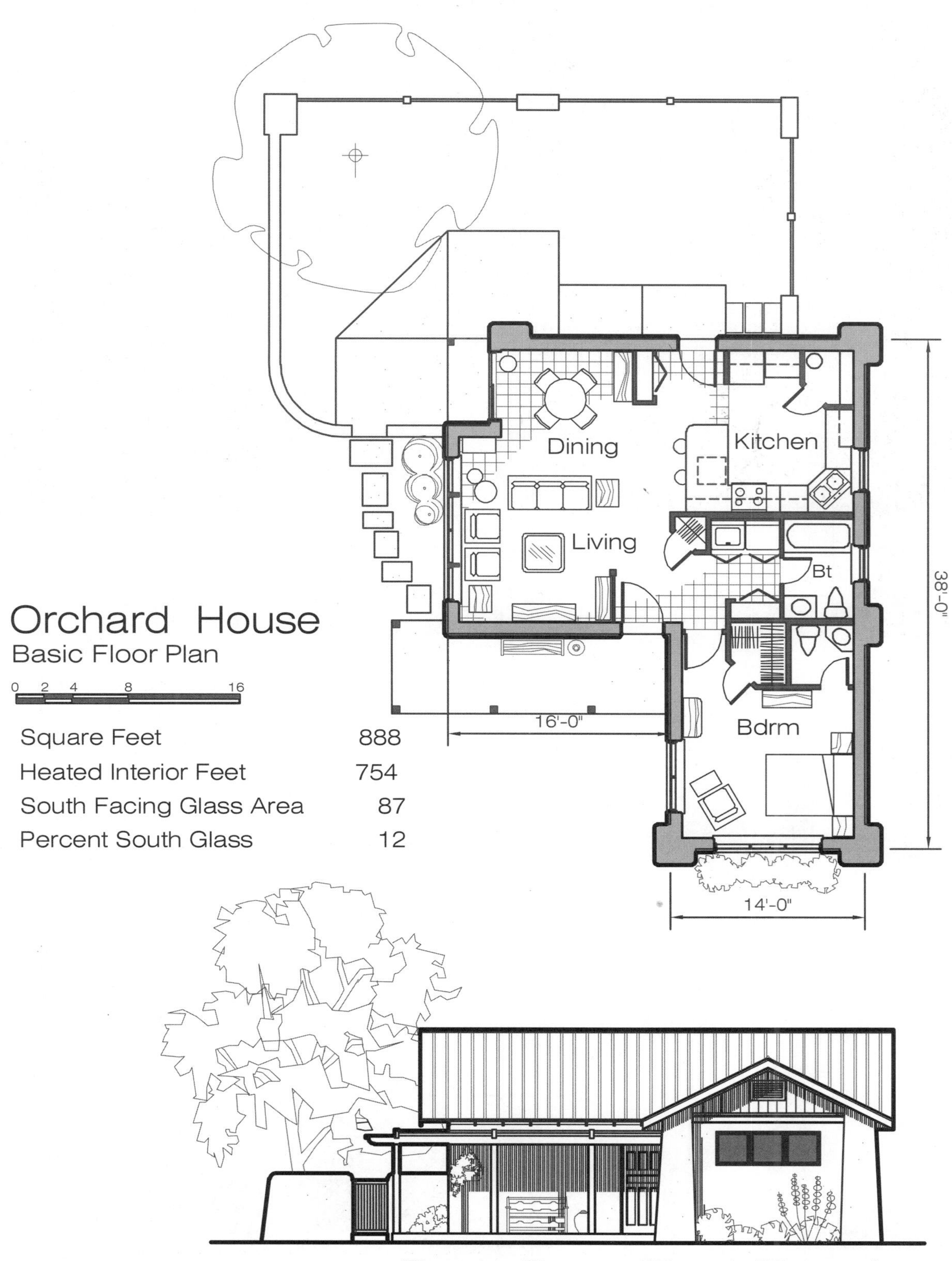

Orchard House

Basic Floor Plan

Basic Front (East) Elevation

The expanded house stretches back to accommodate plenty of south-facing glass and a sunny courtyard accessible from the dining area, the large new family room, and the main bedroom suite. The extra bedroom has its own half-bath, which is also convenient for gatherings in the family room. A garage fits into the northeast corner with access to the kitchen through the family room.

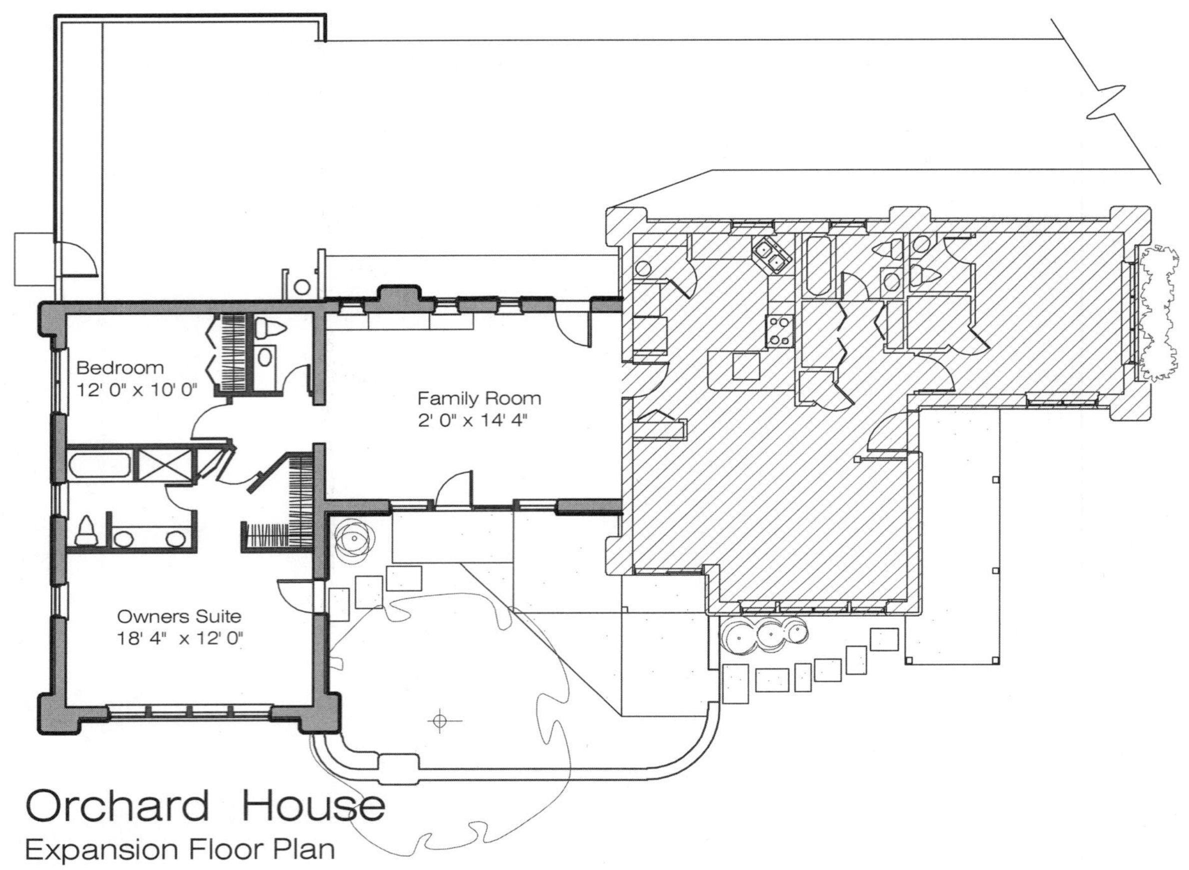

Orchard House
Expansion Floor Plan

Side (South) Elevation, Expansion

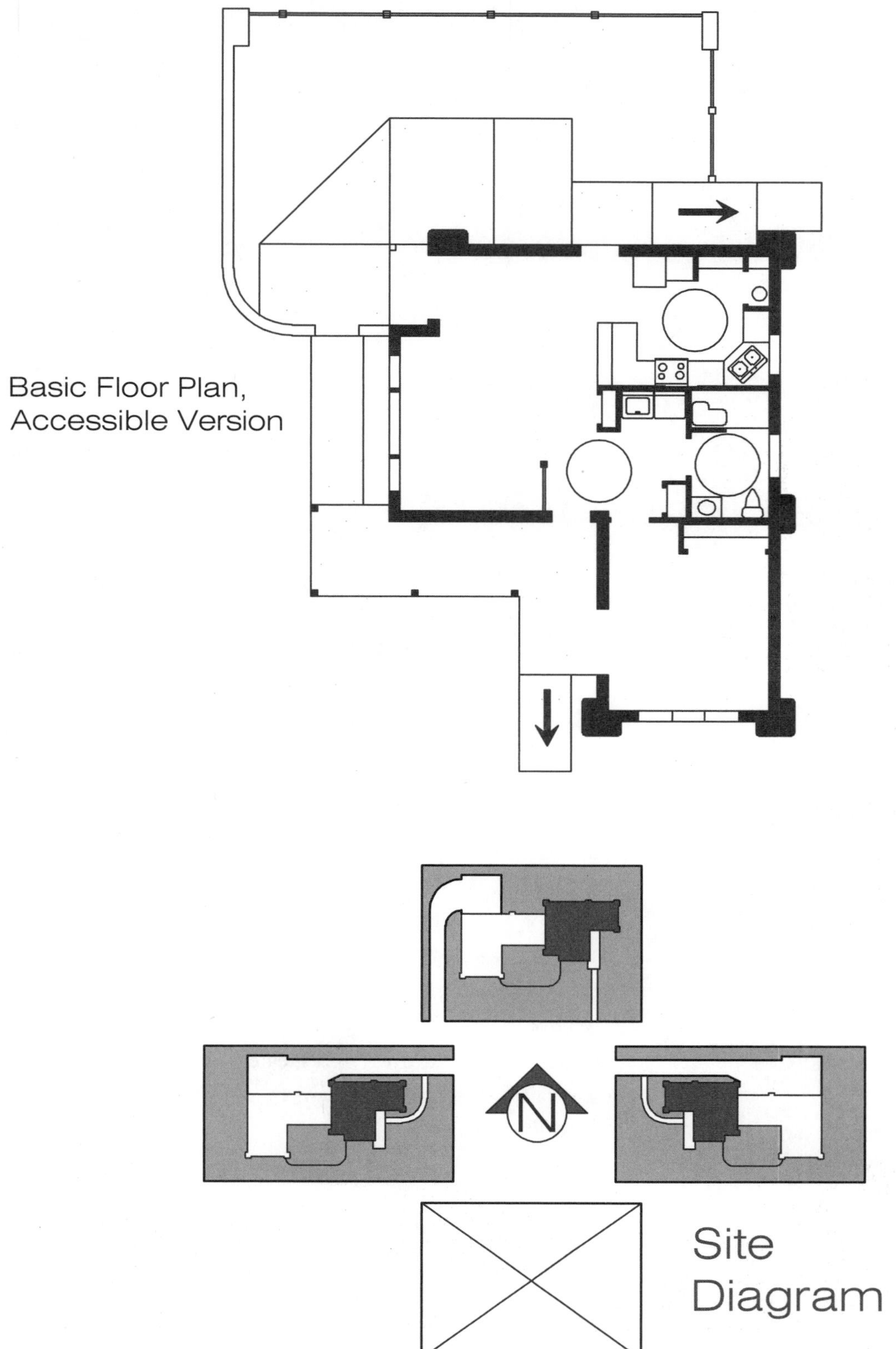
Basic Floor Plan,
Accessible Version
N
Site
Diagram

PLAN 4
CORBEL HOUSE

In the version shown, Corbel House includes a separate dining room and an eating counter screened by a stepped adobe wall. A more informal arrangement substitutes a table for the counter and wall, creating a country kitchen in the high-ceilinged living area. A study or second bedroom can fit in the space shown as a dining room.

Carved corbels support an entry porch and shading overhangs across the south front of the house and trim a back porch large enough for cool relaxing in the summer. The patio wall shields the house from the street and creates a welcoming approach. The house can face south as shown, or west if the patio gate is moved around the corner.

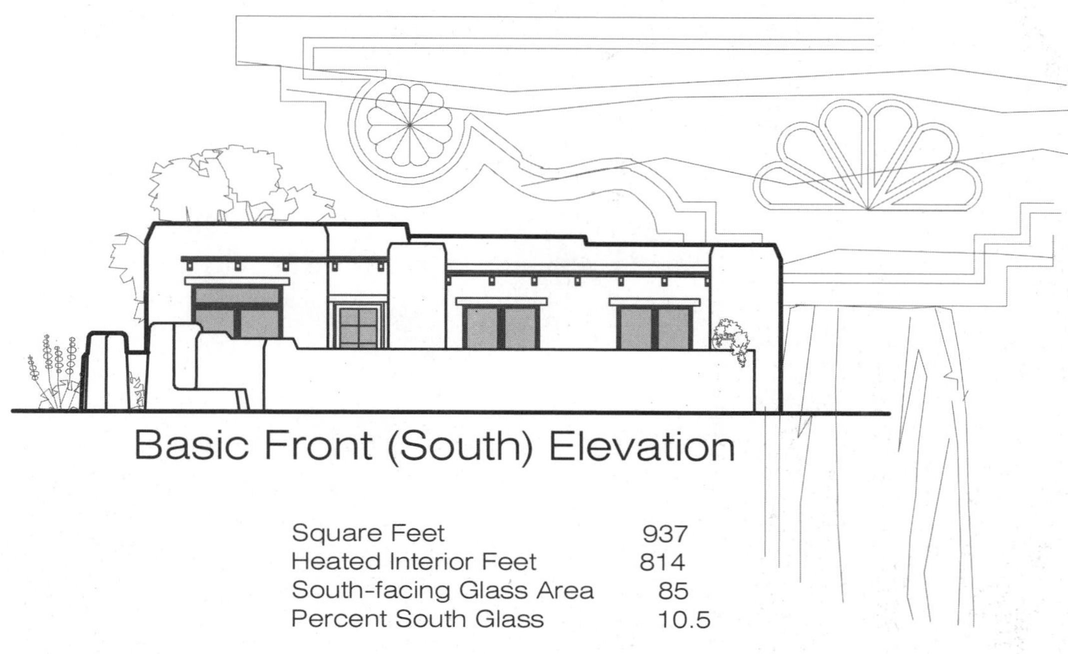

Basic Front (South) Elevation

Square Feet	937
Heated Interior Feet	814
South-facing Glass Area	85
Percent South Glass	10.5

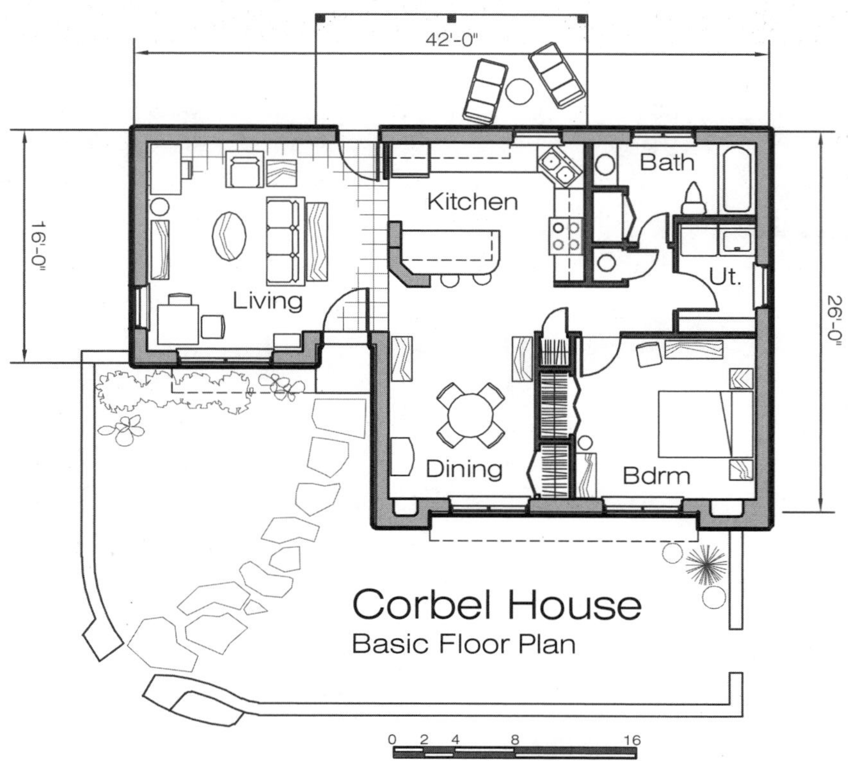

Corbel House
Basic Floor Plan

The house expands with a living room and garage on one end and bedrooms on the other. The new sunroom entry, large enough for lounging, creates excellent circulation to the new step-down living area. The existing south door and window draw warmth into the original spaces.

The former living room can become a large dining room or a family room. The bedrooms can remain as is, or the dividing wall can be removed to make a conveniently located family room. The utility room becomes separate laundry and storage closets, opening the end of the hall into the new bedroom wing.

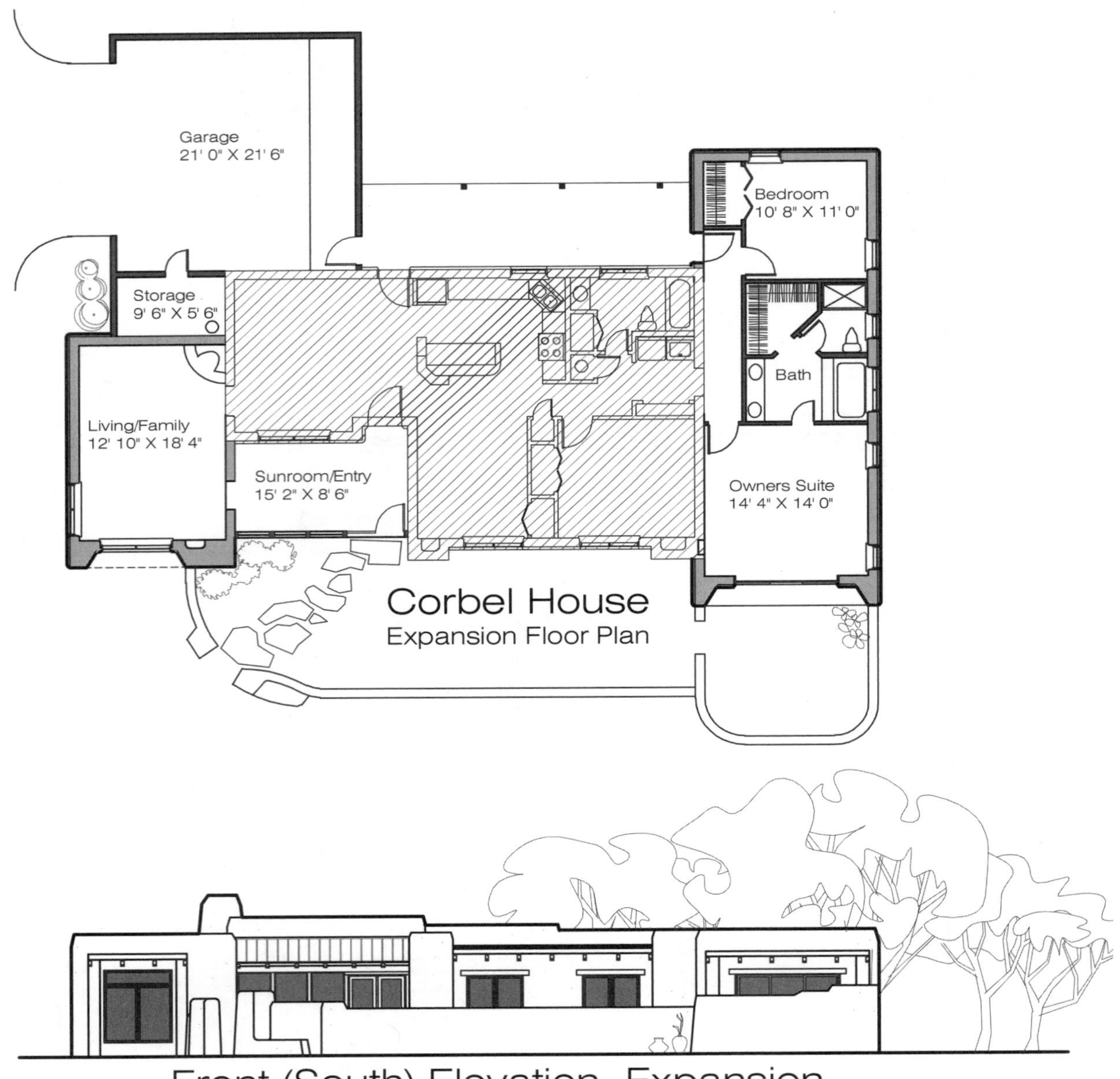

Front (South) Elevation, Expansion

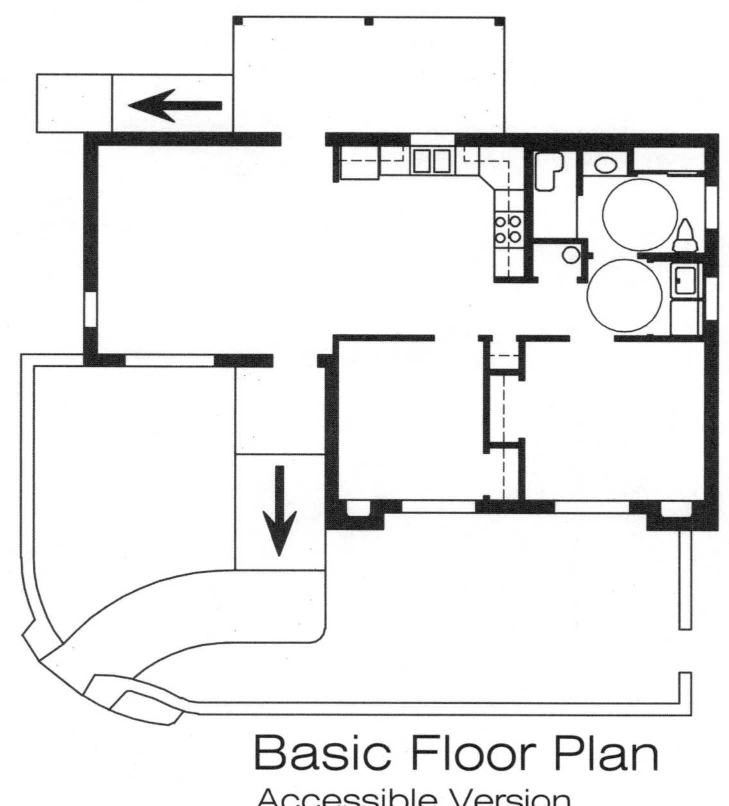

Basic Floor Plan
Accessible Version

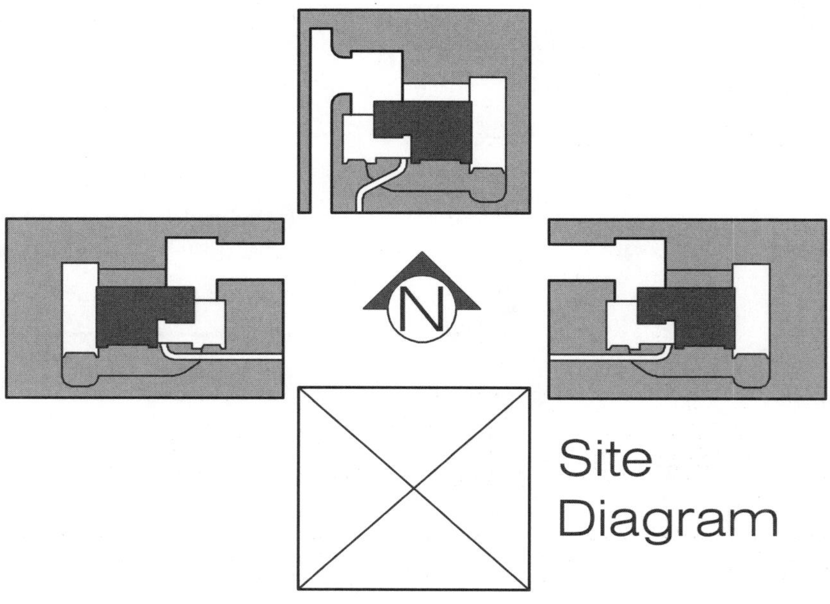

Site
Diagram

PLAN 5
HIGH VALLEY HOUSE

High Valley House resembles traditional homes hidden away in the orchards and mountain valleys of New Mexico. We've borrowed the porch, high-pitched roof and simple, harmonious form but updated the circulation, framing and windows.

The angled entry leads left to the full bath and a main bedroom with half-bath (or an extra closet). Straight ahead is a second bedroom that can also serve as study or office. To the right the ceiling rises to 15.5' over the living and dining room.

The kitchen ceiling drops to an intimate 7' so that a small loft can fit over it. The loft at the top of a ship's ladder can be a storage area, a study, a sleeping place for guests (if they're nimble), or for just getting away from it all. The kitchen includes a pantry, island, laundry center and a north door conveniently near a future garage.

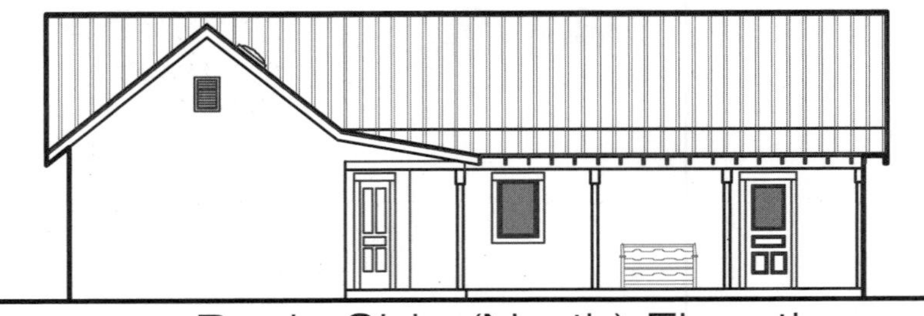

Basic Side (North) Elevation

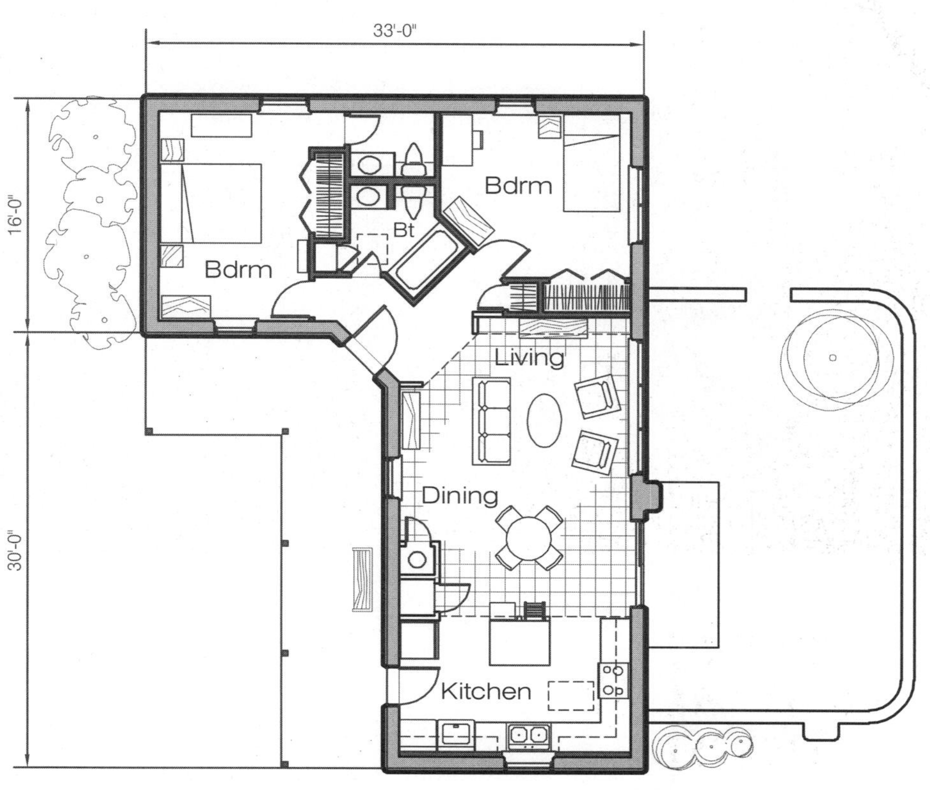

High Valley House

Basic Floor Plan

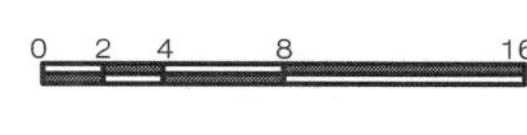

Square Feet	1046
Heated Interior Feet	909
South Facing Glass Area	102
Percent South Glass	11

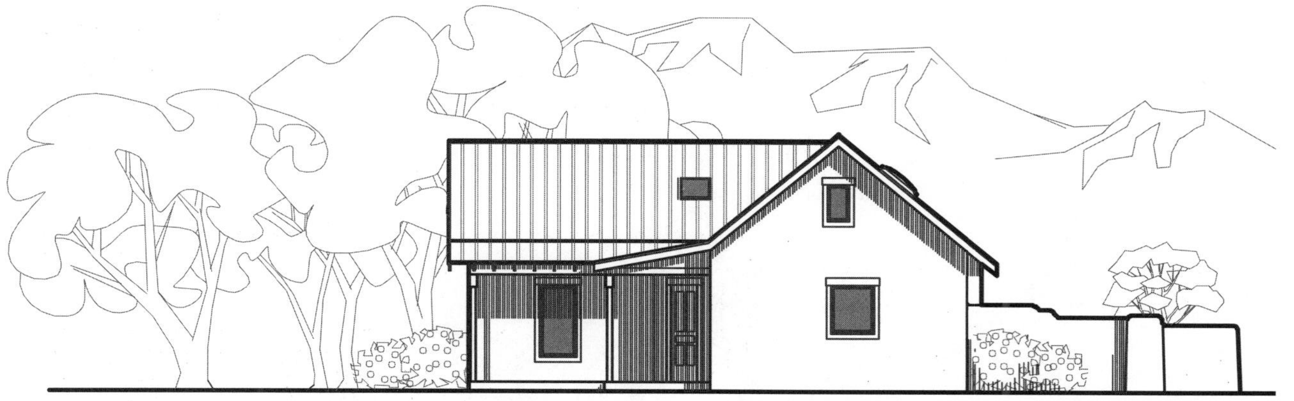

Basic Front (West) Elevation

The fully expanded High Valley House encloses a courtyard, one side shady for summer relaxing while the sunny side invites gardening and winter basking protected from the wind. The hallway to the owners' new suite runs past the existing main bedroom, another bedroom and sliding doors to the courtyard. The suite includes a bedroom with large south windows, a bath and walk-in closet and a door to the private porch on the northwest.

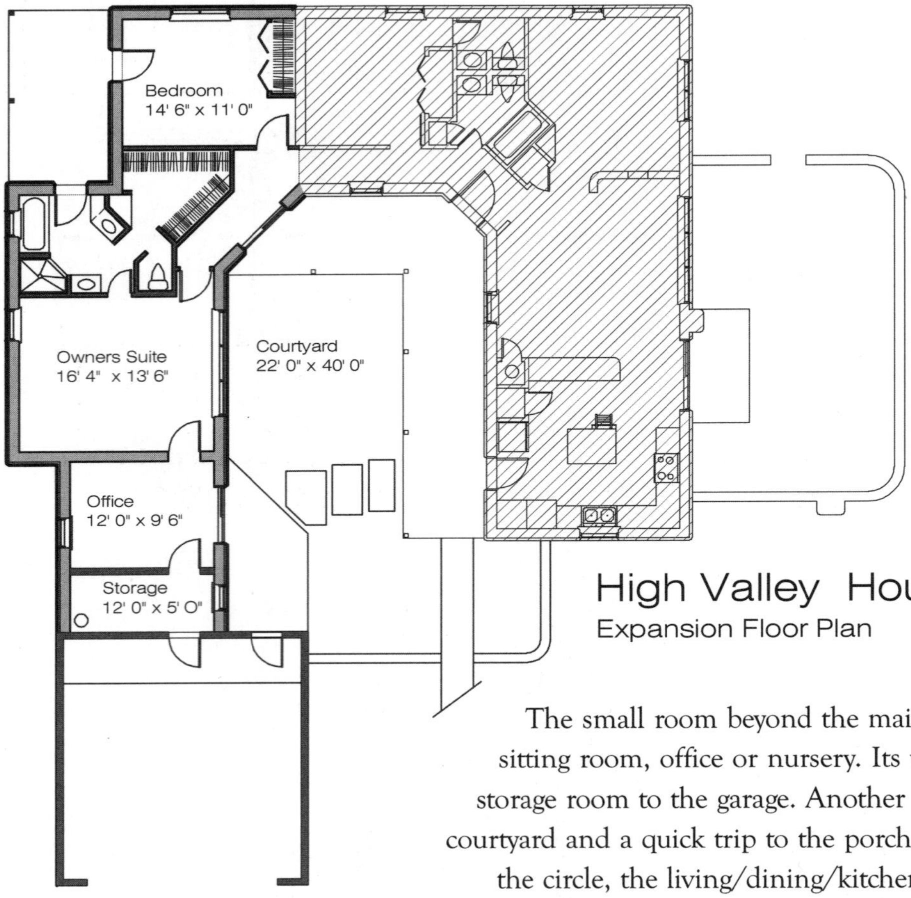

Bedroom
14' 6" x 11' 0"

Owners Suite
16' 4" x 13' 6"

Courtyard
22' 0" x 40' 0"

Office
12' 0" x 9' 6"

Storage
12' 0" x 5' 0"

High Valley House
Expansion Floor Plan

The small room beyond the main bedroom can serve as a sitting room, office or nursery. Its west door leads through a storage room to the garage. Another garage door opens on the courtyard and a quick trip to the porch and kitchen. Completing the circle, the living/dining/kitchen area can remain as is or develop into an expanded kitchen and dining space if the bedroom wall is removed to create a new living area.

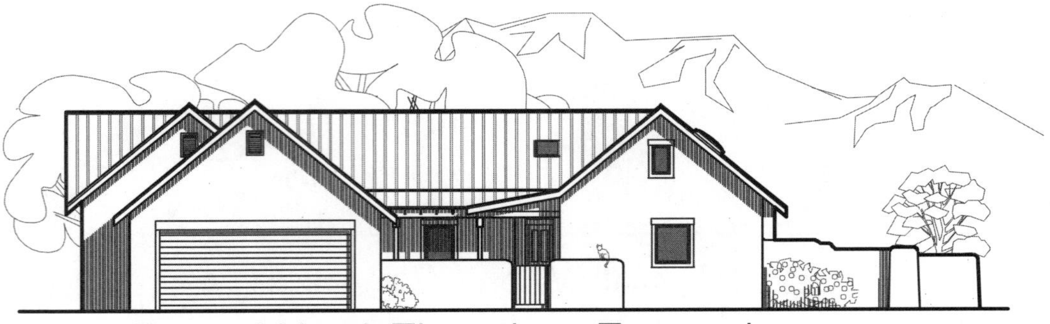

Front (West) Elevation, Expansion

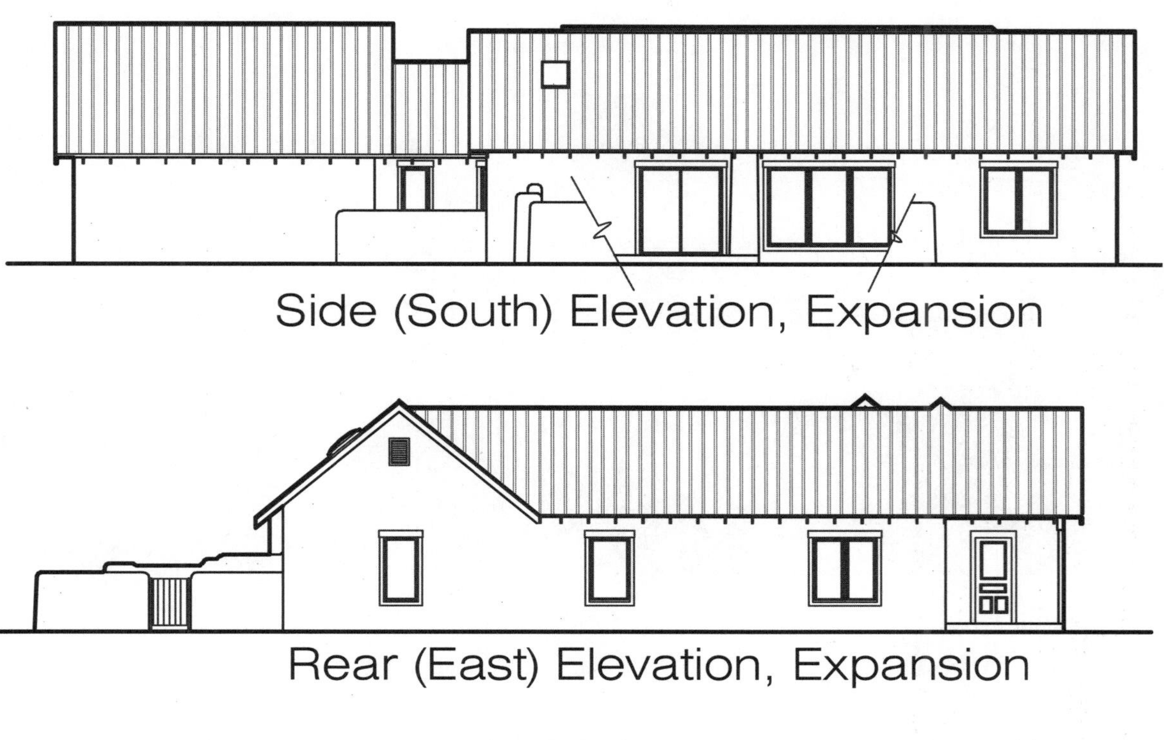

Side (South) Elevation, Expansion

Rear (East) Elevation, Expansion

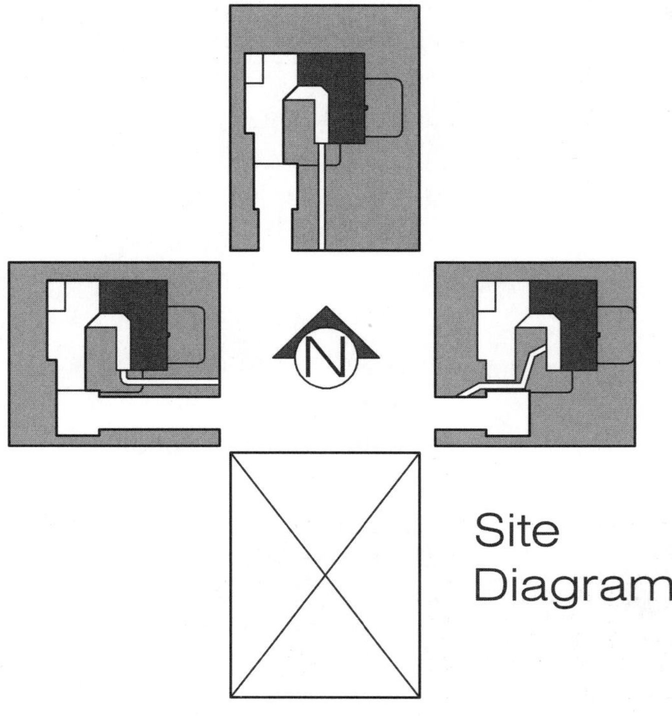

Site Diagram

PLAN 6
SUN HALL HOUSE

Sun Hall House with its generous south-facing glass can stretch along a narrow east- or west-facing lot. The wrap-around wall of the wide front porch blocks the afternoon sun and leads to the south yard. The entry opens onto a long, sunny living and dining room with a 9' ceiling. The kitchen on the north includes an eating counter and pantry.

A hallway jog maintains the privacy of the bedroom and bath zone. The hallway's 7.5' wide sliding door leads to a patio shaded with angled trellis boards that admit sunlight in winter but block it in the warm season.

A laundry center is plumbed into the same wall as the bath. Storage shelves line part of the bath's opposite wall, then moves to the other side to form storage in a child's bedroom. The closet wall beyond buffers the main bedroom at the end of the hall.

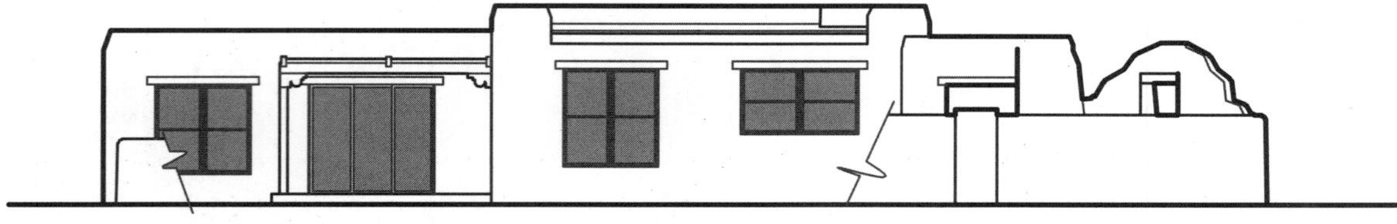

Basic Side (South) Elevation

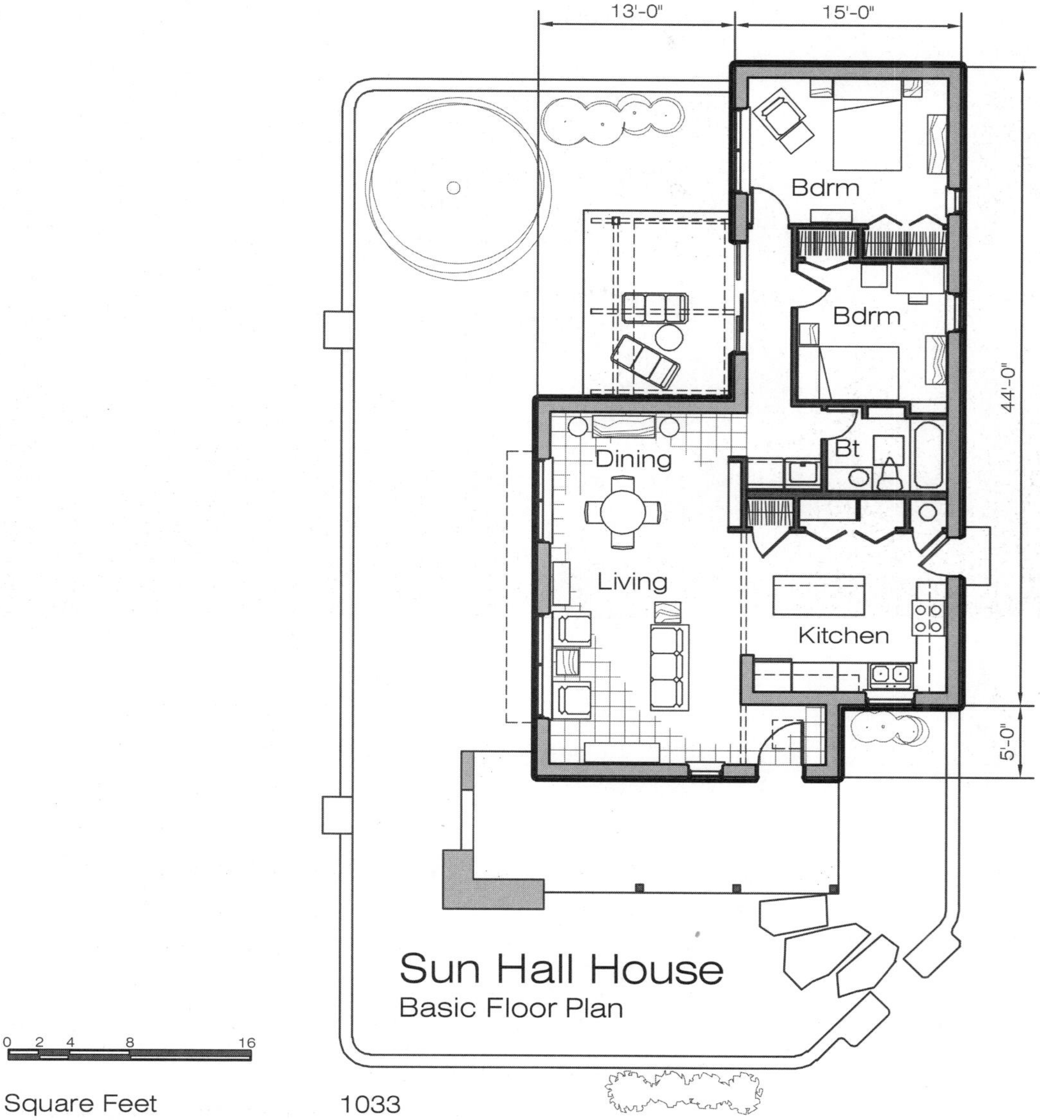

13'-0" 15'-0"

Bdrm

Bdrm

Bt

Dining

Living

Kitchen

44'-0"

5'-0"

Sun Hall House

Basic Floor Plan

0 2 4 8 16

Square Feet	1033
Heated Interior Feet	908
South-facing Glass Area	107
Percent South Glass	12

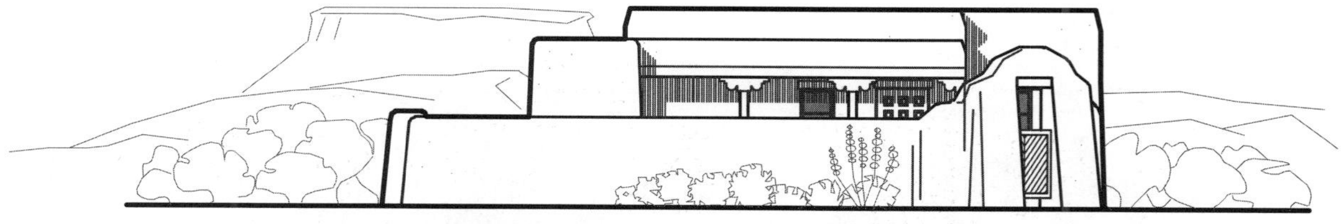

Basic Front (East) Elevation

In the expansion shown, Sun Hall House grows to the front. A corner of the original patio wall creates a small entry courtyard. The original front porch, now enclosed, forms an entry before stepping up to a study defined by a half wall and the original columns and buttress. The study (or small parlor, bedroom, guestroom or nursery) has its own door to the south patio. To the left of the entry is a new main bedroom with large bath and dressing areas, south glazing and a private courtyard.

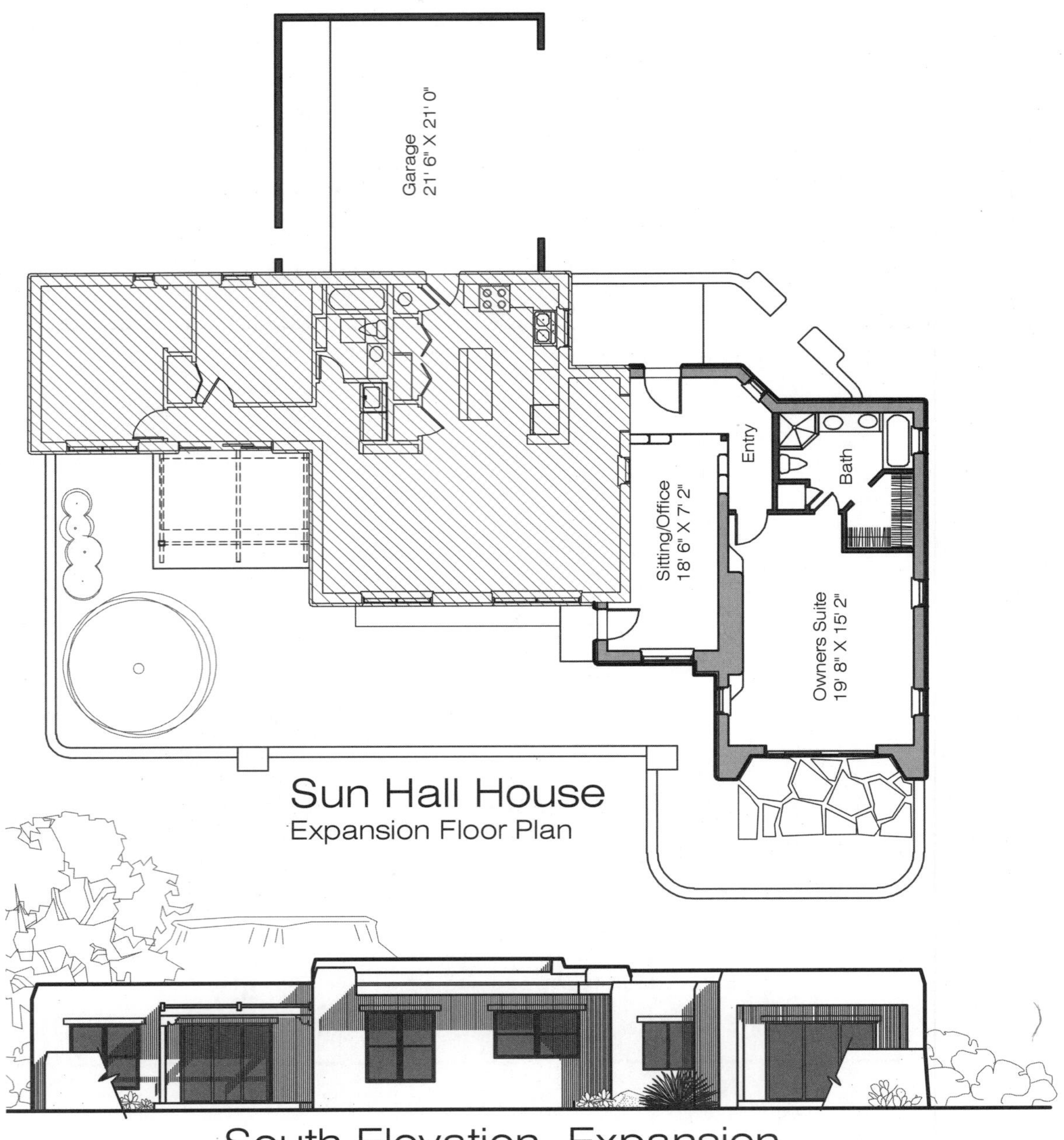

South Elevation, Expansion

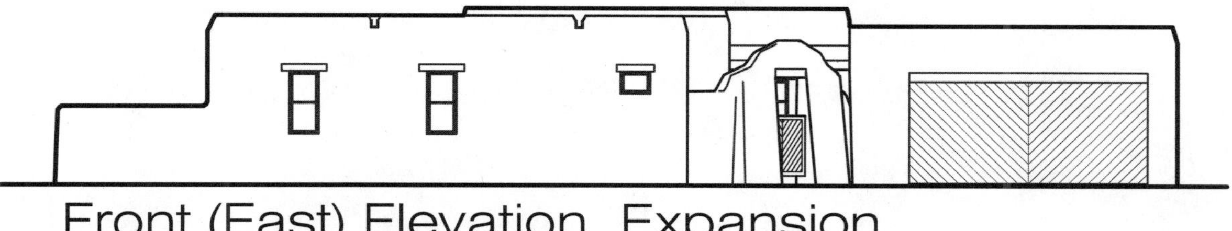

Front (East) Elevation, Expansion

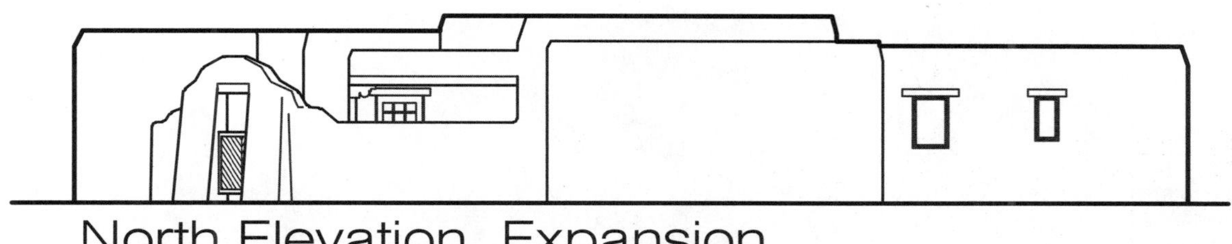

North Elevation, Expansion

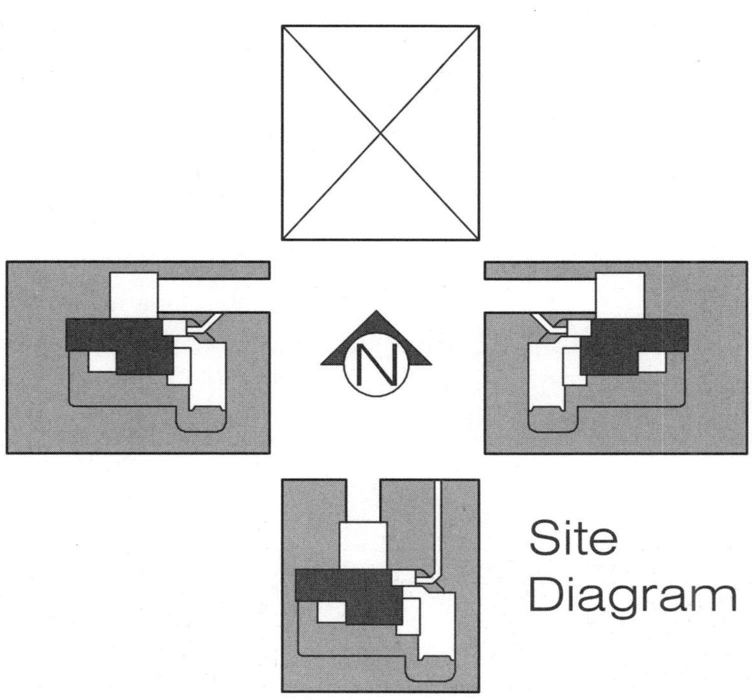

Site Diagram

PLAN 7
GARDEN HOUSE

The patio wall that loops around the east end of Garden House leaves room for growing corn, tomatoes, squash and a few fruit trees. Add a grill or an *horno* (outdoor oven) and you can grow, cook and eat your dinner all in the pleasant southeast courtyard.

The front door opens on an entry and a stepped adobe wall. In the living-dining room beyond the wall, a hearth platform angles around a corner, creating a base for a wood stove or zero-clearance fireplace. You can extend the hearth to create a seating *banco* or cut it short to leave more space for an entertainment center.

The high-ceilinged main room opens to the south with a patio door assembly almost 14' wide and a single door leads east to the shaded patio. A counter on one side and pantry and closet on the other separate the kitchen. To the west, a short hallway leads past a bath and laundry center, separating the bedrooms from the living area for peace and privacy.

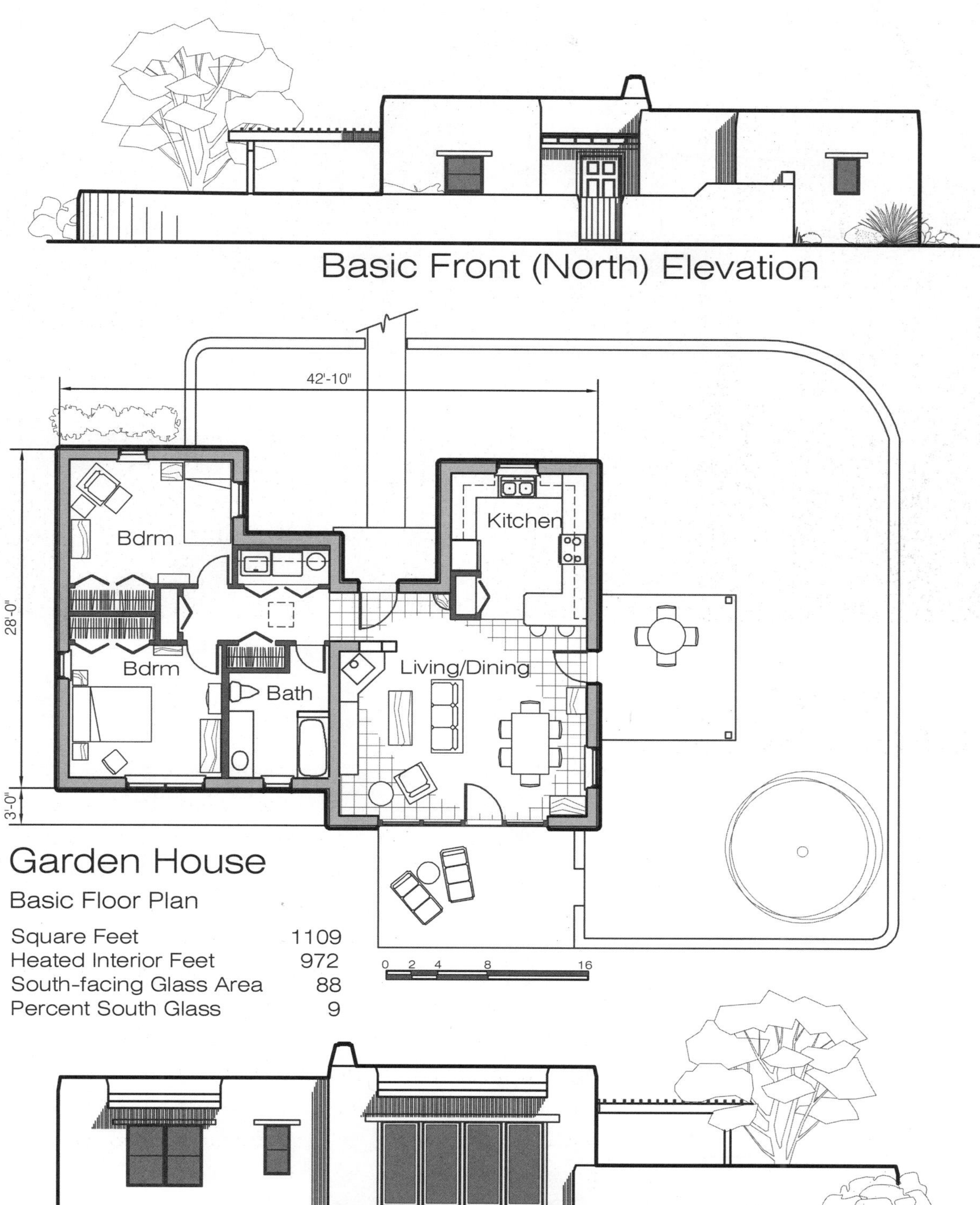

Basic Rear (South) Elevation

In the expanded house, the east patio converts into a tiled sunroom and bath. The sunroom leads to a new main bedroom with double closets and plentiful south-facing glass. A north door opens on a short walkway to the garage.

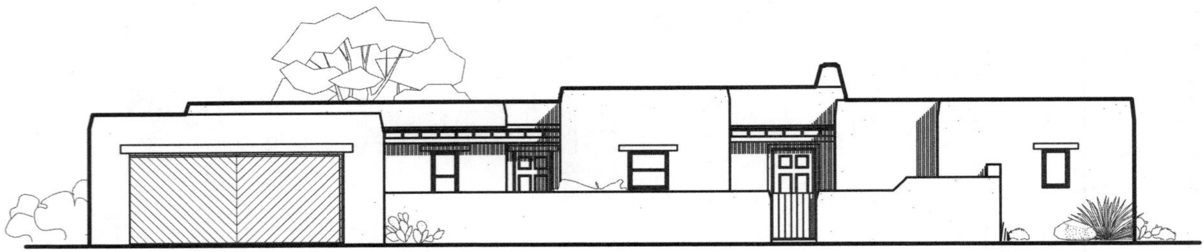

Front (North) Elevation, Expansion

Garage
21' 0" X 21' 6"

Bath

Owners Suite
14' 10" x 14' 0"

Sunroom
12' 0" X 8'

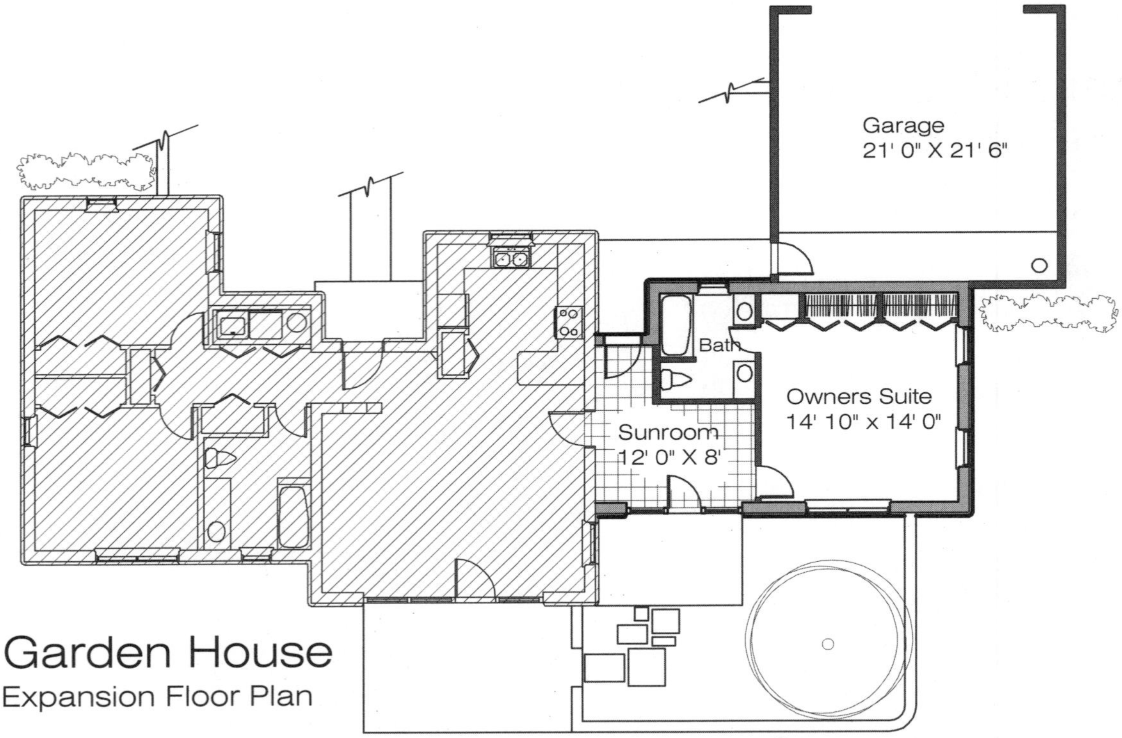

Garden House
Expansion Floor Plan

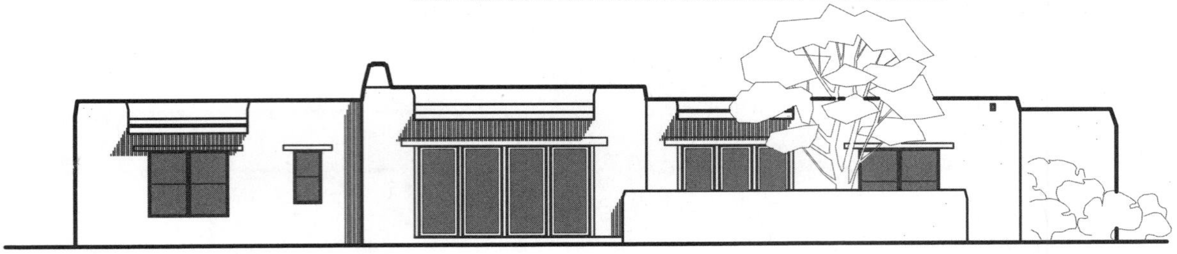

Rear (South) Elevation, Expansion

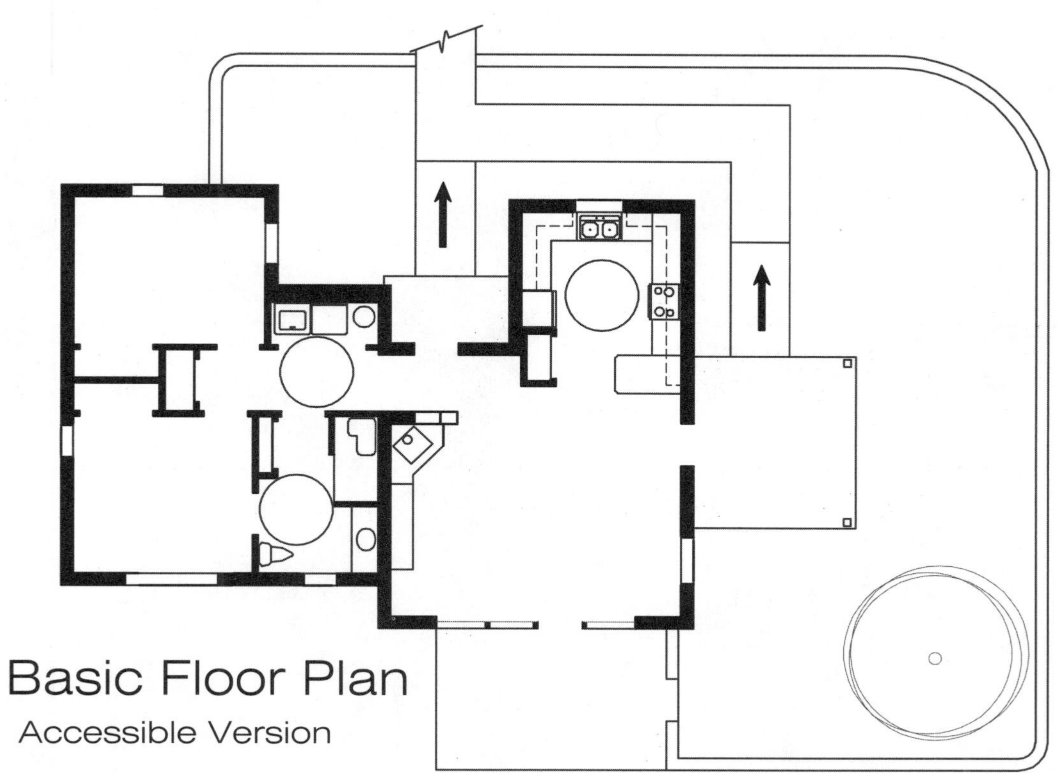

Basic Floor Plan
Accessible Version

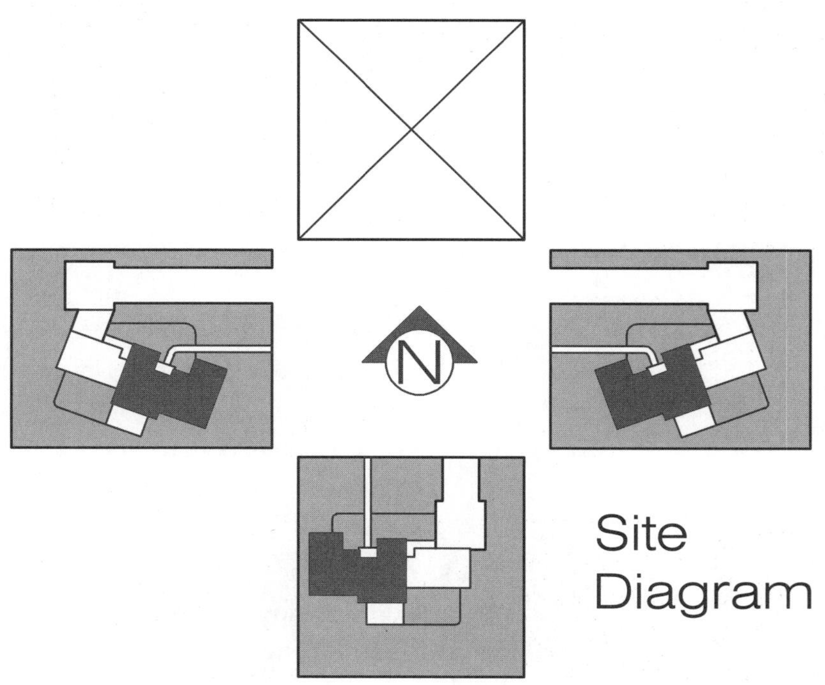

Site Diagram

PLAN 8
RAMADA HOUSE

In the old days people spent much of their time during the warm months in outdoor living rooms called *ramadas*, simple structures built of rustic posts and roofed with branches, poles or slats. In this house, we've combined the ramada idea with the requirements for effective solar heating. Across the private south side of the house angled, removable trellis slats shade a large outdoor living area; in winter, the open frame of beams lets the house soak up the sun. The wall between the interior and the huge *ramada* dissolves into glass.

The front porch of Ramada House greets visitors with a *banco* and recessed front door with transom. Inside, a partial wall reveals the 13' ceiling over the living room, yet screens the private space from public view. Another optional screening partition separates the living and dining areas and provides wall space. Ceilings other than the living room are 9' high.

To the right of the entry the short hall leads between a laundry center and linen closet to a small bedroom for a child (or a private retreat or office). The main bedroom has an optional half-bath and sliding glass doors to the *ramada*.

Basic Rear (South) Elevation

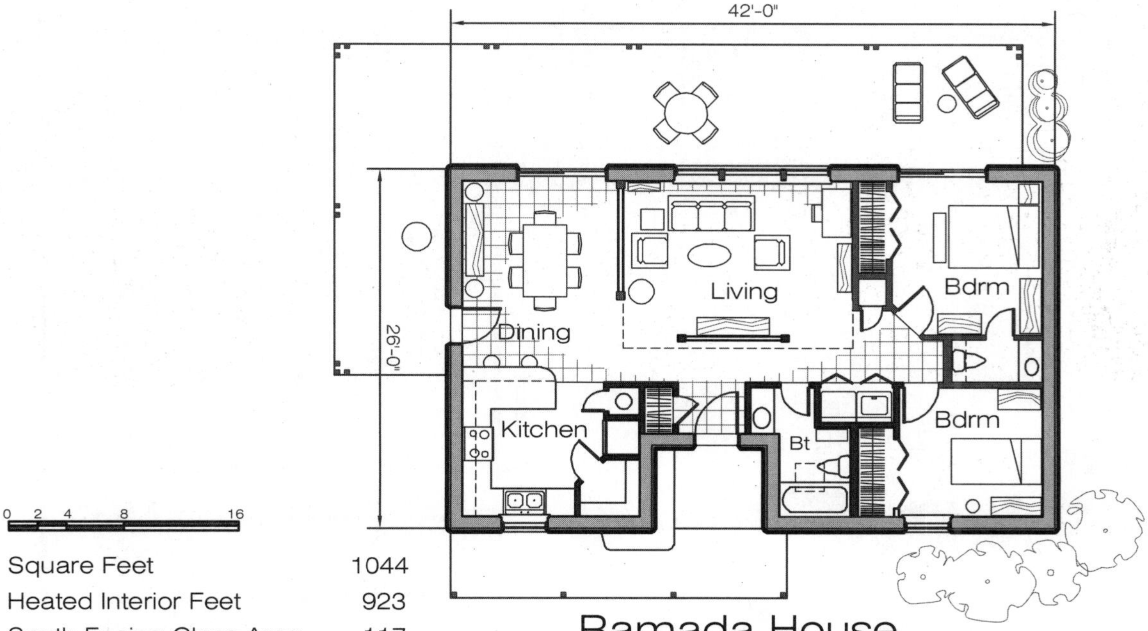

42'-0"

26'-0"

Dining

Living

Bdrm

Kitchen

Bt

Bdrm

0 2 4 8 16

Square Feet	1044
Heated Interior Feet	923
South Facing Glass Area	117
Percent South Glass	12.5

Ramada House

Basic Floor Plan

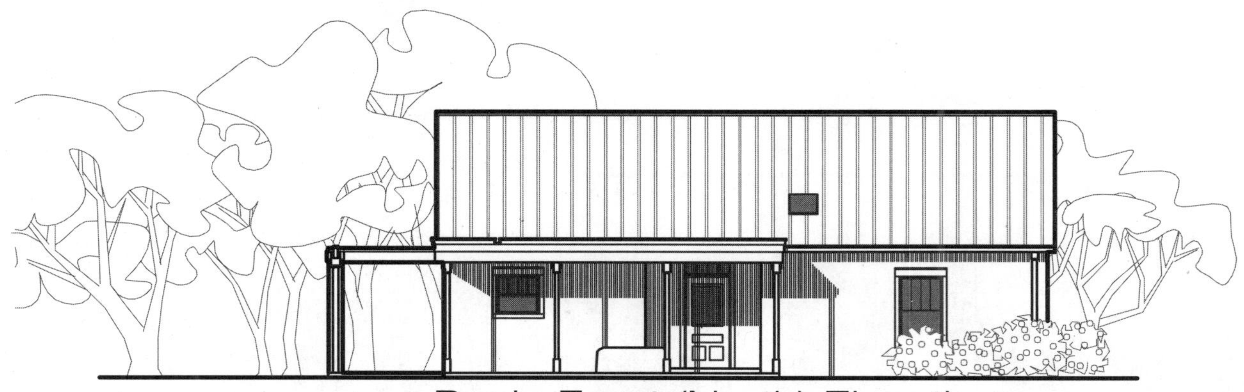

Basic Front (North) Elevation

The house can be expanded as shown by adding a space off the kitchen that serves as a utility or workroom or even small library with storage on the north side. The connecting space leads to a garage and a large bedroom suite on the south that extends the classical symmetry of the main house. You can add a west expansion to the basic plan by using the optional half-bath space as a passageway.

Front (North) Elevation, Expansion

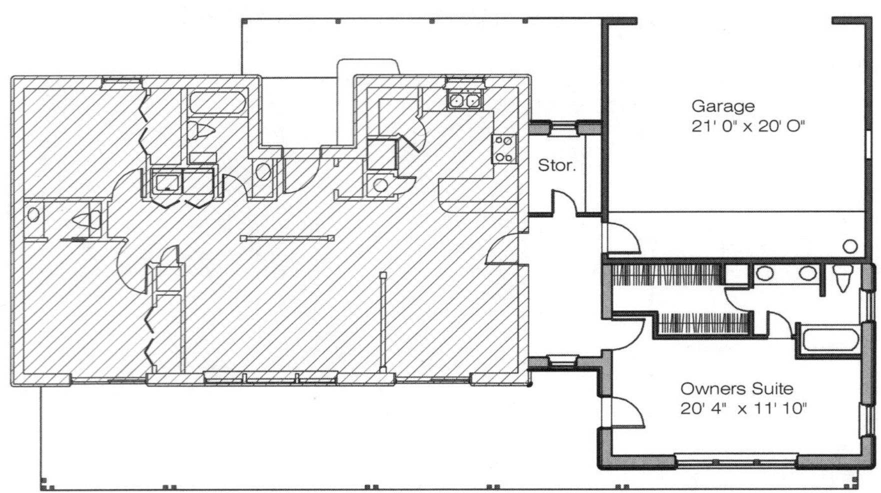

Ramada House

Expansion Floor Plan

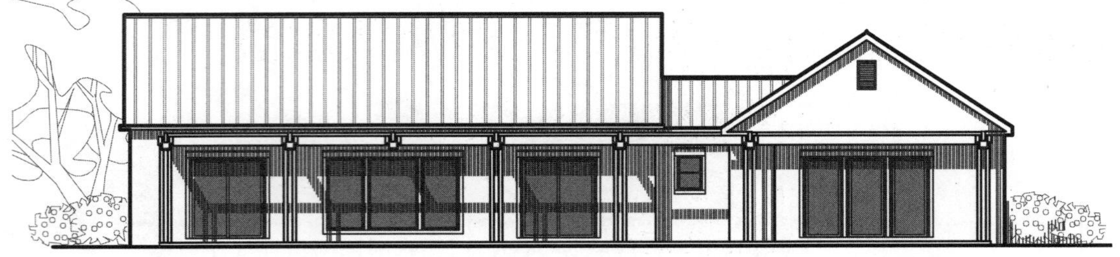

Rear (South) Elevation, Expansion

Basic Side (East) Elevation

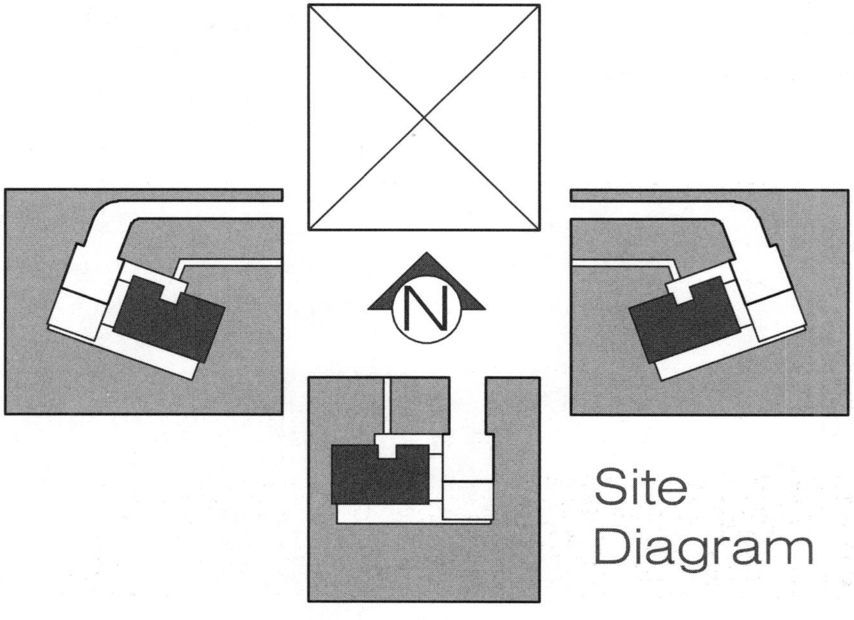

Site Diagram

PLAN 9
FARM HOUSE

Eight-foot wide porches on the north, east and west sides of Farm House provide plenty of room for outdoor living. Open the front door and a short hallway leads past a staircase and closet into the light-filled living area.

The kitchen with its own east door flanks a dining space with a sliding door to the south-facing rear of the house. The ceiling is open above the sitting area, admitting light from the large second floor south window. Smaller dormer windows light the stairway and landing. At the far end of the living area, angled walls form a small private alcove. A short hall gives access to the bath, a washer and dryer tucked under the stairs and the bedroom with a raised ceiling that follows the line of the porch roof.

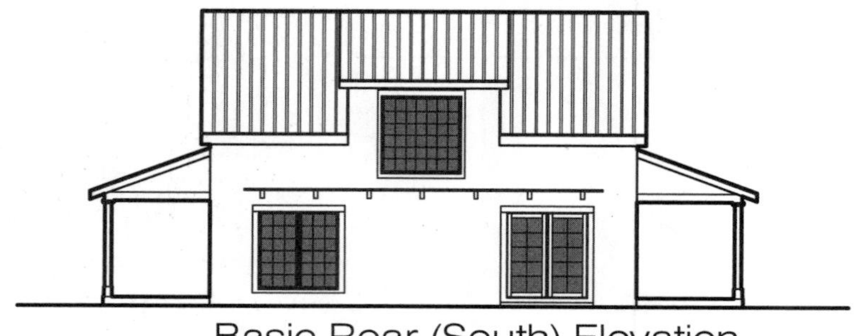

Basic Rear (South) Elevation

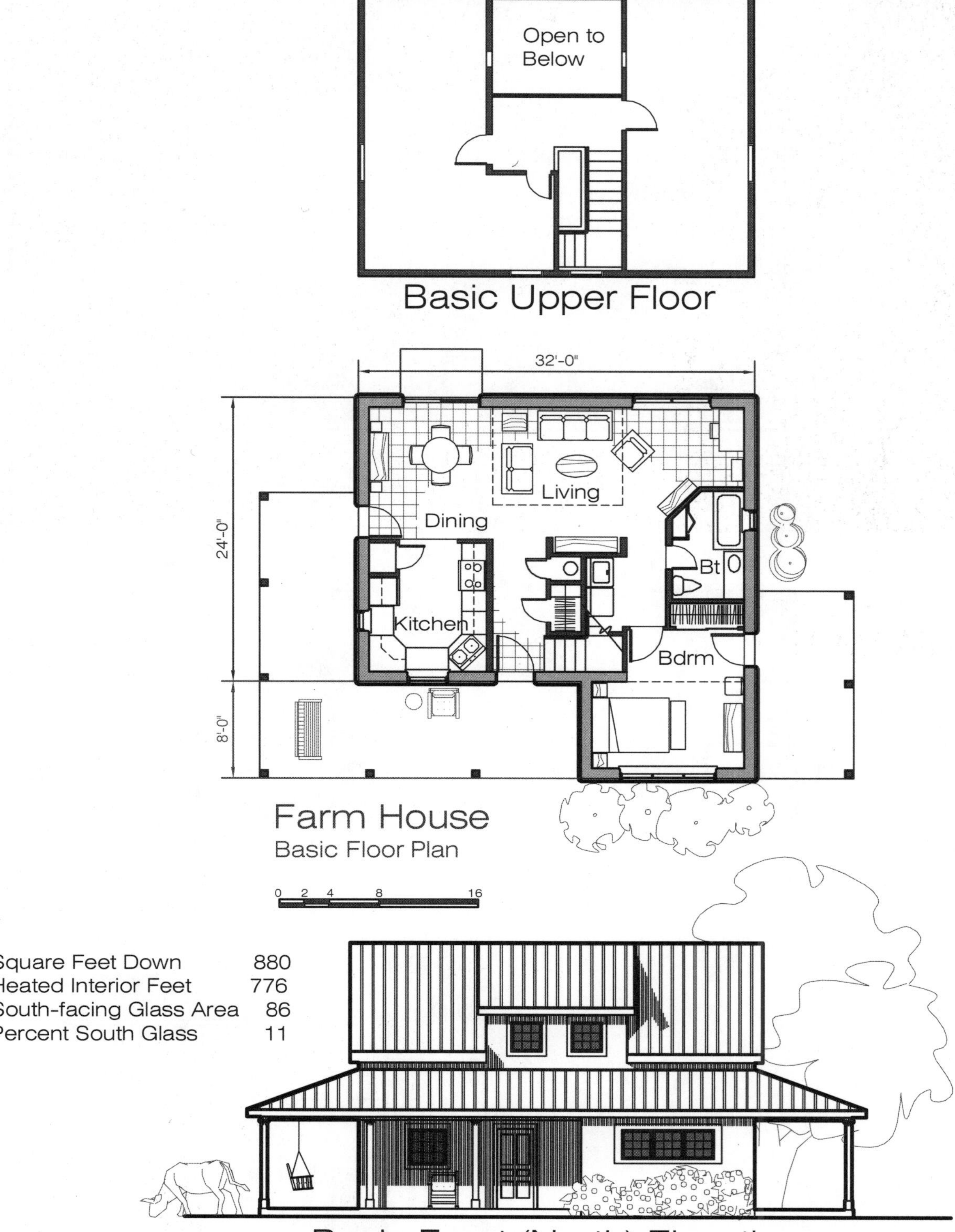
Open to
Below
Basic Upper Floor
32'-0"
24'-0"
8'-0"
Living
Dining
Kitchen
Bt
Bdrm
Farm House
Basic Floor Plan
0 2 4 8 16
Square Feet Down 880
Heated Interior Feet 776
South-facing Glass Area 86
Percent South Glass 11
Basic Front (North) Elevation

The house can grow upwards and to both sides. Upstairs bedrooms flank the balcony landing and feature large storage areas under the low parts of the roof. Plumbing placement allows for easy installation of an upstairs bath with a tub fitted into its own alcove.

The drawing shows a bedroom addition on the west with bath, long closets and doors to a rear patio and the northwest porch. To the east is a large storage-utility room and family room. Alternately, the east unit can add a garage beyond the family room with access through the utility room.

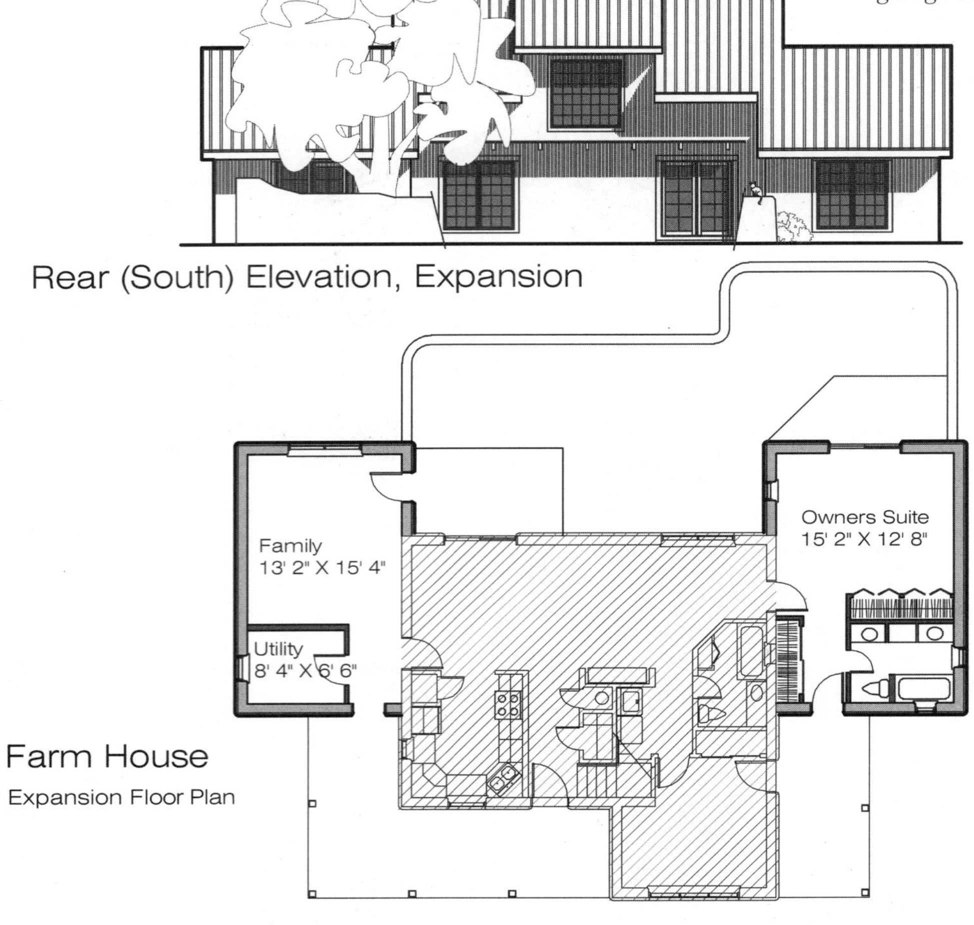

Rear (South) Elevation, Expansion

Farm House

Expansion Floor Plan

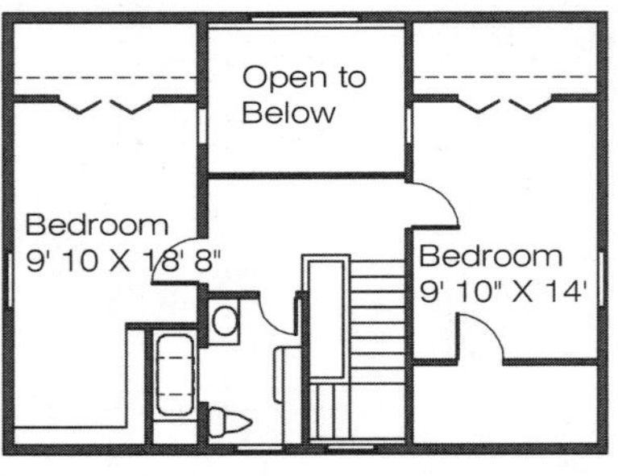

Upper Floor, Expansion

Front (North) Elevation, Expansion

Side (East) Elevation, Expansion

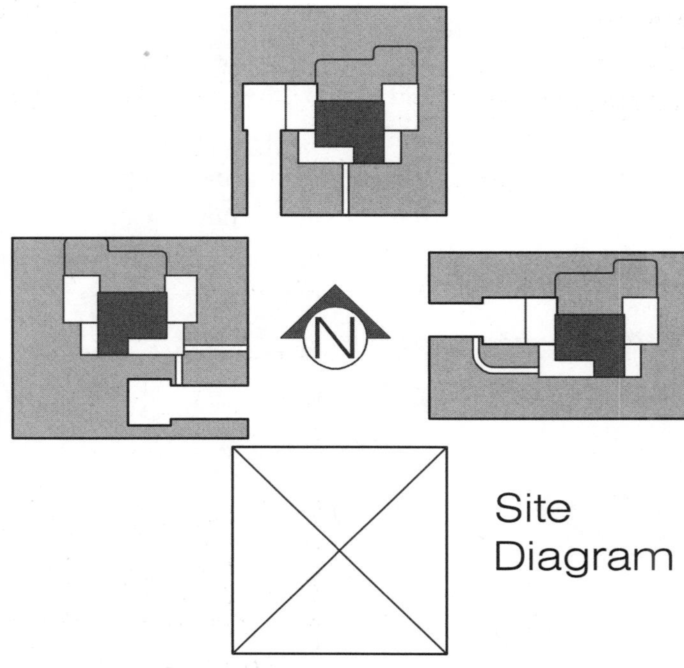

Site Diagram

PLAN 10
BALCONY HOUSE

Maybe views to the south are great. Maybe you like to stargaze. Maybe you have a serenading lover. Maybe you just always wanted a balcony. Balcony House turns a gable end to the south and then uses the balcony structure off the upstairs main bedroom to shade first floor south windows.

The old-fashioned front porch leads visitors to an entry hall with stairs, closet and access to bath and bedroom. The two bedroom closets are separated by space for a bureau, desk or TV. The U-shape of the kitchen keeps it free of passing traffic yet allows easy access to the laundry area and storage under the stairs. The dining space is separated from the kitchen by a half-wall and connected to the east porch by sliding doors.

Basic Front (West) Elevation

The stepped adobe wall between dining and living rooms provides more wall space. The living area can function as one large room or as both a sitting area and a private space defined by the interior buttresses and the high ceiling over the far end.

Square Feet Down 932
Heated Interior Feet 817
South-facing Glass Area 86
Percent South Glass 10

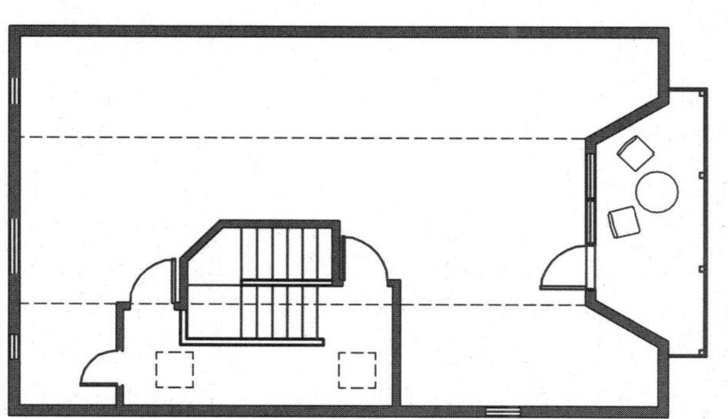

Basic Upper Floor

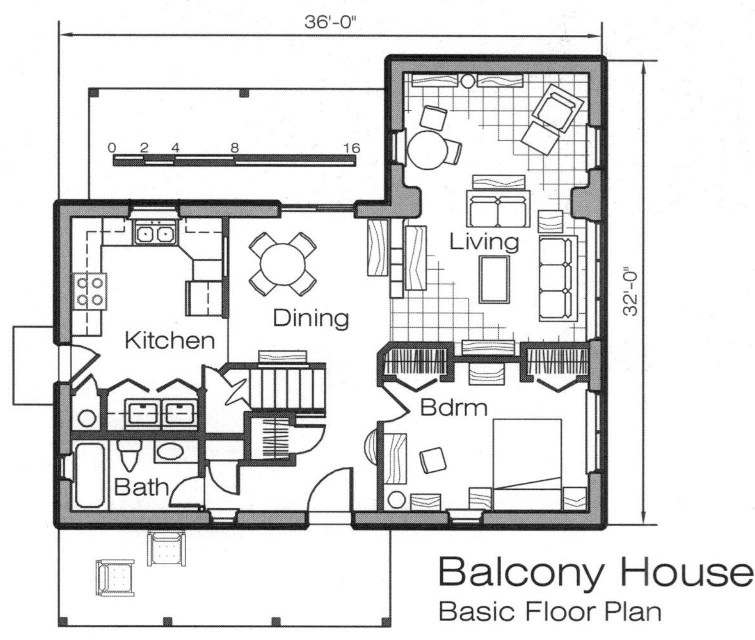

Balcony House
Basic Floor Plan

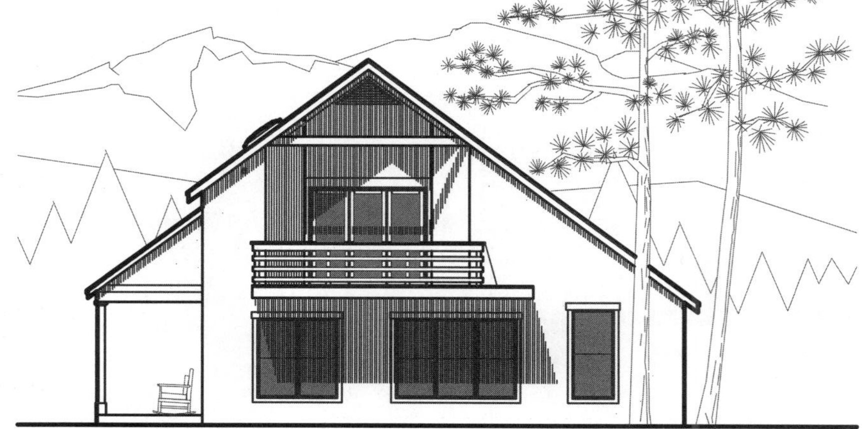

Basic Side (South) Elevation

Finishing the upper floor expands the house to three bedrooms with two and a half baths. The upstairs landing leads to a half-bath, a child's bedroom, and an owners' suite that includes balcony, full bath, two walk-in closets, sleeping, sitting and study areas. The center portion of the upstairs ceiling tops 10'. Once the upstairs is finished, the downstairs bedroom can remain as is or be

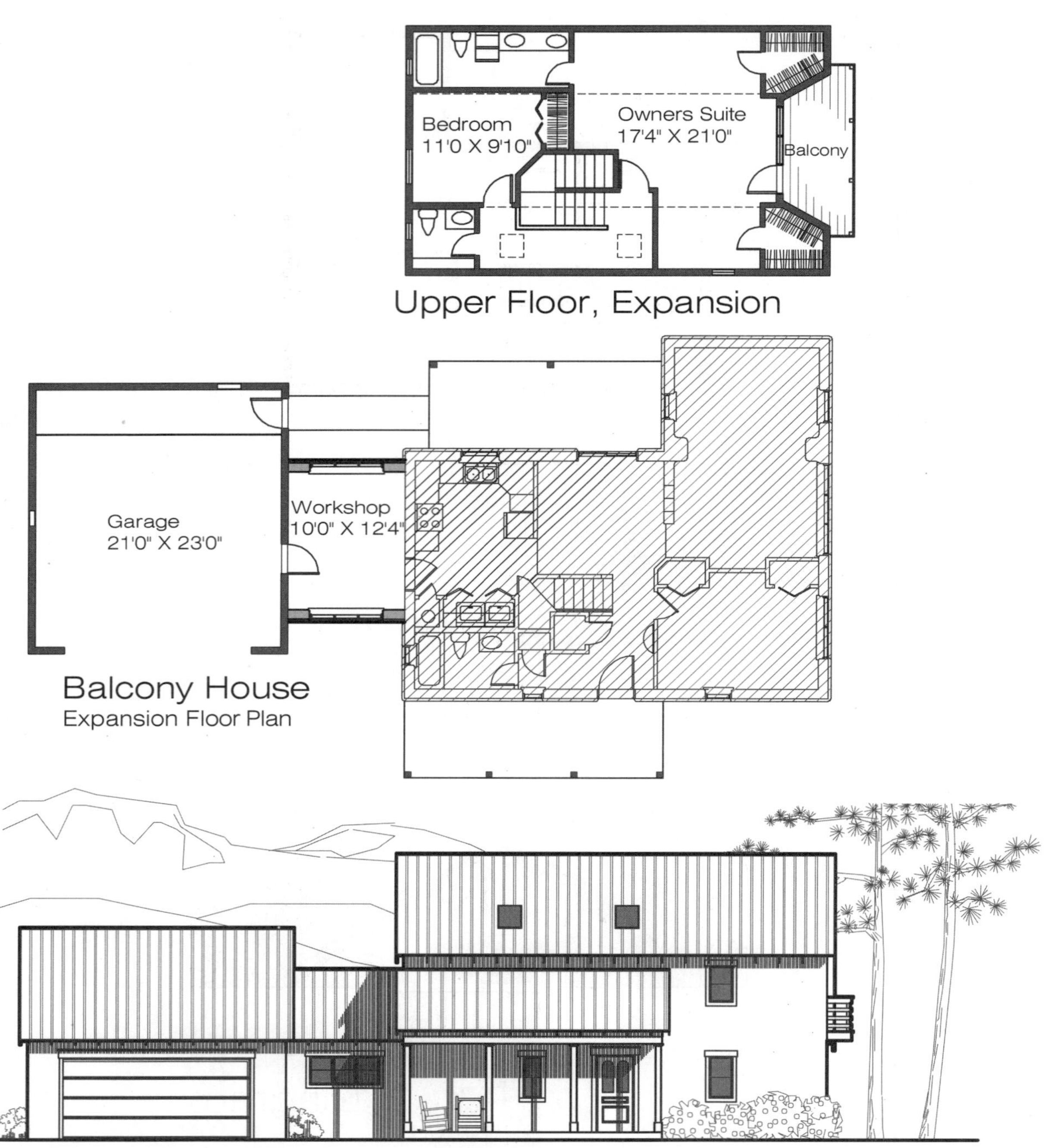

opened up by removing the wall between the closets to form a procession of linked but defined living spaces.

Expansions off the north end of the house can take many forms; the one shown includes a large utility-work room that leads to a garage. Alternately, the house can grow to the east, using the far end of the living area as a passage to more bedrooms or living spaces.

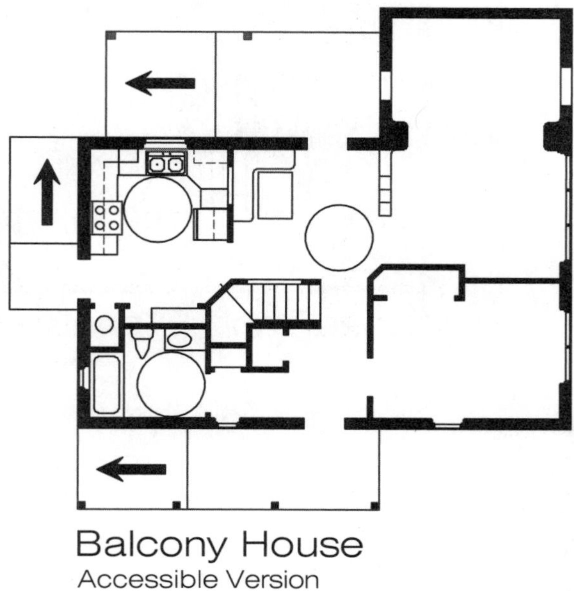

Balcony House
Accessible Version

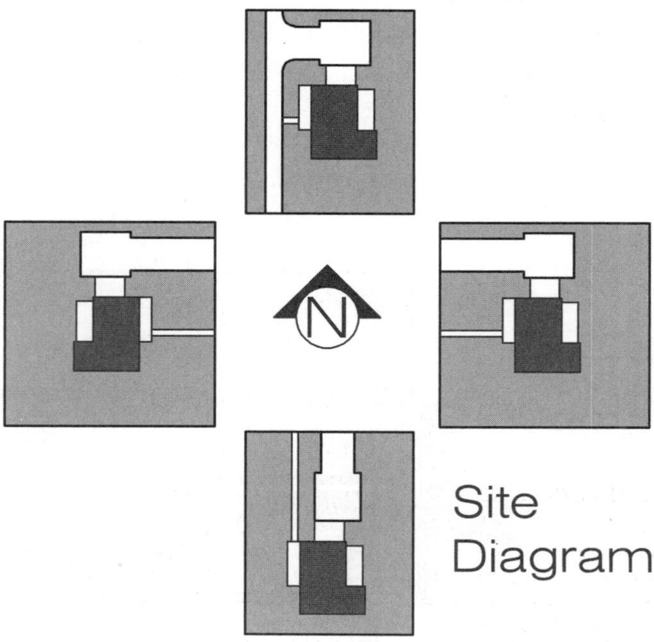

Site Diagram

PLAN 11
DECK HOUSE

Deck House is designed for "zero lot line" properties. Zero lot line covenants allow one windowless wall of a house to run along a side lot line and usually require attached garages. The plan shows a single car garage; alternately the garage can be expanded south across the front of the house to a 22' wide two-car version and still leave room for a porch entrance.

The angled entry with open ceiling leads left to a step-down living room or right to a sunny space for dining and informal sitting. Screened behind the L-shaped stairs, the kitchen is compact yet has 29 square feet of counter-top workspace. A pantry and bookshelves fit under the stairs. Both the dining room and quiet bedroom open onto a private patio on the southeast.

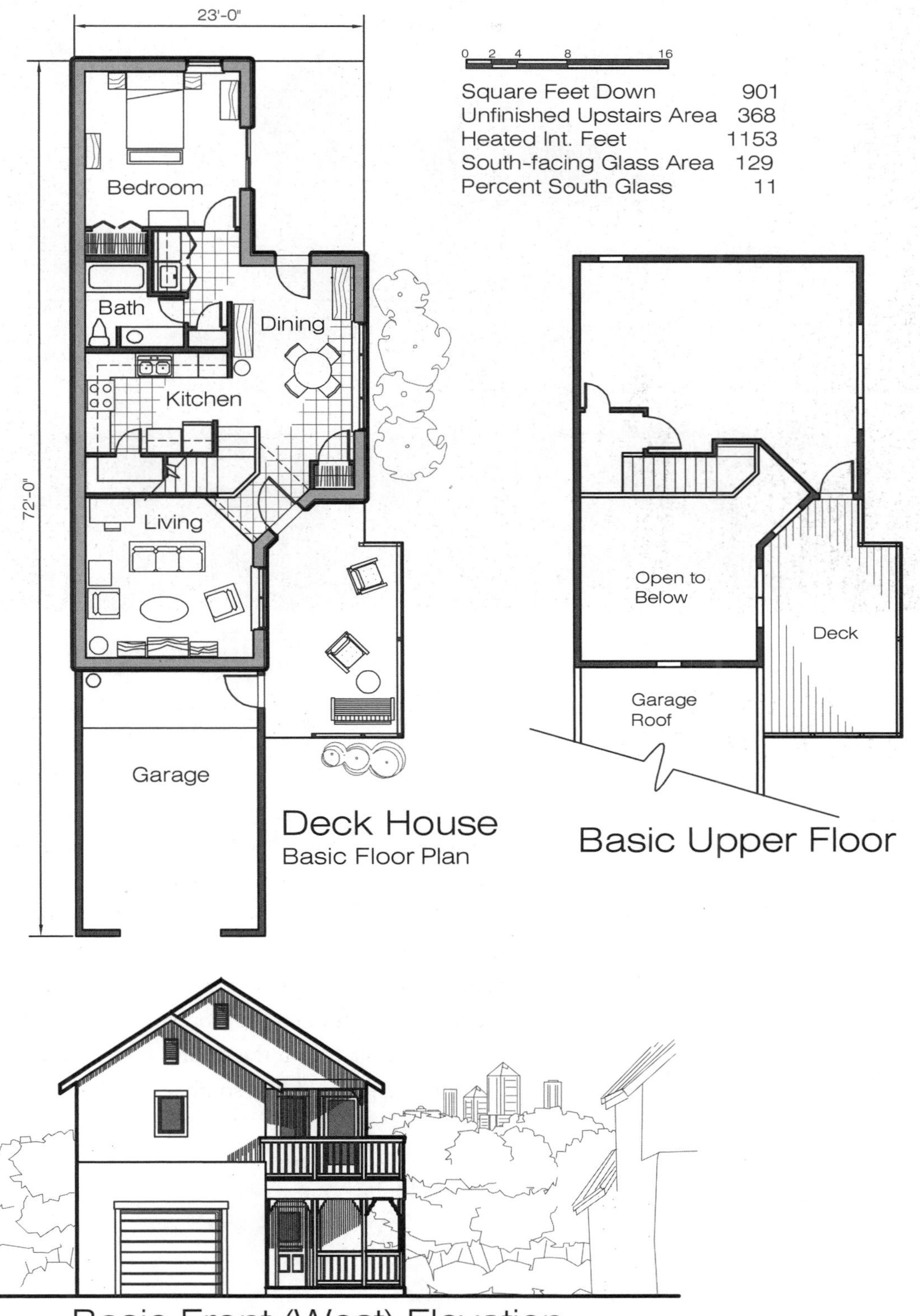

Deck House
Basic Floor Plan

Basic Upper Floor

Basic Front (West) Elevation

Basic Side (South) Elevation

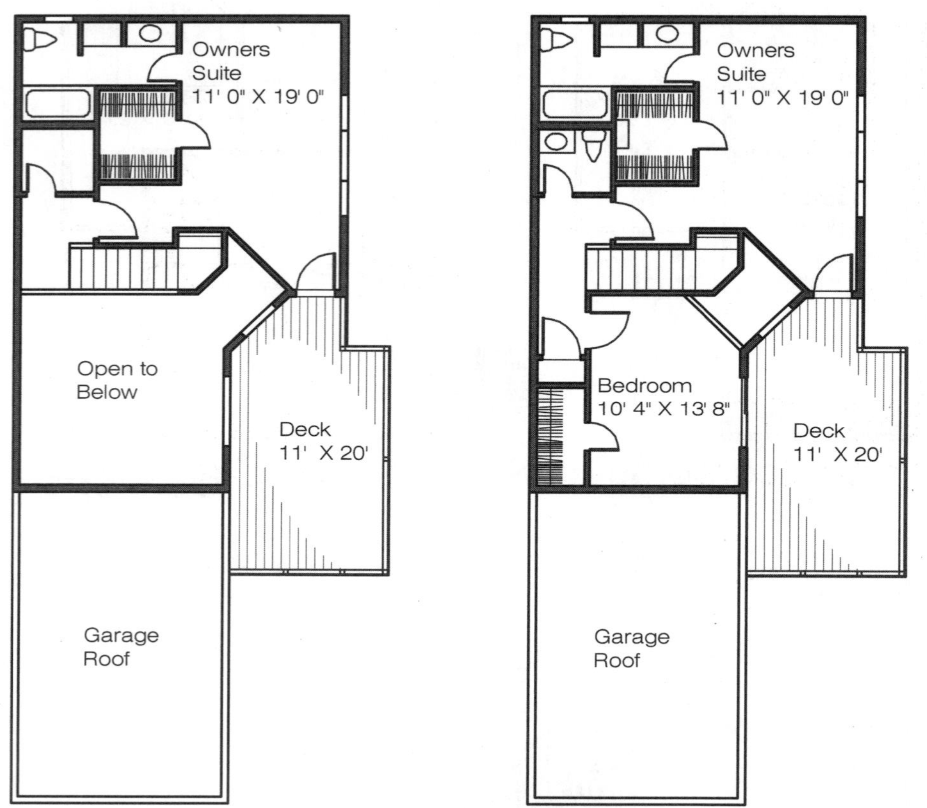

You can build the house, leave the upstairs unfinished and move in. The finished upstairs can contain one, two or three bedrooms (or four bedrooms if you build two over a two-car garage). The main bedroom has its own full bath and walk-in closet. Making the angled wall over the entry half-height creates an open overlook. Alternately, if you want only one bedroom upstairs, the ceiling over the living room can be open. A half-bath serves the second and third bedrooms. If you put in four bedrooms, another bath fits over the back of the garage.

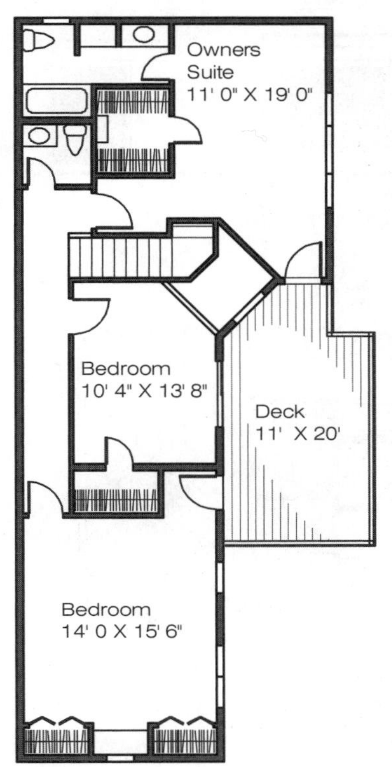

Three Bedrooms

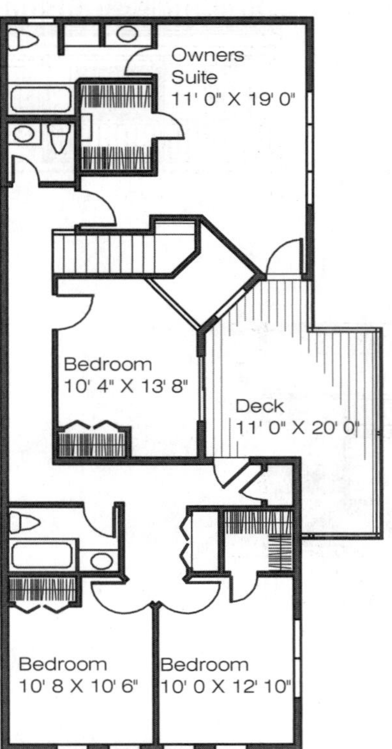

Four Bedrooms

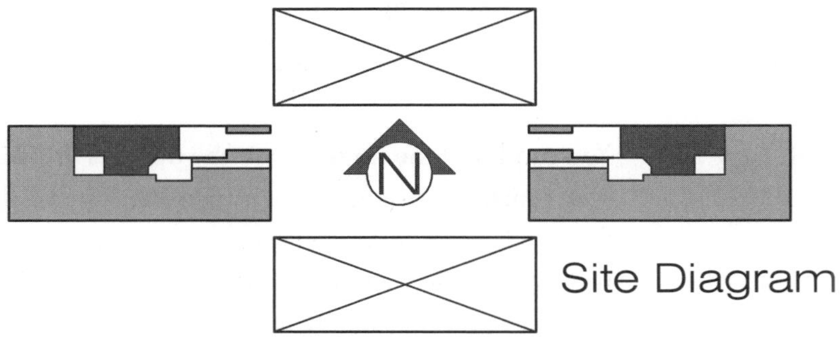

Site Diagram

PLAN 12
PUEBLO HOUSE

Pueblo House is the ultimate adaptable dwelling—adaptable enough to fit almost any definition of family. The house grows around a central core that comprises an entry with *banco* and closet, a large gathering area with corner fireplace, a generous dining room lit by a clerestory, a big kitchen with eating island and a storage/laundry room.

Around these public areas fit one, two or three private modules. (The basic house floor plan shows one module added to the left of the main door.) Each of the modules can be an independent "apartment" with bath, linen closet, large clothes closet, kitchenette, sleeping area and sitting/work area. Each has its own outside door, lots of south-facing glass and a private patio.

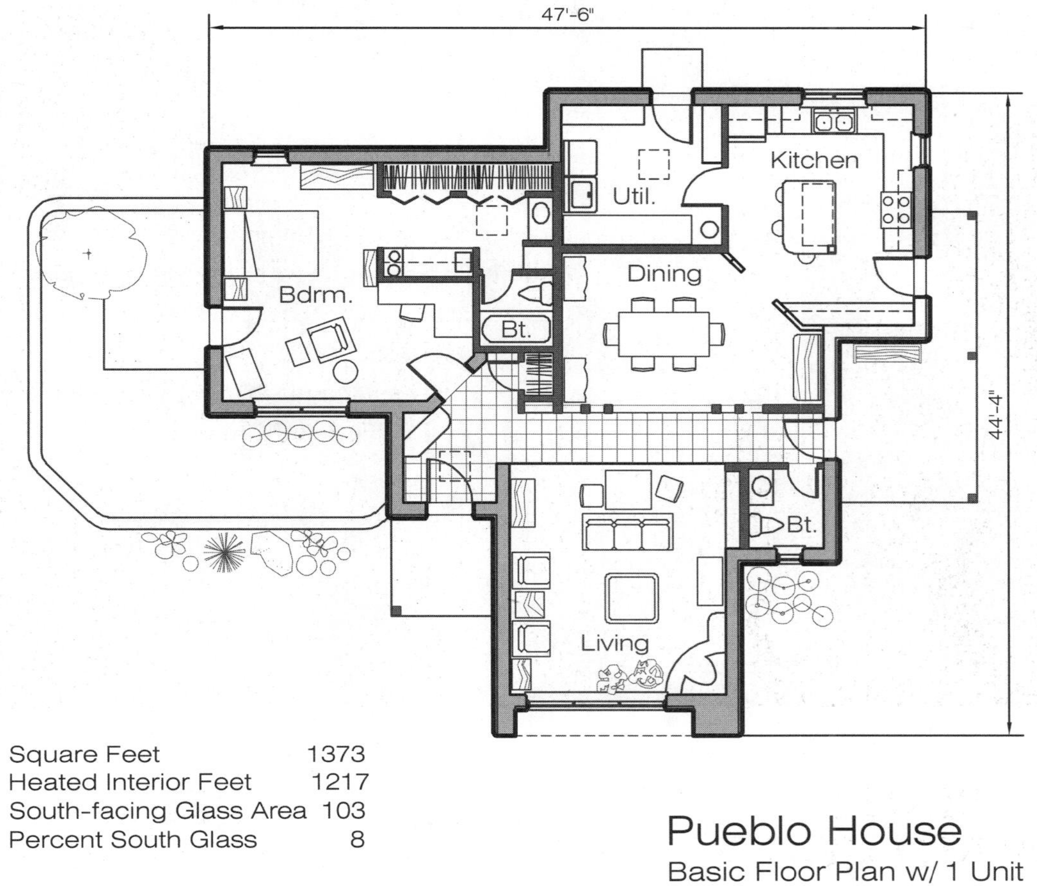

Square Feet	1373
Heated Interior Feet	1217
South-facing Glass Area	103
Percent South Glass	8

Pueblo House

Basic Floor Plan w/ 1 Unit

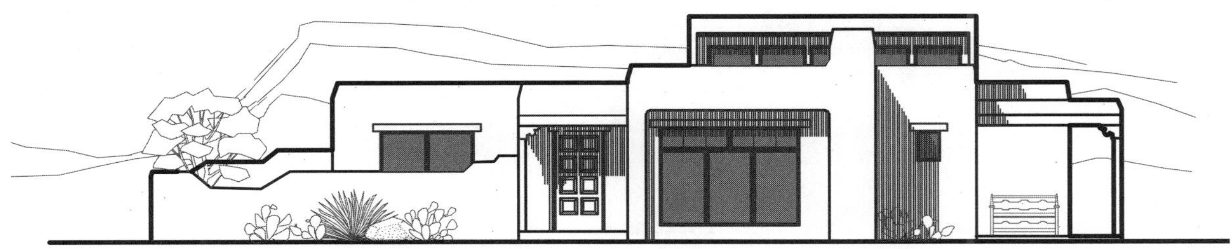

Basic Front (South) Elevation

The expanded floor plan shows all three modules attached to the front and sides of the core and a dining patio and garage added to the rear of the house. While we don't know your personal situation, the modules can accommodate almost any collection of people who want to share living space while maintaining privacy and independence:

- Independent adults who go in together to buy a house
- Adult children who need to live with you awhile
- Older relatives who need a place that is private yet handy to the rest of the family
- A rental unit that can be locked off from the rest of the house (if zoning allows.)

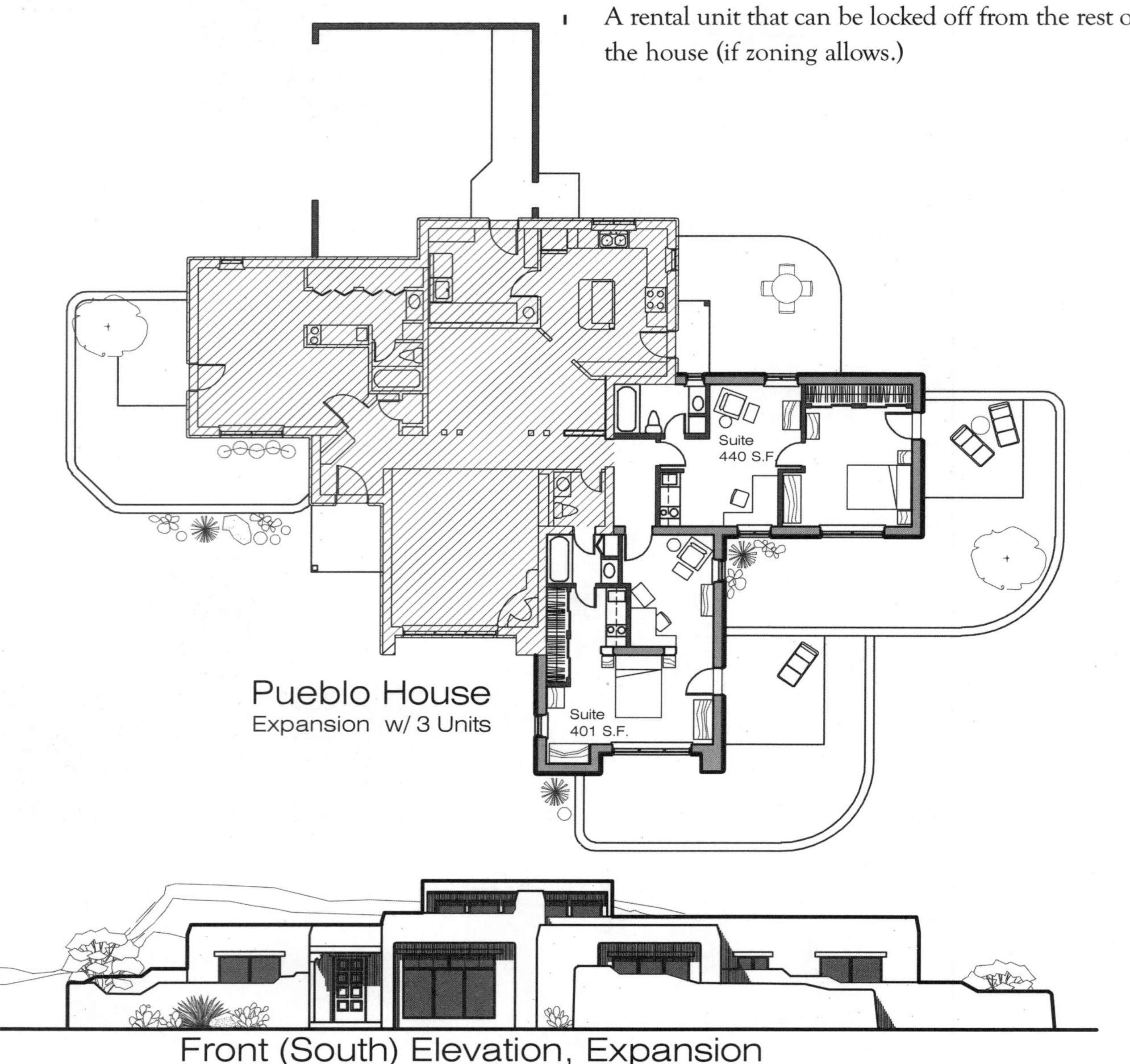

Pueblo House
Expansion w/ 3 Units

Front (South) Elevation, Expansion

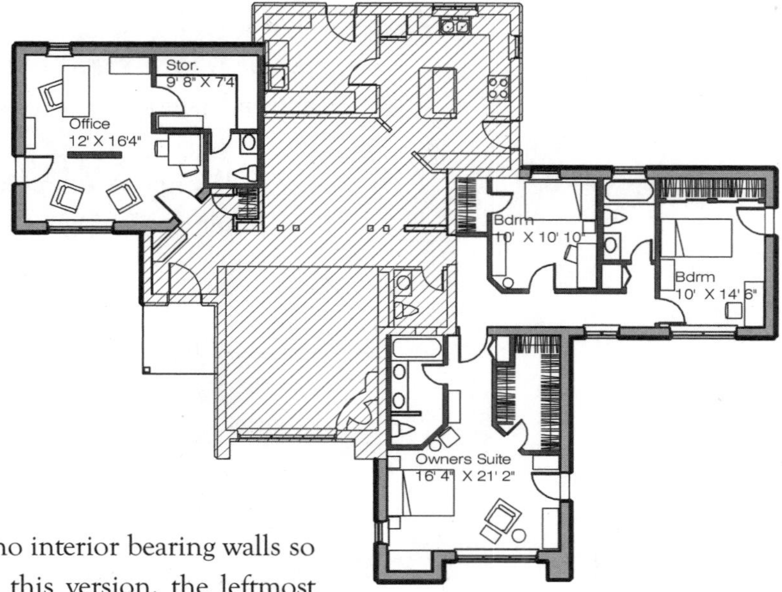

Pueblo House
Alternate Expansion Plan

Finally, the three modules have no interior bearing walls so you can move partitions as needed. In this version, the leftmost module is shown as a home office large enough to include storage and waiting areas. It can be entered through the house's main door without funneling people all through the house or entered from its own exterior door. The rightmost module is altered, as the other modules can be, to create two smaller bedrooms and a bath. The module on the front of the house is shown as an owners' suite with a larger bath and walk-in closets to replace the kitchenette.

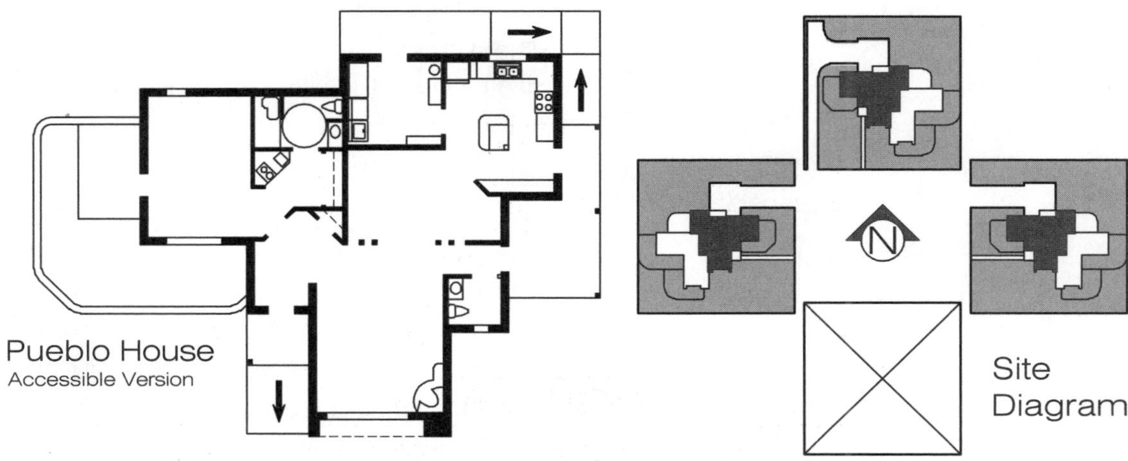

Pueblo House
Accessible Version

Site Diagram

6

ARE WE ALMOST THERE?

Endless car trips with whiny kids, root canals, extreme diets, getting everything lined up to start building—all are cliches for experiences that go on far too long. While everyone's pre-build experience differs, most people have to deal with acquiring land, financing, plans and a contractor. This chapter surveys the critical choices necessary before your house, adobe or otherwise, starts rising out of the ground.

WHERE DO YOU WANT TO LIVE?

Even before choosing a specific building lot, it's necessary to decide whether you'd rather live in a rural, suburban or urban area. Each location has advantages and drawbacks.

Commuting Distance

California developers used to think a 45-minute commute to work was the most that homeowners would tolerate. How quaint. The insatiable demand for detached single family houses has now pushed one-way commutes over the two-hour mark. We see the same thing in New Mexico on a smaller scale as Albuquerque and other metropolitan areas sprout sprawling rings of development.

There are many valid reasons for moving to the "country," but doing it to save money doesn't always work. The initial lower price of outlying housing may conceal financial drawbacks, in particular high commuting costs and inadequate infrastructure.

A 1999 report by the Building Environmental Science and Technology organization, consultants to industry and government, characterizes far-flung housing developments as "requiring long commutes, and big driving distances to shopping, schools, doctors, and recreation sites [that] can cost you over $9,000 per year according to estimates by NRDC (Natural Resources Defense Council)."[1]

While the actual net cost of commuting varies with different wages and different locations, after a few years you're losing serious money by saving ten or fifteen thousand dollars on cheaper outlying land. You can get a rough idea of how much commuting costs you by multiplying your yearly commuting miles by the Internal Revenue Service's current business mileage allowance. (And all those hours you spend driving to and from work could surely be used more productively.) Whatever your personal situation, the idea of "driving till you qualify" is so oversold that you would do well to kick its tires very vigorously.

As well as penalizing individuals, excessive commuting damages the larger community. More open space, farmland and forests have succumbed to urban development in the last 50 years than in all of previous history. Crucial growth issues are usually complex and divisive, with pro-growth positions heavily advertised through local media, governments, business organizations and the surveys they commission.

Opposing opinions often fail to cite hard statistical data. A book that brings balance to the argument is Eben Fodor's *Better Not Bigger: How to Take Control of Urban Growth and Improve Your Community*. Fodor, a professional planning consultant, uses comprehensive data to examine myths about growth. For instance, the belief that "growth makes jobs" runs into data that shows slow growth areas have lower unemployment than faster growing areas. States that pour your tax money into creating a "good business climate" have worse economic outcomes than states with "bad business climates." Prices for median single-family homes in California cities with growth controls did not rise faster than prices in comparable cities lacking growth controls.

Infrastructure

Infrastructure—roads, utilities, parks and services—can usually be taken for granted in urban and suburban areas but small towns and rural areas may be a different story. Discussing outlying inadequate or absent infrastructure, the previously mentioned B.E.S.T. report says, "In theory this added infrastructure will be developed (long) after the new housing is erected, using funding from the new tax base (your tax dollars). Thus, your new 'affordable' home may suffer power outages, traffic congestion, poor water quality, lack of civil services, and other disadvantages while you have to pay higher taxes to compensate for poorly planned development."

Most outlying housing developments are not Subdivisions from Hell, but before buying, it is wise to investigate the following:

- Who maintains roads to your house–you or the county?
- Is there a public water supply?
- If no water, how much have people in the immediate area paid to have wells drilled?
- How is the water quality?
- Is there a sewer system? If not, what are the requirements and costs for a septic system?
- In irrigated areas, do you have water rights and ditch maintenance responsibilities?
- How much will it cost to run electric lines to your property? How long will it take?
- How much and how long for telephone lines?
- Do natural gas lines reach the property?
- If not, what is the usual cost for propane or heating oil delivery?
- Is there public trash pick up? Where's the nearest landfill?
- Is ambulance service available?
- What, if any, fire department serves the area?
- Is police protection available? What is the Sheriff's Department like?
- How much will commuting cost you in time, money and hassle?

Covenants

Various regulations and their associated fees govern building projects at all levels. Whether public or private, the regulations tend to push you toward building exactly what everyone else in the area has built.

Subdivision or neighborhood covenants set a wide variety of rules for builders and homeowners. The stated purpose of covenants is to keep property values high in the immediate area, although the actual agenda may be more complex. Covenants are often linked with homeowners associations that are established by the developer of a neighborhood. The associations levy monthly fees and membership is compulsory for neighborhood residents. Although covenants vary from place to place, the following items are usually regulated.

Usage: Usage sections of covenants regulate the activities that take place on your property. They may limit the time a construction trailer can stay on the property, forbid a collection of junk cars in your yard, or regulate at-home businesses and yard sales.

Design: Design regulations may require a general look, such as "Southwestern," or they may be detailed enough to demand specific roof pitches, finish materials and trim colors. The most frequently required feature is an attached two-car garage.

House Size: Some covenants require a minimum floor area. Depending on how exclusive the neighborhood considers itself, the minimum can vary from around 1,200 square feet to over 3,000 square feet. Covenants may set a minimum total square footage or a minimum square footage for the ground floor only.

Landscaping: In the southwestern United States covenants may require—or prohibit—xeriscaping (landscaping that requires very little water.) Particular species of trees or shrubbery may be prohibited, either because they are considered allergy triggers or their fruit is considered a nuisance.

Subdivisions in which one corporation buys, develops and builds out the land usually have such restrictive covenants that building a home like the ones shown in this book is almost impossible. If you already own a covenant-constrained lot, you might try a workaround. Stretching a room or two on a basic plan may satisfy the more modest square foot requirements. Building a two-story version without finishing the upstairs might work. Building the expanded version of a house without finishing unneeded interior space is also a possibility.

Zoning

While covenants are private rulebooks drawn up by developers, zoning regulations are passed by city or county governments. A city may have dozens of zoning categories and sub-categories. Before buying a lot, read the applicable zoning code very carefully to see if rules concerning the following items fit with your plans.

- Does a property's zoning classification allow adding a rental or "mother-in-law" apartment? What about other accessory buildings and home-based businesses?

- Exactly how does the code define "family" and does the definition allow the people that will be living in your "single-family" home?
- Does the code regulate number and type of pets?
- How is "bath" defined? The number and type of bathrooms often determines requirements for waste systems or parking areas.
- How is "kitchen" defined and regulated? Restrictions against second kitchens might forbid setups such as used in Pueblo House.
- Does the governing body seem particularly amenable or resistant to granting variances and conditional use permits?
- Does the property lie in any overlay zones such as an historical district, urban conservation overlay or airport overlay?

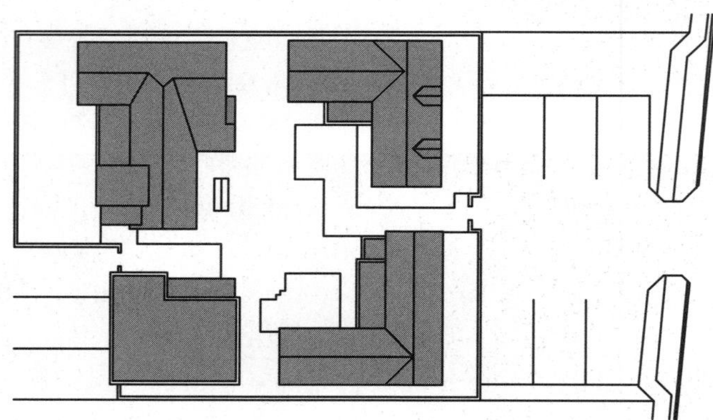

Zoning laws are constantly changing to allow new uses. In the historic area of downtown Albuquerque, New Mexico, a quarter-acre lot has been transformed into a compound of four small dwellings designed by architect Perry Wilkes. In several New Mexico cities, similar high-density in-fill developments are providing a new way for people to take advantage of urban amenities without the usual expense and maintenance burden of standard single-family houses.The energy-efficient, solar-heated dwellings form a quadrangle entered from two gates that lead to parking areas off a street and alley.

Building Codes

On a larger scale you'll encounter regulations set by building codes. Most of the Mountain West and Pacific states use the Uniform Building Code (UBC). Other widely used U.S. codes are the Standard Building Code used in the Southeast and the BOCA code used in the rest of the nation.

None of these mega-codes deals with adobe construction in depth. States, counties and municipalities usually substitute their own adobe codes. Like zoning boards, code enforcement officials may grant variances. Also, officials may allow unusual features if a licensed local engineer approves them. In any event, you will need to check all appropriate government agencies in your jurisdiction to make sure that you are complying with all applicable regulations. The Appendix takes a closer look at the code check and permit process.

The parking area to the north separates the houses, based on New Mexico vernacular styles, from the noise of a busy street.

Each unit has a view of the central garden as well as its own private outdoor space.

Crime

Location implies qualities that are subjective, difficult to assess, possibly short-lived and impossible to separate from larger, politically sensitive issues. Although crime rates have been falling for years, crime is still a subject of great concern to the public. It's not easy to assess an area's crime potential just by looking around. (Burglars like nice neighborhoods—they can rip off better-quality items.)

If you're working with a real estate agent, ask about crime statistics; you may get information although the agent is not obligated to tell you. Neighborhood associations are worth contacting if one exists for the area. You can also try asking the Community Relations officer at the police or sheriff's department. It would probably be worth your fee to consult with a reputable local home security business regarding area crime patterns, aspects of home access and security systems.

Steps you can take yourself to discourage break-ins range from the standard, such as putting lights and TV on a timer and stopping newspaper deliveries if you expect to be out of town for several days, to the extremely creative. One of our deep-cover sources suggests that you leave broken toys in your front yard to deter burglars. Burglars will assume that any extra money is spent on kids instead of easily fenced luxury items, and that everything inside the house is probably trashed out. And obviously this approach will not appeal to everyone.

Property Appreciation

The biggest factor affecting property values is regional economy and there's not much you can do about it. You might, however, have a choice of neighborhoods in which to build. Conventional wisdom says you should build where houses are slightly more expensive so that your house will "borrow value" from the price level of the surrounding properties. Checking out Days on Market (DOM) statistics for available homes gives you an idea of how much demand exists for houses in a particular neighborhood.

If you 're investigating a potential home location on your own, Internet resources offer abundant data. The U.S. Census furnishes hundreds of nuggets of information on a county level such as average income, household composition and number of people with college degrees. The website is www.census.gov. Another rich source is the federal statistics at www.fedstats.gov. The www.homefair.com website offers several tools that describe areas by zip code, including a Relocation Crime Lab tool that lists frequency of various crimes per zip code. However, neighborhoods within a zip code vary greatly.

Neighborhood Sociology

Preferences for a certain type of neighborhood are very personal. We can only suggest that you check your impressions of the following qualities and whether they seem comfortable fits.

- Does the neighborhood contain a mix of uses or is it all single family homes?
- Does the age demographic vary or is every household about the same—couples with young children, retirees or other?
- Do people seem inclined to visit casually back and forth or does each household seem as self-contained as a space shuttle? Do you care?
- Do local people seem welcoming toward newcomers or would they just as soon do without your presence? (Don't go by Chamber of Commerce publications on this one.)
- Do surrounding properties look neurotically neat or maddeningly messy?
- Can you coexist with the neighborhood pet culture, whatever it is?
- Are services and stores within walking distance? Do you care?
- Check neighborhood bumper stickers (or in season, political yard signs). See any kind of herd mentality that will get on your nerves with constant exposure?

IS THIS THE SITE THAT SUITS YOU?

Once you've decided on a general location, it's time to look for a specific piece of land. A house plan that works well for one site might not fit another location. Although plans for the Basic Houses are very flexible, it is still best to choose a building site before making the final decision on a specific plan.

How Big a Lot Do You Need?

Only you can say how much time and space you want to devote to your yard or how much room you need out back for hobbies. Others, however, determine the minimum amount of space required around your house.

Municipalities usually specify setbacks for building lots. That is, each house wall must be a minimum distance from the nearest property line. Setbacks vary by city and by zoning category within a city. In Albuquerque, for instance, R-1 single-family zoning requires a 20' setback from the street and a 15' setback from the rear property line. Side setbacks depend on lot width, solar access, or other conditions.

Think about future expansions as well as immediate plans. The two diagrams show a Basic House on a lot with typical setbacks and the expanded version of the house on the same lot. Note that the basic house must sit farther back and to the right on the lot to leave room for the expansion.

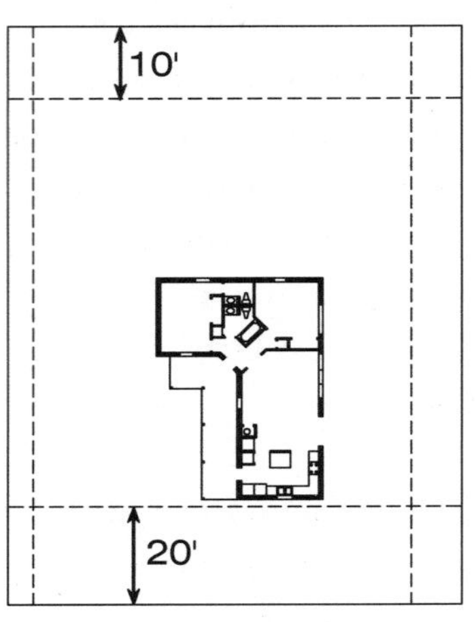

High Valley House on a 90' by 120' lot.

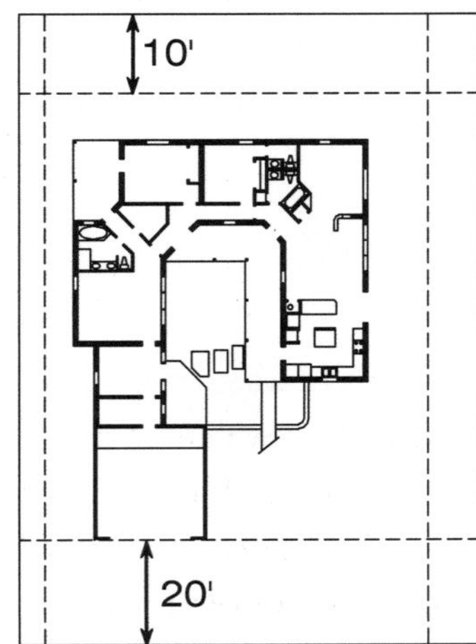

The expanded version of High Valley House on the same lot.

Slope, Soil and Sun

How steeply the ground slopes across your lot affects how much earthwork will be necessary before building. The composition of the soil may affect the design of the foundation. The sun exposure determines how easy it will be to solar-heat your home.

A lot that slopes slightly drains better than one that is completely flat. Even better is a lot that slopes to the south. Avoid lots that slope toward the center, forming a shallow cup that will pond water around your foundations without extensive backfilling. Carefully study nearby terrain. If the ground or streets surrounding your lot are higher, look for drainage channels or other signs of erosion and overflowing that indicate water drains onto your lot during heavy rains.

The foundations for these plans are designed for a soil bearing strength of 1500 pounds per square foot (PSF), that is, each square foot of undisturbed earth will support 1500 pounds of building, a very conservative design load. It is unlikely your lot would require anything stronger unless the soil is almost solid clay (which shrinks and swells depending on its moisture content) or the lot rests on a former landfill or other subsurface disturbance.

If you're buying a lot in a subdivision, ask the developer for a copy of the soils report. The report should note any unusual subsurface conditions. In any case, ask the local building official and any neighbors about the property.

As well as looking for pleasant views, check that solar exposure is (and will remain) unblocked. Communities are beginning to pass solar access laws prohibiting new, tall buildings from blocking sunlight on existing structures. If you're lucky enough to have tall, deciduous trees on your property, try to position your house to take advantage of the trees' summer shading. A stand of conifers on your lot can provide an effective windbreak.

Hidden Drawbacks

It's difficult to learn everything important about a piece of property in one short visit. We don't want to make you paranoid, but investigating certain possibilities can save you a world of hurt. Before you buy, try to determine how a lot might be affected by special designations, seasonal changes, dubious histories or appalling futures.

Land that lies close to a river, coast or other natural drainage route may be designated by the Federal Emergency Management Agency (FEMA) as a flood plain zone. Houses in flood plains usually require extra insurance to cover flood damage, more expensive foundations, and more elaborate well and septic construction if the water table is high. Official flood plain boundaries may be hard to pin down; the designation often provokes heated local dispute.

Because this house is located in the river flood plain of the Rio Grande, it is raised 24" above the natural grade.

Spring is the best time for selling land because everything looks beautiful. On the other hand, winter is the wisest time to buy land. Deciduous trees are bare and you can better see surrounding features. Cold, cutting winds and steep access roads that turn to glassy ice make themselves evident.

Although you seldom have time to visit property in different seasons before you buy, that doesn't prevent you from making a serious effort to visualize any problems that may show up when the weather changes. Once you've bought land, if your construction schedule allows, try to visit the property throughout a year to check seasonal changes before you build.

While a piece of land might look perfect when you see it, its past and future may not be as appealing. Consider a few nightmarish "What Ifs?" The cozy village lies in the path of a future freeway. The alfalfa fields upwind from your lot have been sold for a chicken processing plant. That high fence at the end of the street hides a drag racing track that roars into action every summer weekend. A lovely meadow covers a former landfill. A demolished gas station leaves behind leaking underground tanks. Someone else owns the mineral rights to land you just bought and you're about to have a coal mine for a basement.

Before buying, find out as much as you can about a property's history and about any plans for the area's future. Talk to people living nearby. What they tell you may depend on their own agendas but that's also useful data. Use the Internet for key word searches. Newspaper archives are coming online for metropolitan areas; using names associated with any local land development controversies may turn up information about your proposed land purchase. The archives of newspaper business sections may give you early warning of planned development. At the County Assessor's office you can find out who owns the land surrounding your parcel, which may or may not tell you anything vital.

WHAT ABOUT FINANCING?

Two eight-hundred-pound financial gorillas stalk your home-building project: land cost and mortgage interest. Both greatly affect how much you end up paying. Both vary with time, project and location. Technically, both are outside the scope of this book but we'll quickly look at a few considerations.

Land costs inflate housing costs in two ways. First, as the population increases, land grows more expensive all over the nation. Second, higher land costs affect the "land price to house price" formula. This bit of conventional wisdom says a lot should cost a certain percentage of the price of the house built on it, currently around 30%. As land prices increase, houses must grow ever larger and more expensive to stay at the same proportion of the total cost. Even when the land price/house price ratio doesn't affect you directly, it may provoke lot covenants that require a far larger house than you want to build.

The second gorilla, mortgage interest, grows right along with its twin brother. Whatever your new home's total price, even today's relatively low interest rates will cost you between 2.5 and 3 times that amount if you take the conventional route of a thirty-year fixed rate mortgage.

Pressure, Pressure, Pressure

Obviously we like moderately sized adobe houses. And because you're reading this book, we assume you're willing to consider the concept. But when you start turning your dreams into reality, hold on to your hat. You'll encounter an amazing amount of pressure to build a bigger, more conventional house.

The worlds of real estate, local government, financing and construction are tightly integrated and all are staffed with people who want to help you. The only catch is, they want to help you do it the statistically average way.

Lenders often impose tighter restrictions than building codes. Banks don't want to repossess your house but if they must, they want to resell it as quickly as possible. Therefore, lenders prefer that you build an absolutely average, conventional, median house. Although the situation is changing, banks have rarely cared about the very real advantages of solar heating and adobe. Banks don't care how many extra hours you have to work to pay for and clean up an over-sized house. Banks look for central heating systems, conventional construction, average size and three or more bedrooms.

A friend's mother wanted a small house with one spacious bedroom; her family all live nearby and there's no one else she really wants staying with her. She ended up with three cramped, uncomfortable bedrooms, a larger mortgage and nobody is happy. The culprit was "resale value" with its insistence on a standard number of bedrooms. When you plan to build a small house, you will hear about "resale value" until you want to scream and here's why:

- Local governments want you to build a bigger house so they can collect more property tax
- Lenders want you to build a bigger house so you will pay more interest
- Developers and builders want you to build a bigger house that will yield profit on a larger amount
- Real estate agents want you to build a bigger house on a more expensive lot to pump up the general price level that determines their commissions
- Interior decorators, furniture stores, building material stores, fixture and appliance suppliers—all want you to build a bigger house that will require more of their products to furnish

In short, everyone in the business will pressure you to build a bigger house. They are not dishonest people but the more you spend, the more they make. What they are really saying about "resale value" is that you should build your house to fit another person's wants and needs—the statistically average person. The irony is, the principal and interest you pay to build unneeded, unwanted space would almost certainly bring you better returns invested elsewhere. In the meantime, small inexpensive houses that reach the market are usually snapped up.

Pay Now or Pay More Later—Lots More

The money you pay in mortgage interest dwarfs every other housing cost. Types of mortgages now available are so numerous that even listing them here is impractical. Just one recommendation: when you shop for a mortgage, calculate a deal's total cost for its entire term. Often a "really good deal" with a long term and low down payment ends up costing twice the amount in interest as a mortgage with a larger down payment and shorter term. To put it another way, over the course of a 30-year mortgage the money you pay in interest can almost triple the cost of your house.

We can't say what kind of mortgage will work for you. We're only saying that it's wise to look at the complete picture before putting money down. (And always check whether paying off your mortgage ahead of time carries a penalty.) The bibliography lists further sources for financing information.

How Much Will Your House Cost?

Before you sign a mortgage contract or other financial agreement, you'll need an accurate estimate of your house's cost. Construction costs vary from county to county, from year to year, and from contractor to contractor.

To obtain bids from local builders and financing from local institutions, you will probably need working drawings. Working drawings, often called "blueprints" or "construction documents," are the detailed instructions for building a house. They look quite different from "house plans" or the "presentation drawings" shown in Chapter 5. Working drawings and building permits are discussed in detail in the Appendix. The following illustrations show what is included in a typical set of working drawings.

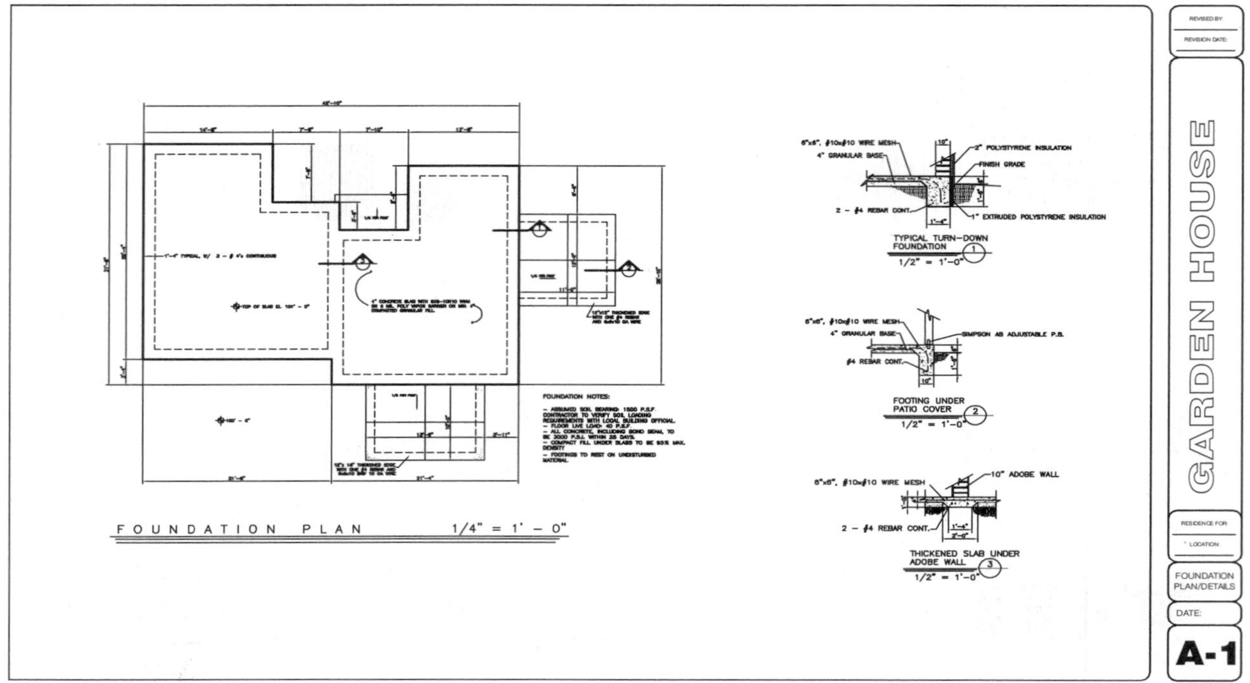

For an average house, a set of working drawings includes from three to six 36" by 24" pages, or sheets. Often the first sheet shows general information, the foundation plan, notes and related details.

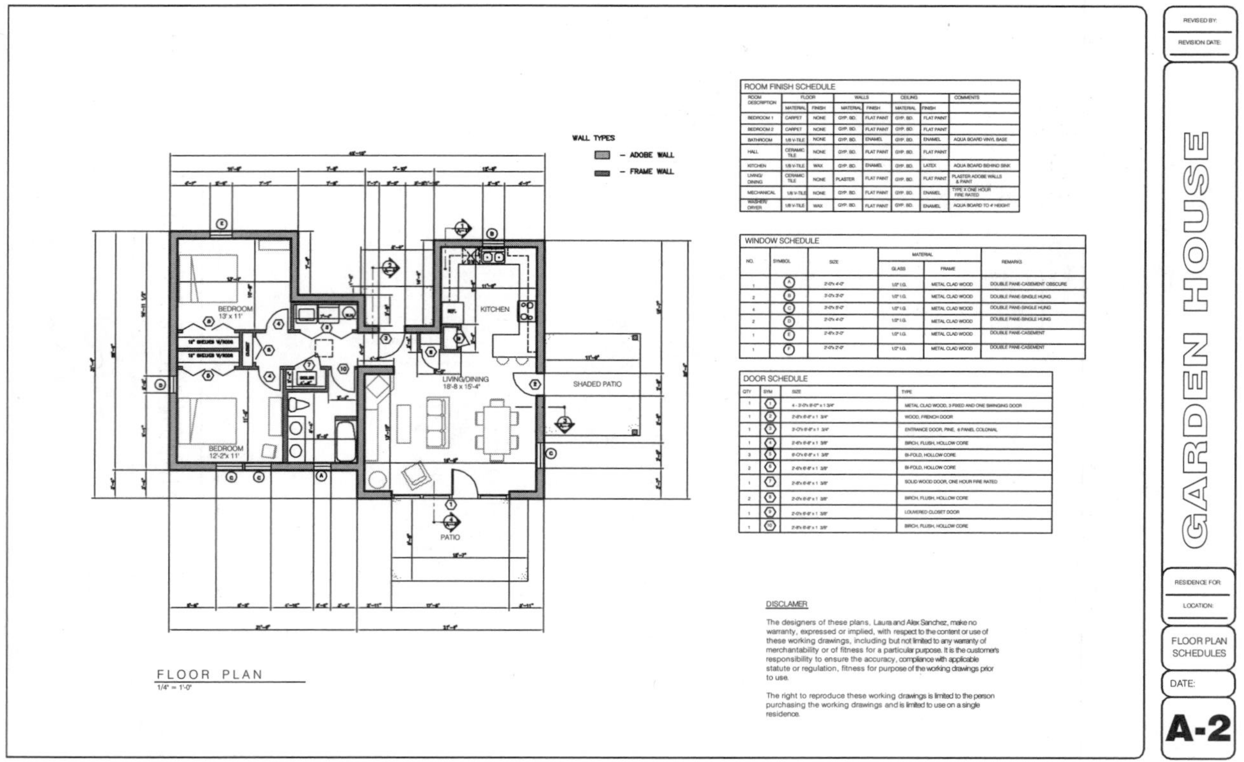

Usually the next sheet shows the floor plan, notes, and door, window and room finish schedules.

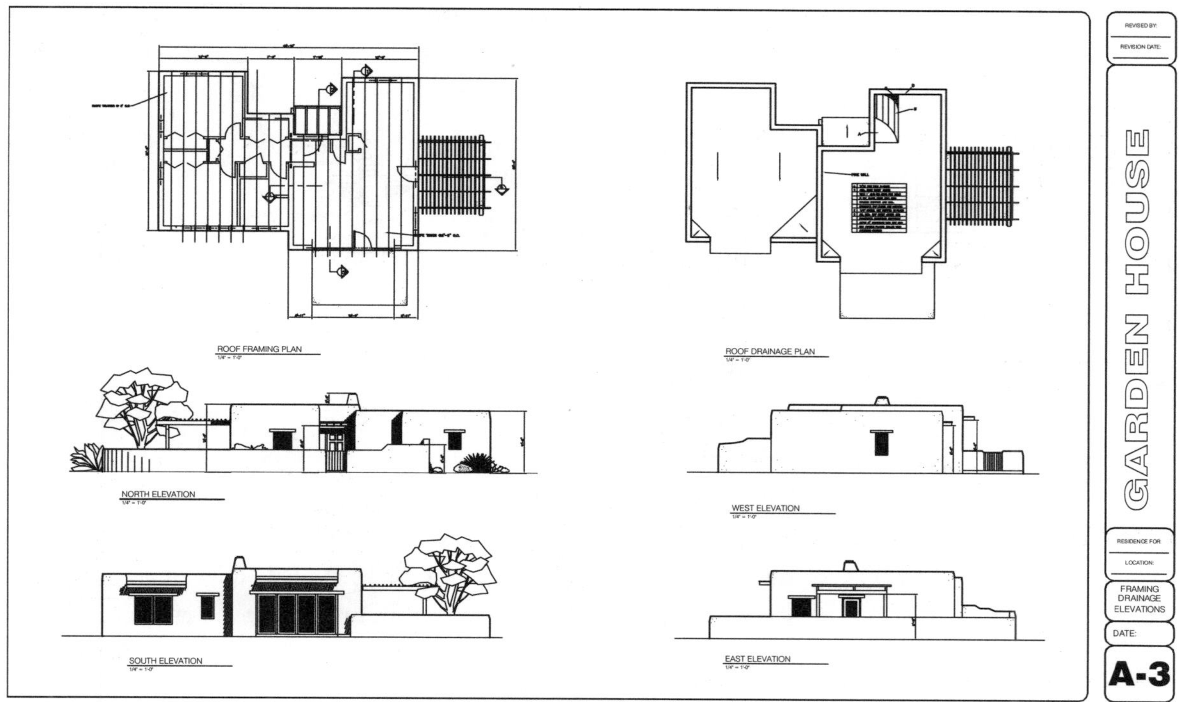

Next come framing plans for roofs and upper floors, as well as roof plans that show drainage slopes and parapets. The elevations show the four sides of the house with necessary notes and dimensions.

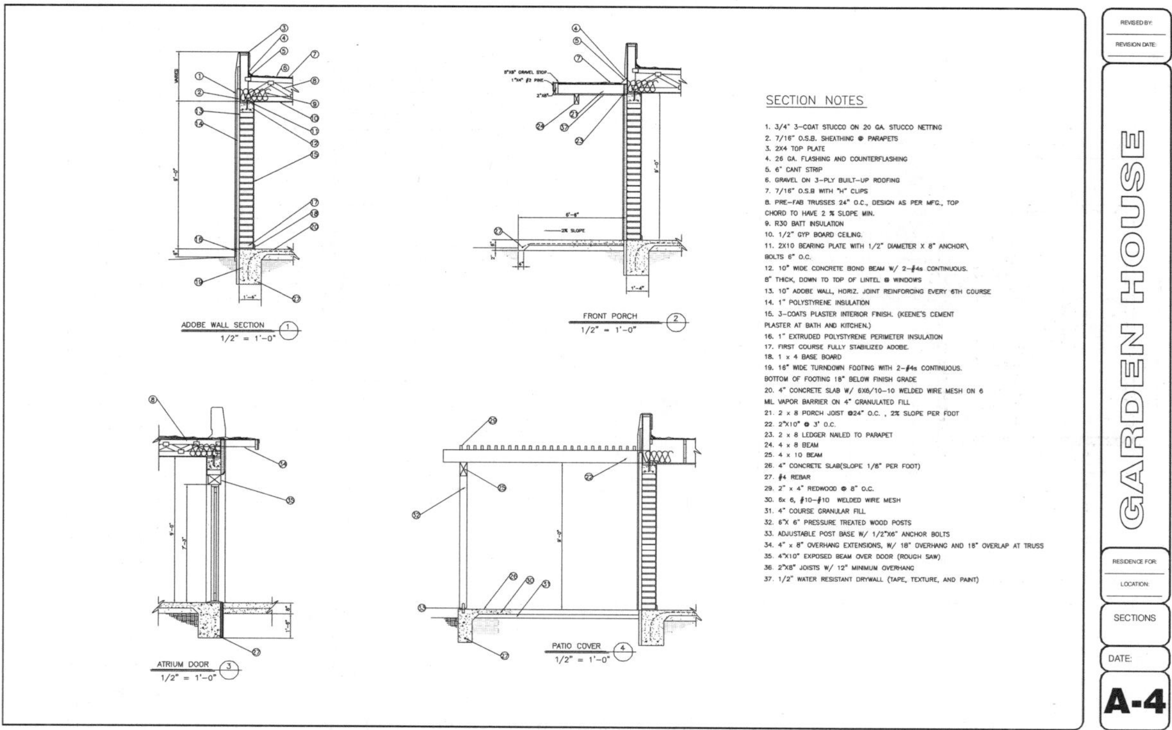

In addition, the drawings include large-scale construction details, seen here, along with building sections as needed.

Location affects construction costs in various ways. Prices vary from one area of the country to another. Labor costs generally run higher in urban areas while materials often cost more when they are delivered to remote rural areas. State and local building codes also affect building techniques and thus costs. For instance, California and Arizona adobe codes require thicker walls, wider bond beams and more reinforcing, making houses intrinsically more expensive. Contractors who dislike building in adobe or who are unfamiliar with the material will bid higher. The same goes for plumbers and electricians.

If contractors in an area are swamped with work, they won't bid as competitively on a small house with its relatively small profit. Conversely, a slower market will bring bid amounts down. Small volume home builders are more likely to bid the Basic Houses. Large volume builders probably won't be interested unless they can build several units at once and benefit from the resulting economies of scale.

Should You Build It Yourself?

You own efforts, either building or serving as general contractor, can cut building costs significantly and add detail work that would otherwise exceed your budget. Still, Doing-It-Yourself can devastate unwary owners with little building experience. Obtaining financing is usually more difficult for a first-time owner-builder than for a licensed contractor.

One option is doing a part of the work. You and your contractor may agree that you will do finish work such as painting, staining and cabinet installation in return for a discount. Some contractors encourage this kind of arrangement to the point of constructing a building shell and turning it over to you. Other builders won't have anything to do with owner-contractor partnerships for several reasons:

- Their insurance may not cover non-employee workers on the job site
- Unless carefully scheduled, novices may get in the way, slowing down the other trades
- Arguments may arise over how much an owner's work is worth
- A contractor doesn't want to risk possibly substandard finish work on a project bearing the company's name

Work done by owners following the main construction phase can greatly increase the value and quality of a home, yet avoid the problems mentioned previously. Woodworker Michel Richard added finishing touches with gable-end brackets and window trim. Engineer John Finger turned a narrow north-side yard into an appealing outdoor living area with deck, landscaping and adobe wall.

While doing construction work offers the side benefit of getting in great shape, beware of the accompanying temptation to acquire a "healthy" tan. If you're working in the sun, wear SPF 30 sunscreen, a hat and nonporous clothing with long sleeves and pants. (T-shirts and gauzy fabrics don't do the job.) Even if you Do-It-Yourself all the way from making your own adobes, you'll still come out behind if you develop malignant melanoma in the process.

Doing-It-Yourself is often associated with another appealing idea: you and your friends can erect your house walls in a couple weekends of "barn raising" and thus reduce your home's square foot cost to about half that of conventional construction.

A couple of things to consider. The average labor and materials cost of building the exterior walls for one of the houses shown in this book is 9%. When you add the costs of land, financing, site development, fees and permits, wall cost shrinks to approximately 4% or 5% of the total home cost. By saving half the cost of your walls, you save about 2% of the cost of your home.

As for using your friends—if it works, it's a wonderful experience. But make an honest assessment before you base your budget on an assumption of competent free labor:

- Do your friends have experience in construction or any other manual craft?
- Do they own the necessary tools or will you have to buy or rent for everyone?
- Will your friends' schedules mesh with those of subcontractors on the project?
- Do your friends have roughly similar ideas about acceptable quality?
- Can willing friends stand up to physically hard work?
- Do your friends hang on like pit bulls until a job is done?
- Do some of your friends insist on being the boss of any endeavor?
- Will accepting friends' help put you in an awkward position? Will you be able to return the favor?

THE BOTTOM LINE

One day a young acquaintance was griping about his visit to a friend whose parents had just bought a new, very expensive house. He thought the house itself was pretty cool but the money apparently hadn't stretched to furniture. Even worse, their refrigerator was empty. Not that the parents, both working two jobs to pay the mortgage, were home long enough to notice the lack.

The "trophy" house that forces its owners into indentured mortgage servitude and endless cleaning and maintenance has become a cartoon, but it's not funny if you're the one caught in the trap. We hope the Basic Houses can give you the flexibility to avoid a mortgage that controls everything else in your life. The decisions you make about the items in this chapter—land, plans, builder and mortgage—will determine whether you avoid or encounter mortgage slavery.

And after that, the fun begins.

7

ADOBE FROM THE GROUND UP

Once the maddening preliminaries are finished, take a deep breath, celebrate and then watch your house rise from the ground. In this chapter, we'll track an adobe house as it grows from a foundation trench to a finished home.

The construction world often breaks down the work of building a house into "assemblies." An assembly includes all the labor, materials and costs that make up one particular phase of a project, such as building the foundation or finishing the interior of the house. We'll follow the house's progress through the following assemblies:

- Site Work
- Concrete
- Adobe Walls
- Framing
- Stucco and Plaster
- Insulation
- Windows and Exterior Doors
- Roofing
- Interiors and Kitchens
- Mechanical
- Electrical
- General Job Costs, Overhead and Profit

SITE WORK

The nature of the building lot controls the cost of site work. The price of a level subdivision lot with infrastructure in place is usually higher per square foot but that price includes finished features such as access roads, clearing, rough grading and utility lines to the property. Still to be done are excavating for the foundations, replacing backfill, finish grading and installing utility lines from the street to the perimeter of the house.

While a typical subdivision lot may not be inspiring, it's usually ready for construction with rough grading and utility lines in place.

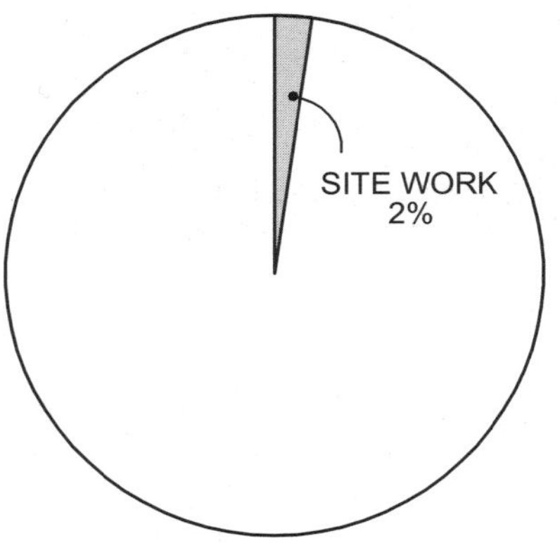

For a developed lot, site work makes up about 2% of the total construction cost. The approximate percentages shown on the pie charts throughout this chapter are averaged from the one-story Basic Houses.

The first time you see your foundation trench, don't panic! Because of a perceptual kink in the way our eyes and brains operate, a flat area on the ground such as that defined by a footing trench or a slab always looks much smaller than the actual finished house. In fact, your slab will look about the size of a walk-in closet, but your house will grow miraculously larger as it approaches completion.

The calm before the storm.

An area under and immediately around the house site is cleared of vegetation and graded. It's usually best to keep the demolished area as small as possible to reduce erosion, destroyed topsoil, blowing dust and other ills of stripped earth.

Trenches in place for pouring the house and porch foundations. After the walls go up, dirt is backfilled around the foundations and graded to slope away from the house.

CONCRETE

The concrete assembly includes all slabs and footings for the house. Houses shown in this book use turndown footings, common in temperate climates. A turndown uses slightly more concrete than a separate footing and stem wall, but it saves a great deal on forms and labor. It is essential that the bottom of a footing lie below the frost line, a depth of about 18" below the surface of the ground in central New Mexico. Local codes will specify the frost line depth in your area. If your frost line is significantly deeper, it may be more economical to build a separate footing and stem wall of poured concrete or block.

Of all possible Do-It-Yourself jobs on a house, pouring concrete is probably the most dangerous choice. It requires strenuous, fast, skilled work, lots of equipment and is very unforgiving.

A footing trench with wood forms and steel reinforcing bars in place. *Photograph courtesy of Jim and Lefty Folkman.*

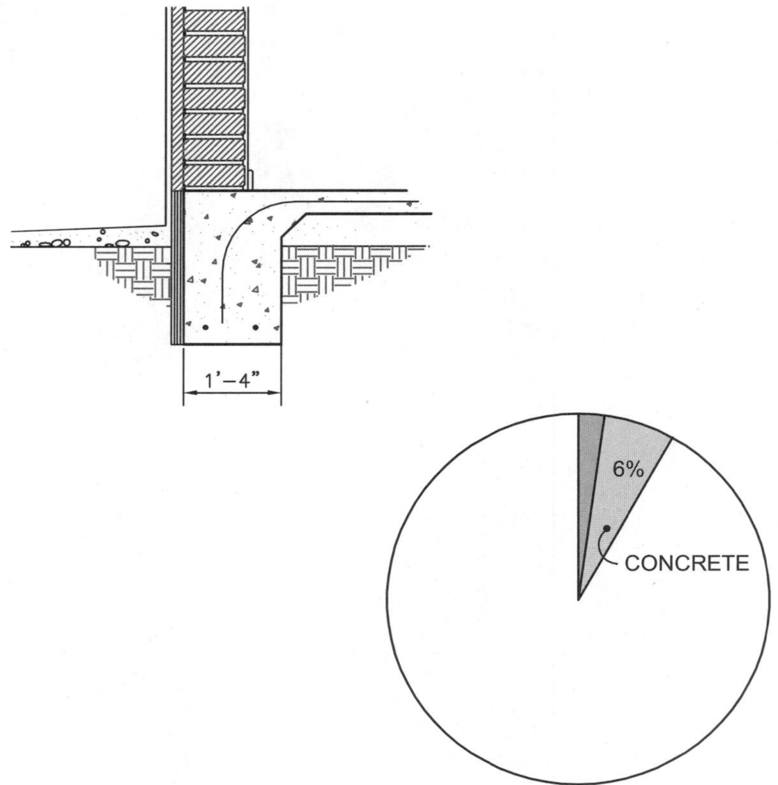

A foundation section from the Basic House working drawings shows the relation between slab, footing, insulation, natural and finish grades.

For houses shown in this book, concrete work makes up about 6% of the total cost of construction.

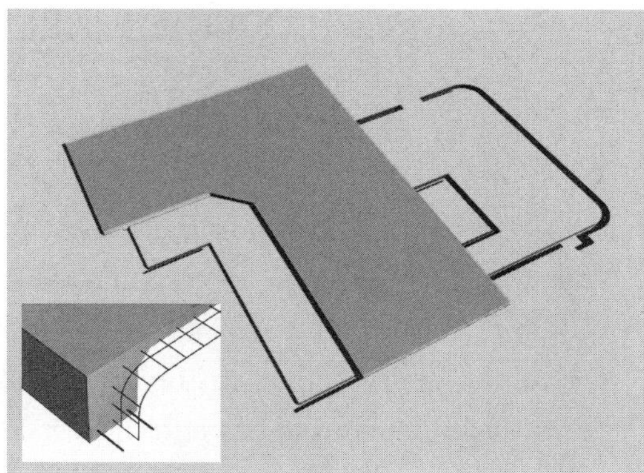

The 4" thick slab is poured continuously with the turndown footing. The inset shows the 6x6/10-10 wire mesh reinforcing, along with two #4 steel reinforcing bars along the bottom of the footing.

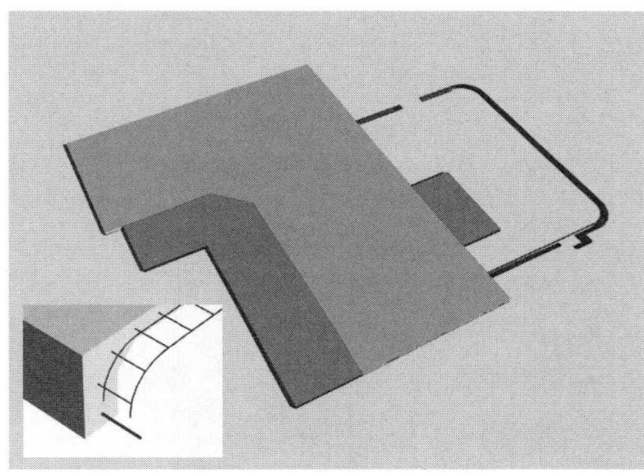

After the slab under the heated area is poured, perimeter insulation is placed around the vertical edges. The insulation prevents cold from seeping through the slab. It also serves as an expansion (or control) joint where needed to separate the main slab from the porch slabs. The inset shows the smaller footing used under roofed porches.

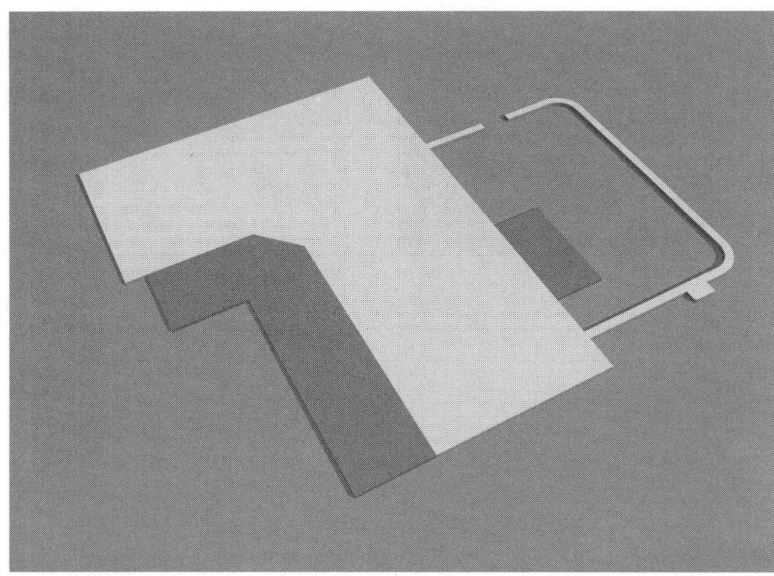

Usually foundations under garden walls are poured separately. They can be built when the house goes up or put off until later.

ADOBE WALLS

In New Mexico, Texas and southern Colorado, a 10" thick adobe wall—one built from bricks laid end to end—suffices for a single-story house or the lower level of a two-story house. Alternately, bricks can be turned sideways to make a 14" thick wall or doubled up for 20", 24" or 28" walls. The thicker walls, of course, boost costs for labor and materials. Adobe costs can vary dramatically depending on characteristics of the local pool of skilled masons. Costs also depend on the season; freezing weather prevents traditional adobe manufacturing, reducing supply and driving up prices.

Adobe Haiku.
First course going down./Masons laying, dog sleeping./Please don't rain again.
Photograph courtesy of Jim and Lefty Folkman.

Adobe walls with box-shaped wood nailers at the sides of door and window openings. The nailers provide a firm surface for attaching boards called rough bucks which anchor door and window jambs. Wooden forms are in place to contain the concrete poured for the bond beam.

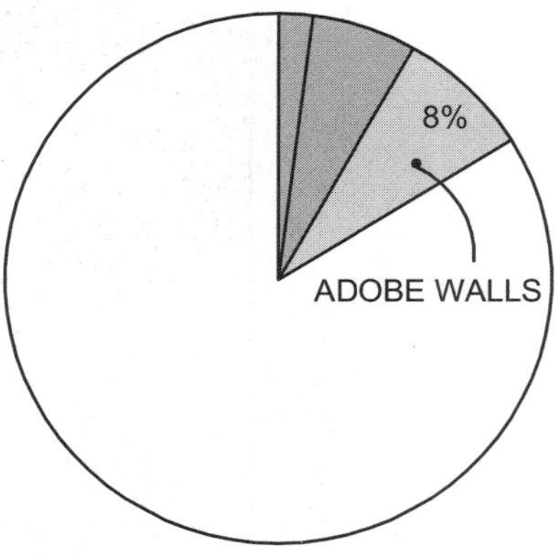

The adobe walls and concrete bond beam make up make up about 8% of construction cost.

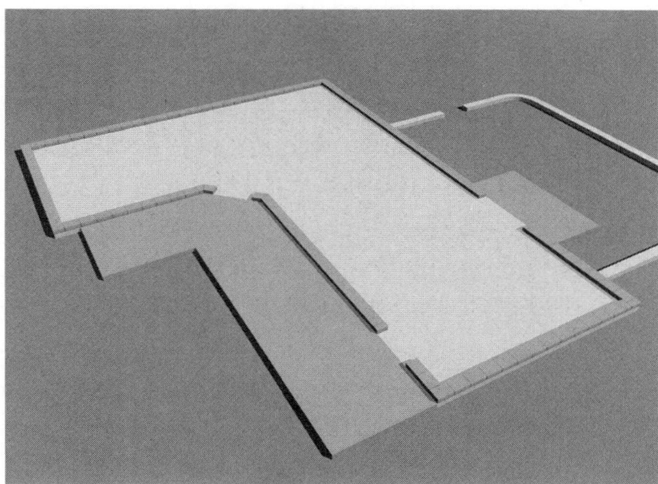

The first course of adobe goes in, leaving openings for doors.

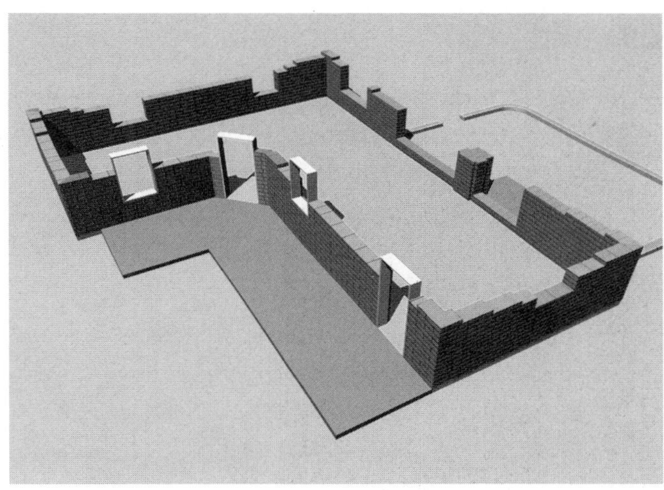

Masons usually lay up corners first so they can stretch lines to mark the level of a course. Door and window bucks are installed as the courses rise.

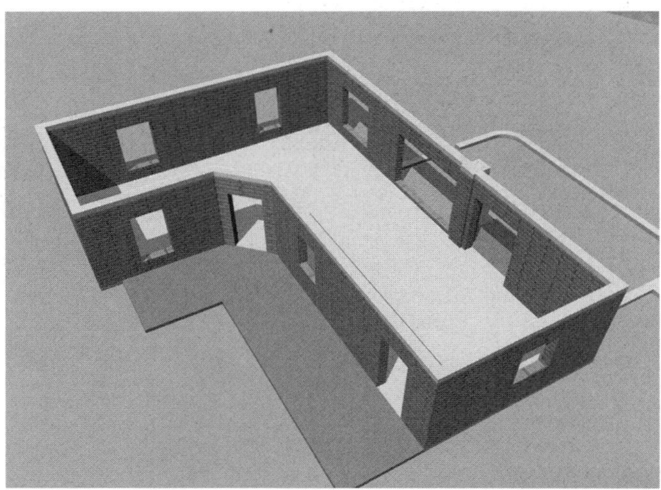

The continuous concrete bond beam around the top of the wall helps tie the adobe together so it resists lateral stresses. The beam also anchors the wood plate to which the roof attaches.

FRAMING

"Framing" includes work classified as rough carpentry in contrast to the finish carpentry included in the assemblies for interior finishing and windows. Even adobe houses include a lot of wood construction. The major framing elements are interior walls, decks, porches, roofs, upper floors, second floor walls and the lintels and girders across the tops of doors, windows and other open spans.

Decks are delightful but they present economic and environmental problems. We've used them only on Balcony House and Deck House. Two factors affect deck costs regardless of size or design: whether the deck lies over interior space, in which case it must be insulated and rendered watertight; and what material is used for decking—traditionally redwood, cedar or pressure-treated pine.

Pressure treated pine can be aesthetically unpleasant and many people don't want to lounge on wood impregnated with chromated copper arsenate (CCA) which tints wood green and ammoniacal copper arsenate (ACA). Wood products treated with less-toxic substances such as ACQ (alkaline/copper/quat) exist, but may be costly and hard to find.[1] Redwood and cedar are horribly expensive, and using them puts more logging pressure on dwindling supplies. As a compromise, we've used these woods as sparingly as possible.

An alternate material worth investigation is decking made from recycled plastic and waste wood. Its environmental benefits, low maintenance and lack of splinters offset its lack of mystique.

A wall with lintels in place over door and window openings. The New Mexico adobe code requires door and window lintels 6" deep by 10" wide that extend a minimum of 12" on either side of an opening. Other than timbers required by code, the Basic Houses use large-section timbers sparingly to reduce both costs and old growth lumbering.

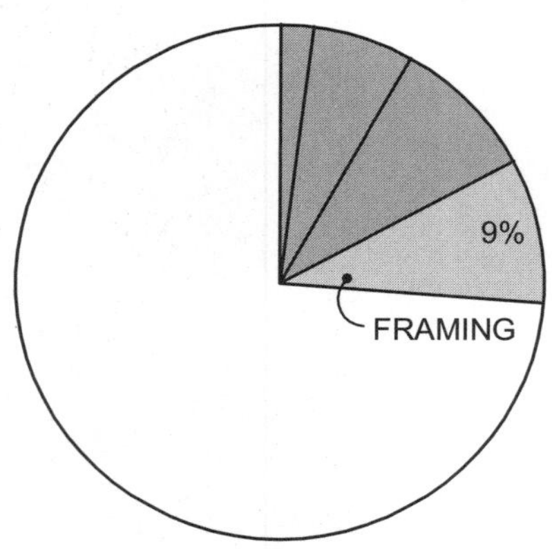

The average framing cost for single-story Basic Houses is 9%.

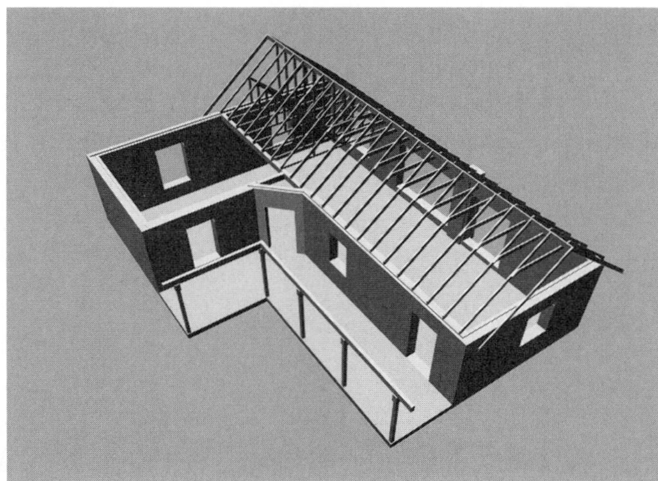

The main portion of High Valley house combines a site-built roof of 2x10 rafters over the high-ceilinged living area with a pre-manufactured truss roof over the bedroom.

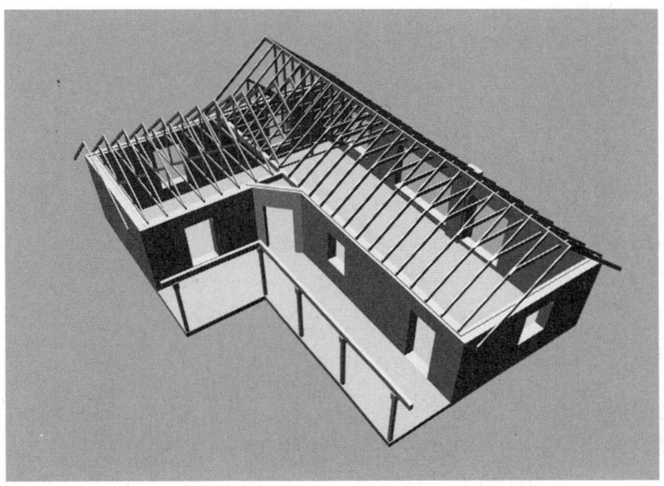

After the main area is roofed, the roof is built over smaller wings, with "valley jacks" marching up the trusses of the main roof.

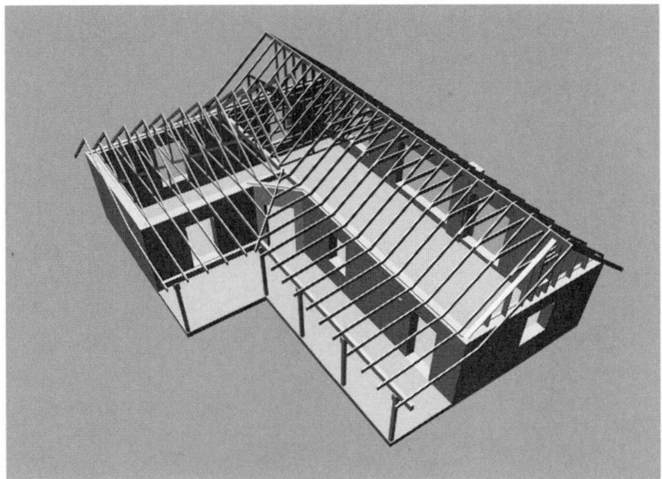

Porches are often the last element framed because they are usually supported by other components of the house. A contractor's bid may include porches as an optional item, meaning that you can decide whether to build them now or later.

INSULATION

Most houses today are built with a skin of insulation that effectively controls thermal change. Types of insulation vary according to the material they cover.

Foundation Perimeters

Perimeter insulation reduces heat loss through foundations. Two-inch thick extruded polystyrene, or "blue board," covers the concrete from the bottom of the foundation to the bottom of the adobe wall. Blue board has an R-value of 4 per inch. The insulation also serves as an expansion joint between concrete porch slabs and house foundations. If you use a radiant floor heating system, it helps to add insulation under the slab around the building perimeter.

Adobe Walls

Adobe walls are generally insulated with 2" expanded polystyrene, or "white board." A greater thickness of polystyrene is difficult to install. In a moderate climate polystyrene on a 10" adobe wall yields an average effective R-value of R-19 for medium-color walls or R-22 for darker walls.

"Effective R-value" is a measurement developed to more accurately assess the insulating ability of a wall. While a "steady state R-value" total includes only the R-values of the physical components of various wall layers, an "effective R-value" total includes all factors that affect the thermal performance of a wall:

- How much the sun heats a wall, which depends on which direction the wall faces
- Whether the wall is a light color that reflects heat or a dark color that absorbs it
- Whether the wall is massive enough to store significant heat

As mentioned in Chapter 3, enormous wall R-values are usually pointless but if you live in a severe climate, consider changing to 2" of polyurethane or isocyanurate, materials with twice the R-value of polystyrene.

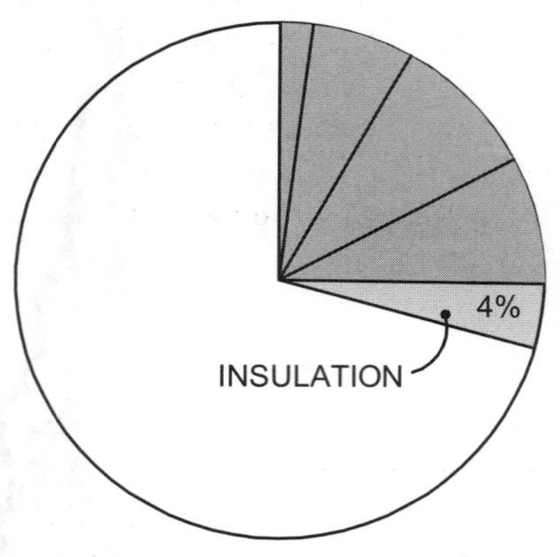

Insulation for the Basic Houses averages about 4% of construction cost.

Roofs and Gable Walls

The plans shown in this book specify R-30 undyed fiberglass batt insulation for ceilings and R-19 for the upper story frame walls. Undyed insulation is less environmentally offensive than the bright pink variety. Colder mountain areas may require thicker ceiling insulation.

We've zoomed into the rendering of High Valley House to show how insulation is applied to the foundation, wall and ceiling. The foundation insulation abuts the lighter colored wall insulation so there is no thermal gap. The wall insulation runs up past the end of the batt insulation in the ceiling for the same reason.

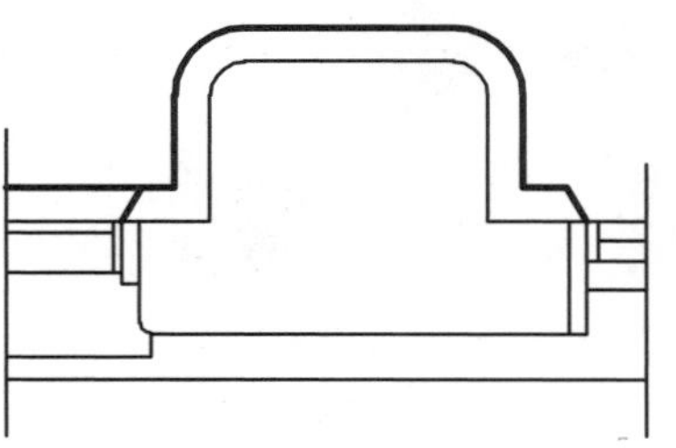

The exterior wall buttresses often used on adobe houses are too thick to need insulation for thermal purposes. This drawing and the following one show a buttress on the floor plan of High Valley House, illustrating different approaches to buttress insulation. Above, the 2" thick insulation is wrapped completely around the buttress, which costs more but offers a continuous surface for the stucco finish.

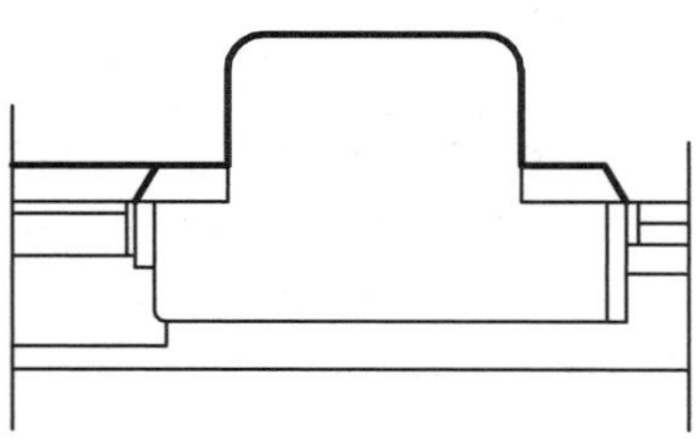

In this approach, the insulation stops at the buttress—cheaper but more likely to cause expansion cracks in the stucco where it bridges two different materials.

STUCCO AND PLASTER

Together, stucco, plaster and wall insulation cost more per square foot than the adobe walls they cover. Although the words "plaster" and "stucco" are often used interchangeably, plaster usually refers to an interior finish made from gypsum. Stucco refers to an exterior cement-based coating. The first coat, or "scratch coat," of stucco is applied over a mesh backing that anchors the mix to the wall. The next coat, or "brown coat," evens out irregularities and provides a smooth base for the finish, or "color coat." Finish colors can range from the usual tans to apple green, grayish blue or oxblood red.

Steeply sloped porch roofs on the Basic Houses have ceilings. Low-slope porches don't. Stucco is so expensive that installing a porch ceiling cuts costs if it hides a large wall area that would otherwise require stucco. Porches without ceilings can be decked with tongue-and-groove boards, *latillas* (peeled sticks laid side by side to form a ceiling), hardboard siding with the finish side turned down or rough-sawn lumber as shown here.

Many custom mixes are used for plastering interior walls. Portions of this house are plastered with mica-flecked mud covered by a sealer.

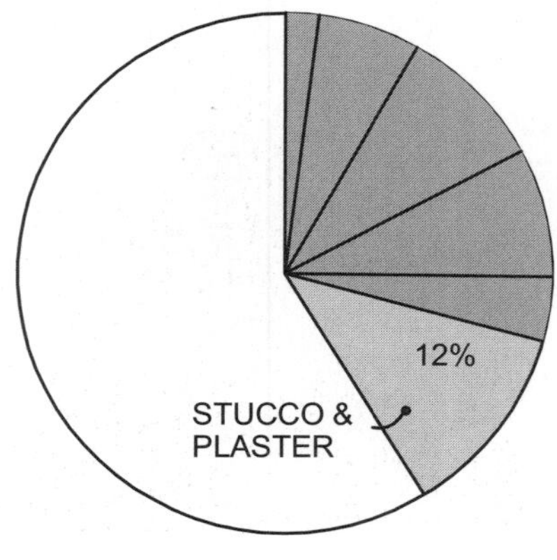

Stucco and plaster gobble a 12% chunk of the construction pie.

An exposed adobe finish is frequently used on interior walls. As masons lay up the wall, they take extra care to smooth the mortar joints and then score a brick pattern in the concrete bond beam. The completed wall receives a rubbing with burlap or a "slurry coat" of drywall compound. Then the wall is sealed and painted. While adobes left their natural color look warm and appealing, a white-painted finish makes an interior seem much brighter. *Photograph courtesy of Laura Burr.*

Plaster and stucco don't take up much space, but they greatly affect the look of the finished house. A single color of stucco unifies a house visually.

On the other hand, using a different stucco color for each block of a house as shown in this rendering of Garden House gives the appearance of a small compound of dwellings.

WINDOWS AND EXTERIOR DOORS

Windows are poetically called the eyes of a house, perhaps because their cost approaches that of bionic eyeball implants. Good windows, however, repay their extra cost fairly quickly. As mentioned previously, plans for the Basic Houses specify metal-clad wood for quality and durability.

The styles of windows shown vary from double-hung to casement to fixed depending on which works best with the house's style and the window's function. You may prefer another style but before changing, check code compliance. Bedrooms and baths require windows with minimum opening areas for emergency exits and ventilation. Substituting a double-hung window for a casement of the same size cuts in half the area that can be opened. The Uniform Building Code requires a bedroom to have either an exterior door or a window that opens a minimum of 20" wide and 22" high with a total opening area of 5.7' square feet or greater.

While you're deciding on windows, you may want to comparison shop. We asked friends who have a window company what single thing customers could do to ease the process of window-shopping. Their answer? The ideal customer understands exactly what items a window bid includes. The following checklist of window questions can help you verify that competing window bids include the same items.

- How many operable units in a mulled window?
- Exactly what size is the window?
- Any special glass or glass coating, and what are its benefits?
- Are grilles included? What type and material?
- Are screens included? What material?
- What about warranty and service?
- Finger-jointed or clear wood on the interior?
- U-value and infiltration specs?
- How much solar heat do the windows admit (heat gain coefficient)?

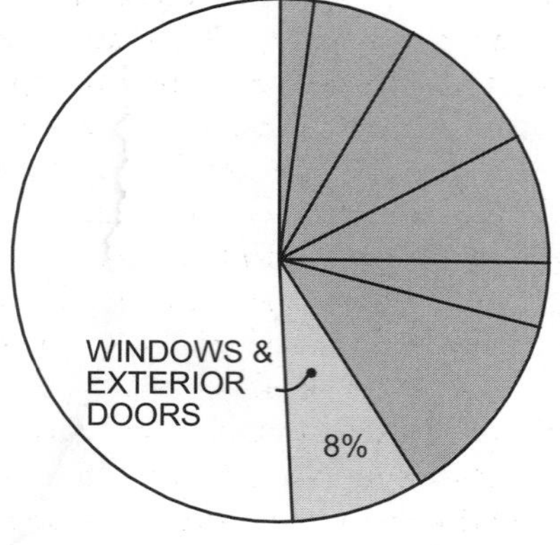

Good quality windows and exterior doors cost approximately 8% of the construction budget.

Most houses in the United States used double-hung windows until the early 1900s when Frank Lloyd Wright popularized casement windows. Wright despised double-hungs, which he called "guillotine windows," and would not use them on his buildings. Less doctrinaire people often use whatever styles work best. To the left of the corner is a double-hung unit. To the right, casements line this house's north wall.

Awning windows control air flow effectively. Installed over casement or fixed units as shown here, in summertime awning windows dump the hot air that rises to the ceiling in living areas.

The patio replacement units across the south wall of this home help reduce heating fuel needs to about one cord of wood each winter. Patio replacement units (PRUs) are double-glazed, sealed glass panels used to replace broken glass in patio doors. For years, solar home builders framed in PRUs as fixed windows. The relatively inexpensive door-height panels are available in widths from 2'4" to 3'10". PRUs can be cost-effective if you do the tricky installation job yourself. (And check the seal warranty before purchase.) If a contractor frames in the panels, they may cost as much as factory-finished fixed windows. A bank of carefully installed PRUs separated by posts usually looks better than PRUs framed into the same rough opening with doors or operable windows.

ROOFING

The pitched roof houses in this book use metal roofing that effectively has a lifetime warranty. Metal roofing styles and prices vary considerably. Plans for houses with flat roofs specify 4-ply built-up roofing. Skylights are fixed, double-glazed units designed to fit between framing members without cutting joists or trusses.

Ladders hung from the ridges of steeply pitched roofs provide safe footing for roofers. Often the ladders are left on the pitched roofs of traditional houses for future maintenance. *Photograph courtesy of Jim and Lefty Folkman.*

Flat roofs usually require *canales*, or roof scuppers, for drainage. This metal porch roof *canale* will receive a decorative wood sheathing. The Basic Houses with flat roofs are framed with trusses that have a slope of 1/4 inch per foot along the top chord to ensure that a roof drains effectively.

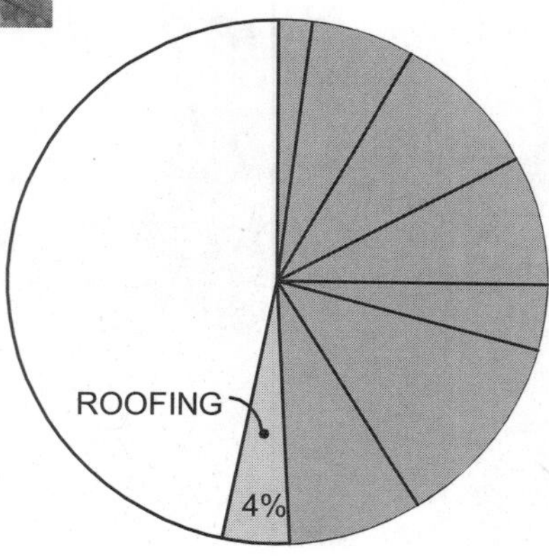

The pie chart shows the 4% average cost of 26-gauge ribbed roofing such as "Pro-Panel."

Although metal roofing is more expensive per square foot than built-up asphalt, pitched roofs don't necessarily cost more than flat ones. The cost of a flat roof's trusses and stuccoed frame parapets often offsets the cost of a pitched roof's greater enclosed space and more expensive roofing. However, using trusses eliminates some interior bearing walls and reduces the need for large-dimension lumber. If you choose a heating system that requires ducts, a truss roof makes them easier to install.

The builder of this studio, also shown in Chapter 1, wanted to use traditional corrugated steel to roof it. Unfortunately, most "tin" manufactured today is very thin, 28 or even 29 gauge. He finally located good, heavy-gauge tin on an old house some miles away. He designed his new building to fit the old tin, lining up rafters and purlins under the existing nail holes.

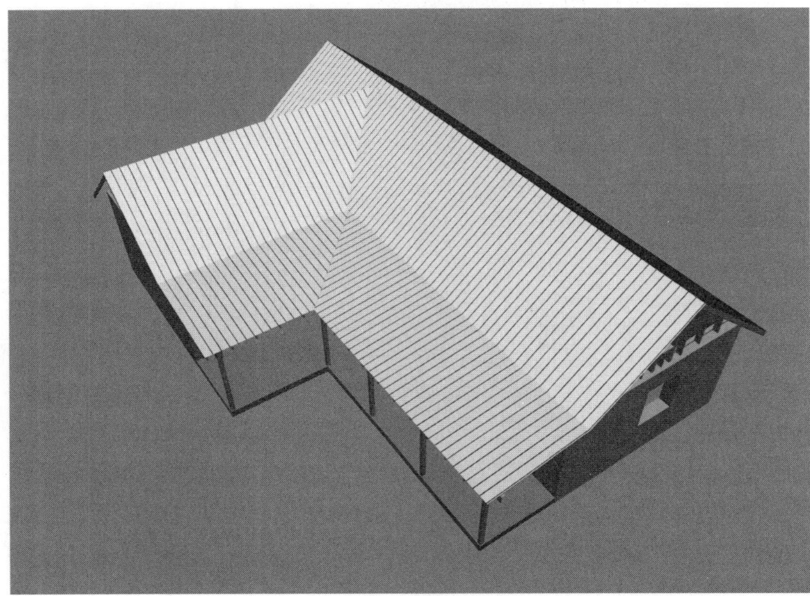

The rendered house acquires roofing.

INTERIORS AND KITCHENS

This ship's ladder leading to a loft is similar to the one specified for High Valley House. For houses with a full second story, however, codes require a standard staircase. The staircases in the Basic Houses use gypsum board on 2x4 framing, hardwood caps and railings and carpeted treads. *Photograph courtesy of Jim and Lefty Folkman.*

While you've watched your adobe house go up rapidly to this point, it may seem that progress screeches to a halt when interior finish work begins. Interior finish work can easily take longer than all other jobs combined and cost more than any other single assembly. But just look at what the category includes:

- Installing and finishing moldings and coverings for walls and ceilings
- Laying and finishing floor coverings
- Hanging doors and adding interior door and window trim,
- Finish carpentry for shelves, stairs, closets and cabinets
- All interior painting and staining.

The finishes specified for the Basic Houses are simple and inexpensive, yet of good, durable quality. The pie chart percentage shown allows for ceilings and walls covered with 1/2" gypsum board. Interior doors are flush, hollow-core birch. Most closet doors are bifolds, less costly than bypass doors and less frustrating to operate because they open the full width of the closet.

Interior trim for doors and windows is made of 1x4 boards. Per dollar spent, nothing boosts an adobe house's look of quality more than using custom door trim instead of stock "clamshell" or "colonial" molding.

The floorings are sheet linoleum in the bathroom and kitchen, carpet in the bedrooms and halls, and stained and sealed concrete in the living areas and entries. The concrete floors can be further embellished by stamping patterns that make the concrete resemble tile of various styles.

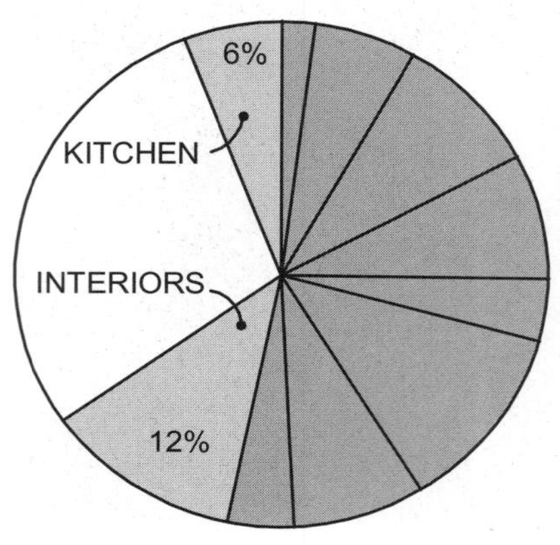

Interiors and Kitchens are often bid as separate assemblies. The pie chart shows 6% as the average cost for kitchen work and 12% for the other interior labor and materials.

A contractor's bid for installing a kitchen can cover a wide variety of items. The bare minimum, the percentage shown by the pie chart, usually includes labor and materials for a double sink, wall and base cabinets and counter tops. When you get bids, check exactly which appliances are included, and how their brand and quality are specified.

You may get bids that treat cabinets as an allowance so you can scout around for the best value. Standard cabinets come in 3" increments of length—12", 15", 18" and so on. Longer cabinets are more economical per linear foot; one 48" long base cabinet costs about half as much as four 12" long cabinets.

Check the small print in advertisements for kitchen cabinet packages offered by home and building stores. The large, full-color photographs seem to show luxurious, full-sized, lavishly equipped kitchens. However, the "amazingly low" advertised package price usually includes less than 10 linear feet of base and wall cabinetry, with no counter tops or installation.

Installing a small kitchen. *Photograph courtesy of Jim and Lefty Folkman.*

Wood corbels can embellish interiors as well as exteriors. Originally used to help long beams carry the weight of roofs, corbels have shown up all over the world. These are from New Mexico (top) and the Middle East and Asia (left).

MECHANICAL

Plumbing

The mechanical assembly covers waste and supply lines at the point where they cross your foundation line and become building mains. Also covered are branch waste and supply lines that run from the mains to each plumbing wall, fixtures and their installation, associated fittings such as faucets, and miscellaneous plumbing such as lines to refrigerator ice-makers and hose bibs. Several of the one-story plans show half-baths adjacent to the main bedrooms. The half-bath spaces offer owners several options.

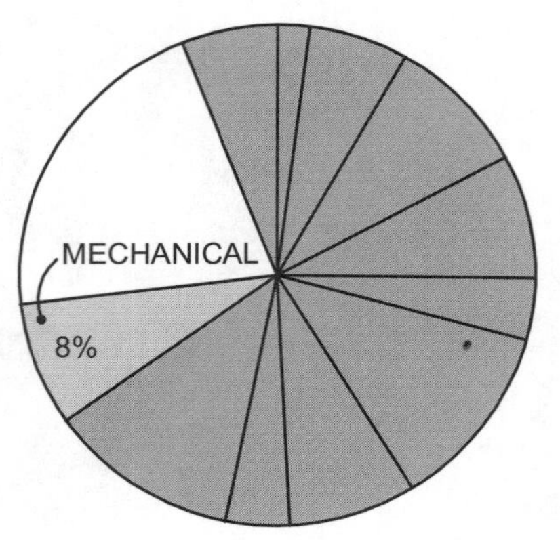

Mechanical costs for plumbing and a single boiler hydronic heating system average 8%.

What to do with a half-bath space? The space shown as a half-bath on the Ramada House plan can be used in several other ways. From the top, as an extra closet, to add extra space to the bedroom, or as a passageway to a west-side addition.

To save floor space, we first designed the Basic Houses with stacked laundry appliances, but then we started talking to people in the business. Unless a stacked dryer has a 220-volt connection, it takes two hours to dry a half-size load. But hey, no problem—the washer will only handle a half-size load. Stackables seem a poor solution for households of more than one person, so all the plans show space for side-by-side washers and dryers.

Heating and Cooling

The Basic House plans specify a hydronic radiant floor system that uses an ordinary domestic water heater as the "boiler." Potable (suitable for drinking) domestic hot water flows from the water heater through sealed tubes and back to the water heater. We chose the system for several reason

- The system cost is competitive with low-cost forced air systems because you don't have to buy a boiler.
- Radiant floor systems are the most comfortable heating available. The concrete floor becomes a whole-house radiant heater.
- Because the system has no blower fans, it doesn't spread dust, pollen and other airborne pollutants.
- Radiant floor heating can reduce an already small heating load by 25% to 35% compared to convective systems, according to studies done by ASHRAE (American Society of Heating, Refrigeration and Air Conditioning Engineers). Radiant systems achieve the same comfort level as other systems while operating at a 6 to 8 degree lower air temperature. Infiltration losses run 10% to 20% lower than with forced air systems.
- Solar heating works well with radiant floor heating. Both systems require storage mass and conductive floor coverings.
- The lack of a heating system boiler or furnace frees up space in the Basic Houses for larger rooms or more storage.
- The system makes it easier to expand the houses. All the plan expansions include bathrooms, which will require additional hot water capacity. To heat the expansions you simply add the new water heater and connect it to in-floor tubing. Thus the original system can be economically sized only for the core house.

Hydronic tubing in place before the slab is poured. *Photograph courtesy of Geri Rhodes.*

ELECTRICAL

The Electrical portion of a bid usually includes:

- Electric service (the service cable, meter socket, panel box and associated items)
- Any electric heating
- Wiring, switches and outlets
- Light Fixtures

Unless your house has an electric range, dryer or heating, 100 amp service is sufficient. Otherwise, you'll need 200 amp at a considerably higher cost.

The most variable component of electrical cost is lighting. Light fixture prices vary from under $100 to thousands—not counting bulbs or installation. Your contractor may supply fixtures or include a fixture allowance that you can spend as you wish. Alternately, you may purchase fixtures completely outside the bid.

Light fixtures and installation for one of the Basic Houses, using inoffensive fixtures with simple lines and decent-quality materials, amounts to between 1% and 2% of construction cost. Later you can upgrade individual fixtures if you wish; fine lighting has a great impact on the appearance of a home. However, if you want to change the number or position of fixtures, add recessed lights, or wire the lights to switch differently, discuss the changes with your contractor before construction begins. The changes may increase the initial bid, but they will be much costlier if done later.

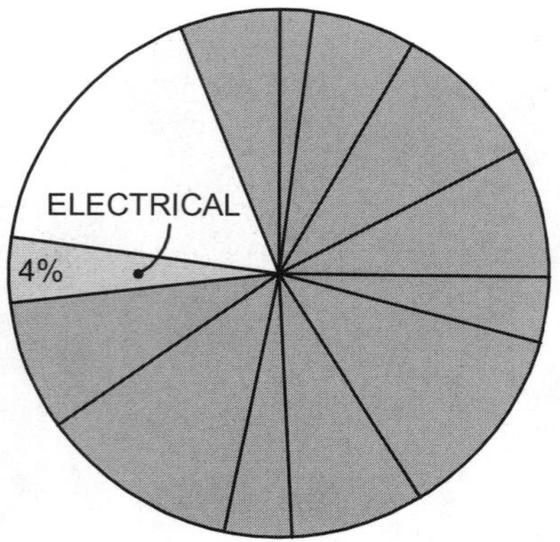

Electrical work takes approximately 4% of the pie.

GENERAL JOB COSTS, OVERHEAD AND PROFIT

Our construction cost pie chart still has a wedge missing. That final wedge is filled by the general contractor's job costs, overhead and profit.

General Job Costs

General job costs are tied to a specific job, yet they do not become part of the building. Nor are general job costs covered by a contractor's overhead. For example, the total cost of electric power needed to complete a particular job falls into three categories:

- Utility bills for a contractor's office fall under "Overhead"
- The cost of wiring the building project falls under "Electrical"
- Running temporary power to the job site falls under "General Job Costs"

Bids may list general job costs separately or add them as a percentage to other assemblies. The category includes what the contractor pays for supervision, permits and fees, construction loan financing, insurance, transportation and utilities. The location of a job greatly affects these costs. A cabin up a pot-holed mountain road 90 miles from the builder's office produces much higher job costs than a house on a developed city lot ten minutes away.

Overhead and Profit

Overhead covers a general contractor's ongoing costs such as office and secretarial expenses. Profit accounts for what the contractor makes on a particular job over and above wages, benefits, materials, rental equipment and subcontractors' charges. You probably won't see specific figures for O&P on any contractor's estimate—the costs are usually folded into assembly subtotals.

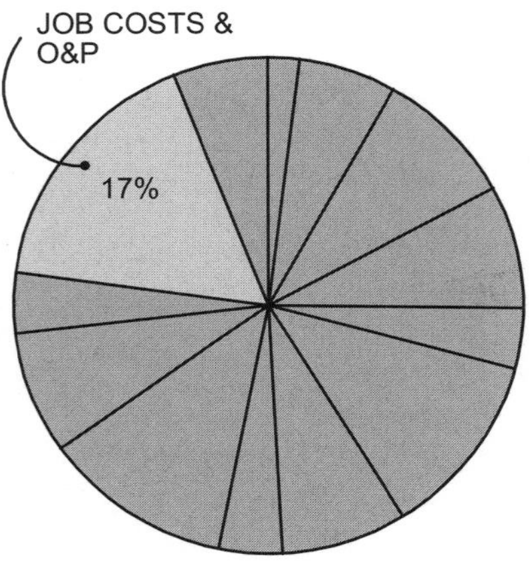

The pie chart all filled in with 17% for general job costs, overhead and profit.

APPENDIX:

WORKING DRAWINGS AND BUILDING PERMITS

Traveling from the point when you decide to build a house to the point when the backhoe moves onto your lot is a long, complicated journey. At some point along the way you will need a building permit unless you're settling in the most remote outback. To get the permit, you will need drawings detailed enough to show that the floor plan and the building's structure meet various code requirements.

"Plans" Versus "Working Drawings"

The term "house plans" can mean two very different things. "Plan books" fill supermarket and bookstore magazine racks, but they limit information about each house shown to a simplified version of the floor layout and views of the house's exterior. "Working drawings" are the detailed, dimensioned documents used to actually bid and build a house. Working drawings are sometimes called "blueprints" or "construction documents." In most locales you must submit a fairly complete set of working drawings to get a building permit.

Even if you don't need working drawings for a permit, the documents prevent problems. Working drawings and specifications provide a clear, detailed basis for the contract with your builder. They also anticipate and solve construction problems on paper, which is much less expensive and traumatic than solving problems in hardened concrete and sawn lumber.

Working Drawings from Where?

Sources for working drawings fall into three general categories: custom plans, builder's plans and stock plans. The working drawings for the Basic Houses combine elements of stock and custom plans.

Custom Designs

Custom plans are drawn by an architect or designer to specifically fit your requirements and building site. Custom plans are probably your best choice if:

- The topology or soil of your building site demands complex engineering
- You require a space arrangement completely different from standard residential layouts
- You want to use an unfamiliar building material
- You are committed to an aesthetic goal not usually addressed by stock plans

The cost of custom plans ranges from several hundred dollars to many thousands. The fee may be based on hours worked, square footage, percentage of the house's construction cost or some combination of the above. The amount of actual design work included in the fee varies greatly. At one end of the scale are drafters who generate working drawings from pictures and sketches you supply; at the other are architects who insist on complete design autonomy.

Builder's Plans

If you have chosen a builder, he or she may offer to supply working drawings. How much design control you have over the drawings varies. Your choices may be limited to a list of standard "custom options" for a stock plan, or the company may have a staff or consulting designer who can draw whatever you want.

The builder may charge you separately for the working drawings or the fee may be folded into the overall cost of the construction bid. As with custom plans, builder's plans should be drawn to meet all local code requirements.

Stock Plans

The "plan books" you see on magazine racks are catalogs of stock plans. Almost all widely available stock plans are for wood frame houses. The cost of ordering the working drawings ranges from a few hundred dollars for one blueprint of a very simple house to over a thousand for several blueprints of a large house. Making changes in the blueprints usually presents problems.

Plans for the Basic Houses

Working drawings for the 12 houses shown in this book can be ordered for the cost of reproduction, shipping, handling and taxes. Each plan package, which can be used to build one house but not resold, includes one full-sized blueprint for you to study and one 3-1/2" disk with the computer files for that entire set of working drawings. The package also includes instructions for taking the disk to a drafting service or print shop to have the files printed, with or without changes.

Having the drawings in computer file format makes it easier for a drafter or CAD operator to change the plans before they are reproduced. Your local adobe code may require structural changes or you may have alterations you wish to make.

Plan Package Components

Most mail order working drawings include all elements that are independent of local conditions. The sample set of working drawings in Chapter 6 shows those elements at reduced scale. You will probably have to supply components that depend on your particular location: site plan, heat-loss calculation, and possibly truss detail drawings and mechanical specifications.

Site Plan

A site plan (or "plot plan") shows how a house is placed on a particular building lot. It usually shows utility line locations, setbacks, rights-of-way, wells and septic systems, any relevant topological features, and site development features such as driveways and walks. It also shows survey information such as the length and compass heading of each property line. If you have the time and experience, you can use the legal survey of your property to draw a site plan yourself. Otherwise, you'll need to have a drafter do it. Take along the survey drawing and legal description of your property and any neighborhood covenants that apply. Photographs of the lot and surrounding area are often helpful.

"Heat Loss" or "U-Value" Calculation

Most locales have enacted energy codes and require written evidence that a building will meet their standard. Usually, the document must list the components of a house's walls, roof, and windows, their respective R-values, and how much area each covers. The figures are totaled to calculate the approximate BTUs lost by the heated building. Ask your city or county building official for any forms that must be filled out and instructions for completing them. Then try to dump the task on your general contractor, heating contractor, drafter, architect or the other agencies listed below.

Failing that, take a deep breath and dig in. The task is not really difficult once you understand it, but the terminology and the reasoning behind the calculations may be unfamiliar.

Truss Drawings

Your building official may require engineering drawings of the specific trusses needed to build your house. The truss manufacturer usually supplies truss drawings. Manufacturers vary in their willingness to supply drawings before receiving an actual order. It is generally the contractor's responsibility to acquire truss drawings.

Mechanical Layout

Permit agencies may require documentation that the layout and capacity of a heating system meets the standards of the local mechanical code. As with truss drawings, it is usually the responsibility of the contractor to supply mechanical drawings.

Engineer or Architect's Stamp

You might like to check with a local licensed professional, such as a licensed Professional Engineer. Some permit agencies require that a local licensed professional stamp working drawings as a guarantee that the floor plan meets code requirements and that the structure is adequate to withstand local conditions such as very heavy snow loads or extreme winds.

LEVELS OF REGULATION

Regional Codes

The working drawings for the houses shown in this book meet the requirements of the Uniform Building Code (UBC), commonly in force throughout the Mountain West. However, variations do exist depending on state, so be sure to check the code as enacted in your state. Other regional codes are very similar. The drawings also comply with the International Residential Code (IRC). At the time of publication, the IRC was still in the development stage. When it is published, each state will have three choices: accept the code with changes, accept the code as is or reject the code. None of these "umbrella" codes cover adobe in any serious fashion, so most states enact their own adobe codes.

Local Adobe Codes

By now you're sick of hearing this, but call your city, county or state building official and request a copy of the local adobe code. Many localities in Texas or Colorado use the same specifications as the New Mexico code.

California and Arizona, however, change codes from county to county and city to city. Most of these codes require thicker exterior adobe walls—12", 14", 16" or even 18". Standards differ for the lintels over doors and windows and for roof design and construction. Many areas require a deeper bond beam, although the thicker concrete may actually perform worse in an earthquake. In seismically active areas, walls must have vertical steel reinforcing although adobe has never been shown to bond with steel.

Local or state energy codes generally specify the capacity of heating and cooling systems and the amount of insulation required for local temperatures.

Your area may have additional building

regulatory codes. Ask your municipal or county building official if the particular area where you plan to build has any further regulations that might apply to your working drawings. Governmental regulations at the neighborhood level usually deal with a building's zoning, size and use.

Neighborhood Covenants

If you already own land, study any relevant covenants and check the house plan you want to use against the covenants. If you're buying land, make sure you study the covenants first. Chapter 6 discusses common features of subdivision covenants.

PEOPLE WHO MAY HELP

A building official's plan review is not a final exam; you don't get penalized for failing the first attempt. Submit your working drawings for review and see what happens. If they are approved, fine. If they are rejected, you should receive an exact list of the items that must be changed to meet local requirements. While it is certainly educational to go through the process of obtaining plans yourself, a wide variety of persons can offer valuable help.

If you have chosen a contractor, discuss whether securing the necessary permits is included in your agreement, and if not, how much extra it would cost.

Call your local building official; the number will be listed as "Planning and Zoning," "Building Inspector," "Plan Checking," or a similar title. Ask whether plans for an adobe single-family residence require an architect or engineer's stamp. (New Mexico does not require a stamp unless the house is very large, three stories or higher or built with unusual construction techniques but requirements vary.) If you must have the plans stamped anyway, use the architect or engineer as a guide through the permit process.

Check whether your state has a "Mortgage Counseling" service for first-time home-buyers. HUD (Housing and Urban Development) is a clearinghouse for this type of help. Their website, www.hud.gov, includes listings for services by state.

Ask your building official for available materials that describe going through the local permit process, particularly any checklists of steps you must follow.

Talk to any friends who have recently built a house. (Take their advice with a grain of salt; they may exaggerate the horrors for dramatic effect.)

NOTES

Chapter 1

1. Rory P. Gauthier and Robin Yeomans Farwell, "New Mexico's Prehistoric Adobe Works," *Adobe Today's Earthbuilder*, pp. 26-28. Issue 40, Summer, 1983.
2. Jerome Iowa, *Ageless Adobe: History and Preservation in Southwestern Architecture*, pp. 78-79. Sunstone Press, Santa Fe, NM, 1985.
3. John M. Taylor, *Our Lady of Guadalupe Parish History Project*, p. 21. Privately published, September, 1989.

Chapter 2

1. Will of Don Ignacio Roybal y Torrado, translated by Jose Antonio Esquibel.
2. Karla Kuban, "An Even Exchange." *The New York Times Magazine,* p. 68, New York, August 16, 1998.
3. Joseph M. Tibbets, "Bullet Penetrations: Adobe & Rammed Earth vs. Straw Bale." *Interamericas Adobe Builder*, pp. 40-48. Bosque, New Mexico: Southwest Solaradobe School, 1999.
4. Joseph M. Tibbets, *The Earthbuilders' Encyclopedia*, p. 52. Bosque, New Mexico: Southwest Solaradobe School, 1989.
5. Andrea Gabor, "From Teepee to Solar-Heated Mobile Homes: Experimental Houses for New Mexican Indians," *Architectural Record*, p.36. November, 1981.
6. "Rastra–Recycled Polystyrene Foam Forms," *Environmental Building News* Volume 5, No.4, July/August, 1996.
7. Ibid.

Chapter 3

1. Rick Nevin and Gregory Watson, "Evidence of Rational Market Values for Home Energy Efficiency," *The Appraisal Journal*, October, 1998. Quoted on U.S.EPA Energy Star Homes Program at http://www.epa.gov.
2. National Geographic Maps, "1998 Population & Resources," produced for *National Geographic Magazine*, Washington, D.C., October, 1998
3. Allan Chen, "Small Appliance Energy Use Surging in U.S. Homes, *Berkeley Lab Research News*, http://www.lbl.gov/ScienceArticles/Archives, August 19, 1998.

Chapter 4

1. In *How Buildings Learn: What Happens After They're Built* (listed in the bibliography) Brand dissects in detail how both residences and commercial building succeed or fail in adapting to change.

Chapter 6

1. Bion Howard, "The Green Home and Development Ties into the Community" in *Green Building: A Primer for Builders, Consumers and Realtors.* 1996-2000 Building Environmental Science and Technology (B.E.S.T.) The Green Building Primer can be found at www.energybuilder.com/greenbld.htm.

Chapter 7

1. Paula Baker, Erica Elliott, and John Banta. *Prescriptions for a Healthy House: A Practical Guide for Architects, Builders, and Homeowners*, p. 81. Santa Fe, New Mexico: InWord Press, 1998.

BIBLIOGRAPHY

The following references include resources for adobe building, solar energy, design, financing, and green building.

BOOKS AND PERIODICALS

Alexander, Christopher, Sara Ishikawa, Murray Silverstein, et.al. *A Pattern Language: Towns, Buildings, Construction*. New York, New York: Oxford University Press, 1977. This classic has spawned many derivative works. Its section on house design shows how our homes' spaces affect the way we live, and vice versa.

Brand, Stewart. *How Buildings Learn: What Happens After They're Built*. New York, New York: Penguin USA, 1995. Brand analyzes what makes buildings work—or not work—by dissecting how well they accommodate inevitable changes in function and design. A provocative, enlightening and entertaining book.

Designer/Builder: A Journal of the Human Environment. Santa Fe, New Mexico: Fine Additions, Inc. Articles that explore the effect of architecture on human society and vice versa. Not the usual industry viewpoint.

Fine Homebuilding. Newtown, Connecticut: The Taunton Press. For twenty years, this magazine has presented excellent, beautifully illustrated articles on building design and techniques.

Fodor, Eben. *Better Not Bigger: How to Take Control of Urban Growth and Improve Your Community*. Gabriola Island, British Columbia: New Society Publishers, 1999. Takes a deeper look at assumptions about the benefits of growth.

The Historic Santa Fe Foundation. *Old Santa Fe Today*. Albuquerque, New Mexico: The University of New Mexico Press, 1992. Informative, well-illustrated tour of historical buildings in and around Santa Fe.

Iowa, Jerome. *Ageless Adobe: History and Preservation in Southwestern Architecture*. Santa Fe, New Mexico: Sunstone Press, 1985. A history of adobe building in the Southwest that is quite detailed, yet enjoyable to read. The book's information on historic preservation is, in effect, a guide to avoiding problems with adobe buildings.

Mazria, Edward. *The Passive Solar Energy Book: A Complete Guide to Passive Solar Home, Greenhouse and Building Design*. Emmaus, Pennsylvania: Rodale Press, 1979. One of the earliest and best passive solar references. It includes many drawings, photographs, and useful appendices. Currently, the book is out of print, but can often be found in used book stores or by Internet searches.

McHenry, Paul G. *Adobe–Build It Yourself*. Tucson, Arizona: University of Arizona Press, 1985. Perhaps the best single book on how to build with adobe. Accurate, detailed, yet clearly written and pleasant to read.

McHenry, Paul G. *Adobe and Rammed Earth Buildings: Design and Construction*. Tucson, Arizona: University of Arizona Press, 1989. Well-illustrated and written, just what the title says.

Molloy, William J. *Save $50,000 on Your New Home: Yes! You Can Be Your Own General Contractor*. New York, New York: John Wiley & Sons, Inc., 1997. While you may not want to be your own contractor, and while following all of Molloy's recommendations may not create the house you want, this book is an exhaustive look at saving money in land purchasing, financing and contracting.

Phillips, Judith. *Southwestern Landscaping with Native Plants*. Santa Fe, New Mexico: Museum of New Mexico Press, 1987. The basic xeriscaping reference. Includes a catalog of plants illustrated with line drawings.

Roy, Rob. *Mortgage Free! Radical Strategies for Home Ownership*. White River Junction, Vermont: Chelsea Green Publishing Company, 1998. Extreme cost-cutting for those who plan to build their own home.

Rybczynski, Witold. *Home: A Short History of an Idea*. New York, New York: Penguin USA, 1987. A surprising look at the development of our modern concept of comfort. Like Rybczynski's other books, *Home* is entertaining, provocative and witty.

Smith, Edward W. *Adobe Bricks in New Mexico*. Socorro, New Mexico: New Mexico Bureau of Mines & Mineral Resources, 1982. A well-written technical manual also known as "Circular 188." Information ranges from desirable adobe soil characteristics to building codes to adobe history to a listing of state adobe yards. Good wall section diagrams and other building details.

Spears, Beverley. *American Adobes: Rural Houses of Northern New Mexico.* Santa Fe, New Mexico: Ancient City Press, 1997. An well-illustrated history of traditional mountain houses, analyzed by locality and architectural forms.

Stedman, Myrtle, and Wilfred Stedman. *Adobe Architecture.* Santa Fe, New Mexico: Sunstone Press, 1987. A book of home designs first compiled in the 1930s, valuable today due to the effectiveness of the floor plans and charm of the drawings.

Tibbets, Joseph M., ed. *Adobe Codes: A Guide to the Adobe Codes of Arizona, New Mexico and Texas–with California Details.* Bosque, New Mexico: Southwest Solaradobe School, 1995. The Southwest Solar Adobe School address is P.O. Box 153, Bosque, New Mexico 87006. The website is www.adobebuilder.com.

Tibbets, Joseph M. *The Earthbuilders' Encyclopedia: The Master Alphabetical Reference for Adobe and Rammed Earth.* Bosque, New Mexico: Southwest Solaradobe School, 1989. A gold mine of information gathered from articles printed over the years in various adobe periodicals. Easy-to-find entries, lots of explanatory diagrams and photographs.

Tibbets, Joseph M., ed. *Adobe News, Adobe Today's Earthbuilder, Interamericas Adobe Builder.* Published since 1974 under various names, these magazines are a good source of trade information on adobe and other earth-building techniques.

Warren, Nancy Hunter. *New Mexico Style: A Sourcebook of Traditional Architectural Details.* Santa Fe, New Mexico: Museum of New Mexico Press, 1995. A photographic gallery of traditional and contemporary details, grouped by building components such as gates, corbels, fireplaces and so on.

WEBSITES

Internet publications are notoriously volatile. Although these websites were active at these addresses at the time of publication, they may have disappeared by the time you read this. If you can not find one, try using its name or other key words in your search engine.

Adobe Building

www.adobe-block.com/
Website for Adobe International, Inc. (corporate office in Milan, New Mexico.) Includes information on hydraulically pressed adobe bricks.

www.adobebuilder.com/
Site for the *Inter-Americas Adobe Builder Magazine.* Contains sample articles on passive solar heating, adobe, and other earth building techniques.

www.claymineadobe.com
Website for a Tucson-based adobe supplier specializing in cement-stabilized adobes. This site also contains adobe-related information and links.

www.earthbuilding.com
Home for The Earth Building Foundation, Inc., a non-profit corporation with information on adobe and a catalog of books on the subject. This site contains online copies of adobe codes for New Mexico and San Diego, California. Also includes a bibliography of more than 1300 entries on earth architecture.

www.epsea.org/adobe.html
El Paso Solar Energy Association website, which includes a wealth of information on adobe homes and passive solar heating. This site includes a detailed example of how to size thermal mass for direct gain systems (www.epsea.org/mass.html).

www.naturalbuilder.com/adobe.html
A website containing information on natural building materials including adobe. This site has an online version of adobe codes for New Mexico; Boulder, Colorado; and Tucson, Arizona.

Green Building and Passive Solar

www.aceee.org/
Home for the American Council for an Energy-Efficient Economy (ACEEE) a nonprofit organization dedicated to advancing energy efficiency. ACEEE also researches and publishes consumer guides, including the Consumer Guide to Home Energy Savings.

www.firstgov.gov
The all-in-one federal government website. When firstgov was launched in 2000, it supposedly consolidated 27 million government web pages. (We didn't count them.) The government has done a vast amount of research on almost every aspect of home building and financing. Use it—you've already paid for it.

http://hes.lbl.gov (At the time of publication, the HES site address does not include the typical "www.")
Lawrence Berkeley National Laboratory's Home Energy Saver online energy calculator. A great site for analyzing energy costs for new and existing houses. Based on your ZIP code, the simulation program uses your climate data and local fuel costs to project energy consumption and costs. Enter your ZIP code to start the energy audit of your house.

www.solstice.crest.org
Home for Solstice, an information service of the Center for Renewable Energy and Sustainable Technology (CREST).

www.ases.org/
Website for the American Solar Energy Society. This site contains an extensive list of publications and links to other solar and renewable energy sites.

www.ccicenter.org/publications/gsd4/gblist.html
Shows green building guidelines in a checklist format as part of the website for Conservation Consultants, Inc., a non-profit organization.

www.BuildingGreen.com
The home site for Environmental Building News, an outstanding online newsletter covering environmentally responsible design and construction.

www.eren.doe.gov/buildings/energydata.html
This site contains U.S. energy consumption data from the Energy Information Administration. The data includes statistics from the 1993 Residential Energy Survey and allows you to generate energy consumption pie charts and tables for specific regions, fuels, and houses in a range of sizes, types and ages.

www.geonetwork.org
GEO (Global Environmental Options) Network, a gateway to online resources for the green design community.

www.greenbuilder.com/sourcebook
A great website with all kinds of information on sustainable building. The site's sourcebook lists physical characteristics and environmental impacts of alternative building materials.

http://www.greendesign.net/greenclips
Home for GreenClips, an email-delivered sustainable building design newsletter.

www.greenera.com
GreenERA home page for sustainable, renewable energy

www.oikos.com
Oikos ("house" in Greek), a site for those working on sustainable design and construction. This site includes a database of 1800 green building companies and products.

www.sbicouncil.org
Home for the Sustainable Buildings Industry Council, which includes a newsletter and links to solar design software and other resources.

Mortgage Financing

www.bog.frb.fed.us/Pubs/Mortgage/MortB_1.htm
Federal Reserve Board website containing a mortgage shopping worksheet and other consumer-oriented mortgage information.

www.homepath.com
Fannie Mae sponsored site containing mortgage calculators and home buying guides in eight languages. This site also has links to your local agencies that provide pre- and post-purchase education and counseling

www.mortgagemart.com
Mortgage financing resource center containing a general mortgage primer that includes information on energy efficient mortgages (EEMs) and a link to an online mortgage application site.

ABOUT THE AUTHORS

Award-winning author Laura Sanchez previously ran a drafting business that specialized in adobe houses. She called it quits sometime after the 250th set of plans but maintains an abiding interest in designing the very best, most cost-effective houses possible. Alex Sanchez, who grew up building houses, has taught courses in adobe construction and solar energy. He founded and currently heads the renowned computer-aided drafting program at the University of New Mexico-Valencia Campus. The authors' previous books and CDs concern architectural computer graphics.

ORDER PLANS DIRECTLY FROM THE AUTHORS

Using this form, (or make yourself a copy) you can order working drawings for the Basic Houses for the cost of reproduction, shipping, handling and tax. The small scale set of drawings in Chapter 6 shows the elements commonly included in the working drawings, which conform to the current Uniform Building Code and New Mexico's Adobe Code. Requirements may vary in your location. Before ordering, please read the Appendix, "Working Drawings and Building Permits," which describes changes and additional items you may need to meet local building requirements. Each $25.00 plan package includes:

- One set of blueprints of the working drawings
- A 3-1/2" diskette with the working drawings in AutoCAD's drawing exchange format, which can be used with a wide variety of drafting software
- Instructions on having the CAD files printed with or without changes

Please check a box for each plan package you want. If you prefer the wheelchair accessible version where available, please circle the word "Accessible" next to the plan you choose.

❑ Plan #01. Round House	
❑ Plan #02. Coyote House	
❑ Plan #03. Orchard House	Accessible
❑ Plan #04. Corbel House	Accessible
❑ Plan #05. High Valley House	
❑ Plan #06. Sun Hall House	
❑ Plan #07. Garden House	Accessible
❑ Plan #08. Ramada House	
❑ Plan #09. Farm House	
❑ Plan #10. Balcony House	Accessible
❑ Plan #11. Deck House	
❑ Plan #12. Pueblo House	Accessible

Number of boxes checked ______ x $25.00 per plan = Total Amount ____________________

If you have questions, contact us at **alexs@nmia.com**
Credit card payments will not be accepted.
Please send this order form with a check or money order for the total amount to:

Plans
P.O. Box 212
Los Lunas, NM 87031

Please fill out the following so we will know where to ship your order:

Ship to: Name____
Street or P.O. Address__________________________________
City___________________________ State ________ Zip ________________
Email:__________________________ Phone:________________________

NOTE: DO NOT SEND THIS ORDER TO SUNSTONE PRESS.